Voice from the Mangrove Swamps

■

A NARRATIVE OF MEMORIES, STRUGGLES, AND TRIUMPH

by Bassey E. Essien, Ed.D.

DORRANCE PUBLISHING CO., INC.
PITTSBURGH, PENNSYLVANIA 15222

Dorrance Publishing Co., Inc.
701 Smithfield Street
Pittsburgh, PA 15222
Visit our website at www.dorrancebookstore.com

ISBN: 978-0-8059-7420-1
Library of Congress Control Number: 2006929131

This book is dedicated to:

MY FATHER, the late Mr. Edet Essien Asuquo, for his untiring energy and persistent effort to succeed as a fisherman, despite all the obstacles along the way; for his competitive spirit of seeking to stay ahead of his peers in the fishing industry; and for his courage to try again and again, without losing hope for success.

MY MOTHER, the late Madam Arit Effiong Udoh, for her faith in God and her persistent inspirational prayers calling on God to shower her children, including me, with His spirit of protection and blessing; for her selfless and heavy-laden duty on and off the farm to secure food for her children, even in the hardest of times; for instilling in us the sense of God's love and service to the community. She believed that, given a drop of water, you should first pass it on to your more thirsty neighbor before yourself.

MY DEAR WIFE, the late Mrs. Elizabeth Okon Bassey Essien, for helping to lay a strong foundation for the growth of the Essien family and her strong support of the children's education; for her love, care, devotion, and patience during the days of my graduate school in Albany, New York; and for her well-rounded positive spirit and contribution to the community. Elizabeth believed that only individual and group collaboration can assure more positive community growth and development.

MY FOUR DAUGHTERS—Dr. Eno Essien-Ebong, Dr. Ime Essien-Lewis, Ms. Anniedi Bassey Essien, and Miss Iquo Bassey Essien—for the pride and honor they have brought into my family through their outstanding academic achievements; for having initially prompted me to write about my life and for their contributions toward final completion of the book; and for the love they have for me, the support they give to each other, and the help they have given, and will continue to give, to the family relatives, particularly in Nigeria.

MY DEAR NIECE—Mrs. Mercy E. Umoren, for her services and devotion to the family; for the time she spent caring for the girls right from the City of Albany to the South Colonie; for the love, care and interest, that she has shown; for being a strong moral support and adviser to the girls; and for being a positive role model that they can look up to.

MY OLDER BROTHER, Mr. Offiong Edet Essien, for having been the first person to recognize the need to teach me how to read and write, in the absence of formal schooling; and for having been able to create the opportunity for me to leave my place of birth for the first time, in order to better prepare myself for the greater challenges of life.

MY DEAR FRIEND, Mr. Akpan John Esenyie, for being the only one to physically assist me in many ways during my early days of struggle to become a professional photographer in Lagos; for having taken the action of obtaining travel papers for me to leave Nigeria for the USA in 1969; and for helping with my resettlement upon my arrival in Washington, DC.

A SPECIAL APPRECIATION IS EXTENDED TO THE FOLLOWING:

To Dr. Ekpo M. Ossom, Campus Director and Head, School of Agriculture and Food Technology, the University of the South Pacific, Alafua Campus, PMB Apia, Samoa, for his ideas and assistance in editing the manuscript right from its inception.

To Dr. Peter N. Kitonyi of the NYS Department of Correctional Services, Albany, NY, author of *From Where the Lion Roars* (2004), for his inspiring words of encouragement, wisdom, and direction on important aspects of the book.

To Barbara Casey of Albany, New York, for all her helpful suggestions and help in proof-reading and editing the manuscript.

To Mr. Muhammed Owusu, B.A., M.B.A., Associate Treasurer, Office of Finance and Treasury, Government of the District of Columbia, Washington, DC, for his help in proof-reading and editing the initial story concept drafts.

To Mrs. Monica Gutierez-Quarto, the artist who designed the Mangrove Forest Wetlands (on the cover), for authorizing me to use her work on the cover.   Monica and her husband, Mr. Alfredo Quarto, operate the Mangrove Action Project (MAP), P. O. Box 1854, Port Angeles, Washington State 98362.
www.mangroveactionproject.org.

TABLE OF CONTENTS

FOREWORD

Though humankind has made a lot of progress in the modern world, one of our major failures is the inability to make patently accurate and infallible predictions of the future, be it of weather, of political developments, or of the outcome of a war. It is even bewildering to try to predict the type of adult the child of today will become tomorrow. I am full of awe and admiration for the author of *Voice from the Mangrove Swamps* for undertaking the mammoth task of writing this exceptionally interesting biography. I feel deeply honored and privileged to be asked to write this foreword.

Only a few African children are ever born with silver spoons in their mouths. If they are born with any spoons in their mouth at all, such could only be wooden spoons. The author of the *Voice from the Mangrove Swamps*, using words that evoke tears in the reader, has painstakingly and carefully narrated the story about his humble birth in a non-sterile village home shared with domesticated goats. At the time of his birth, the author was not welcomed into the world by obstetricians and midwives as might happen in modern hospitals. This inevitably set the pattern for his subsequent difficult upbringing.

Young Bassey Essien was not sent to any formal school that others of his age attended in other parts of the world or even in the same country. He grew up serving his father in the old man's sea-going fishing expeditions. Leaving behind his three wives, the fisherman would take his young son along on most of the fishing voyages that took them beyond the shores of Nigeria and into the Republic of the Cameroons.

Alternating between the hectic work scenes of his father's fishing vessel and his mother's farms, Bassey experienced a series of mind-boggling childhood sufferings that today would be termed "child labor" by psychologists and social welfare workers.

As a lump of gold may be refined when put through a fiery furnace, or a sapling is hardened by gradual exposure to the sun's heat, Bassey was unconsciously undergoing body- and mind- shaping ordeals that would physically and psychologically prepare him for the future of what can only be characterized as the school of hard-knocks.

While the author might not have enjoyed any benefit of being nurtured and groomed for the purpose of intellectual and cognitive learning and enrichment, he certainly utilized many cognitive and psychomotor skills that enabled him to survive the hazardous fishing trips and risky farm duties.

From the rugged and dangerous mangrove swamps of the West African coast, Bassey was whisked off to Lagos through a collusion that was carefully coordinated by his concerned mother, much to the chagrin of his father who recognized too late the imminent loss of an unpaid but useful crew member of his fishing team. After arriving in Lagos, though fascinated by the bright city lights, Bassey did not let his relative freedom becloud his vision and determination to succeed in life.

Guided by his older brother, Bassey entered the glittering world of professional photography—that magic world of freezing images on film or paper, not only for today's viewing but also for countless generations to catch glimpses of the past. After completing an apprenticeship in photography, he briefly worked as a journeyman before setting up his own photo studio, the Bassey Essien Photo Company (BEPCO).

That photo studio filled a vacuum in the social circles of Lagos, and soon the young manager and proprietor of BEPCO became much sought after by the Indian business community, members of the diplomatic corps, and other Nigerian residents of Lagos. BEPCO's Lagos operation was, however, cut short by Bassey's sudden departure for the USA where he would take on new challenges in education, personal development, and family life.

Arriving in Washington, DC, as a prospective student, Bassey was more determined than ever to make a name for himself. By dint of hard work, he started formal adult education, steadily progressing through the ranks. He studied in the day and worked at night to make ends meet. Sometimes, just as he was about to make ends meet, somebody or some unforeseen circumstance moved the ends and he was back to square one. No longer serving as a farm worker, a boat crewman, or a professional photographer, he then became a porter, cab driver, teacher, counselor, and, lately, a civil servant.

In the course of all these, Bassey met his soul-mate, a lady with the same family name as Bassey's first name, Elizabeth Okon Bassey. Subsequent to their marriage after a brief courtship, Elizabeth became Bassey's pillar of moral and financial support, defender of his rights, his companion, and mother of his children, all rolled into one. Together with his wife, Bassey Essien raised and nurtured his children with the fear of God, that the Bible tells us is the beginning of wisdom. Wisdom has indeed visited him as the challenges of life have taught him the lessons of perseverance, determination, patience, and hope even when hopelessness stared at him in the face. Eventually, Bassey climbed to the pinnacle of academic achievement by earning a doctorate degree in education.

Judging from his community and work experiences, Bassey's past struggles, endurance of various excruciating pains and hardship, have combined to mold the finest gentleman and role model that he is today, as exemplified by his writing of this book. The book is a beacon of hope for all whose early circumstances in life are anything but promising. The author has invited us to peep into his life and hear, conceptually, his originally lost voice. He has held our hands and guided us through the winding paths to that invisible world where the helpless receive help, the hopeless see and grasp audacious hope, the fearful have courage, and the weak feels much needed strength.

By writing this book, Bassey has shown us that one need not be born with a silver spoon in the mouth before he or she can succeed in life. Indeed, one may be born blind but may have more insight than those with eyes. Bassey has demonstrated that, though disaster may unexpectedly strike and one's health may fail at any age, when one's spirit and hope are alive, determination and perseverance can pull one through any man-made barriers.

To the underprivileged, the author is a hero who has spoken for them. He has examined events and situations and asked relevant questions many avoid or dread to ask. He has challenged the privileged members of society to live up to the expectation of children who are brought into this world and left to toil.

The question, therefore, is will the message of this book be

heard and the condition of children in the developing world be rec-
tified to the author's satisfaction? May the message in *Voice from
the Mangrove Swamps* not only be heard loud and clear; may its
yearning and aspirations be transmuted to the golden opportunity
for the children of today and those of tomorrow, without regard to
race, religious affiliation, or nationality.

Dr. Ekpo M. Ossom, CPAg
Professor of Agriculture,
Campus Director & Head,
School of Agriculture & Food Technology
The University of the South Pacific,
Alafua Campus,
PMB Apia, Samoa

CHAPTER 1

INTRODUCTION

I want to open this introduction with a quick reference to the King James Version of the book of Jonah chapter 2 in verse 2 which states: "...I cried by reason of mine affliction unto the Lord, and he heard me; out of the belly of hell cried I, and thou heardest my voice." This book is all about my voice having been heard, after it was lost. I just could not come up with a better defining statement from any other source to support my story than that cited above from the Bible. *Voice from the Mangrove Swamps* is an attempt on my part to share with the world my personal story of survival in America after early periods of unpleasant, difficult, and sometimes deadly struggles and suffering in the mangrove swamps, as well as in my village and in Lagos, Nigeria, West Africa. This book is a narrative of how I discovered my inner voice and feelings which were, heretofore, suppressed, neglected, and isolated due to ignorance and extreme poverty. During the early days of my life, I benefited from no structured educational activity for my intellectual growth and development; instead, I was preoccupied with working on the farm in one season and working on the fishing port in another season.

This period of my life was filled with despair and isolation. There was little or no room for me to express my desires, my hurts, and my needs, because such expressions could not be heard. Indeed, what could have been the loudest part of my voice, in all likelihood a voice of cries, was overshadowed and covered by the mangrove swamps and by endless physical struggles.

Indeed, because it was buried, literally, in the mangrove swamps, my voice could not be heard. If my voice were heard, the early beginning of my world could have been different. I could have spent time working on my intellectual development, instead of struggling to survive one traumatic experience after another. For example, there were occasions when I was part of the fishing team on the high sea, and the storms were raging forcing the ocean waves to rise up high, tumbling the canoe from left to right and the waters were rushing into the canoe and nearly causing the canoe to capsize and sink to the bottomless sea. In those occasions, I was asked to bravely rise up and bail out the waters with a hand bowl, even as I was full of fear for my life, wearing no life jacket, and wailing to God almighty for rescue; but no one could hear my voice. Again, my voice was literally drowned-out and lost in the mighty waves of the Atlantic Ocean off the east coast of the Cameroons and Nigeria; otherwise, how else could no one hear my cries of hurt, my cries of injuries, hunger, and pain? How come no one came to my rescue—rescue from physical suffering, mosquito bites in the remote mangrove swamps, ignorance, and isolation?

When my lower right knee was lacerated and nearly severed by a machete in the muddy swamps, leaving me nearly dead or disabled, all that was left for me to do were my cries for help and treatment, but none of my yelling and humming could be heard by anyone in the outside world, because my voice was buried in the mangrove swamps. Those who could have heard my voice and seen what was going on did not seem to understand, mainly due to the fact that most of them either knew not what they were doing or were incapable of meaningful intervention.

Of course, my voice was lost in the mangrove swamps and nobody could hear my cries for help, especially when a good part of the cries took place in my veins, my facial expressions, my body language, and, in some cases, my intellect. In the depth of the mangrove swamps, where I found myself at my early age, these emotional and psychological manifestations meant nothing. When I was left alone in the canoe at night fall on the Calabar shore of Nsidung, Cross River State, when the canoe strayed away with the rising tides and was almost torpedoed by passing ships, when I became disoriented and didn't know where I was late into the night, the most I could do was to cry out to the Lord, "*Abasi mi, Abasi mi.*" "My Lord, my Lord." I called on the Lord to lead me safely back to the shore of Nsidung and bring me back into the hands of my father. The good Lord hearkened to my prayers, though my voice could not be heard by the outside world.

When my father contracted me out, at the tender age of fourteen, to serve his friend on a fishing trip to Inua Abasi, during which I narrowly escaped death from intensive fishing labor night and day, both on the swamps and on the high seas, no one asked how I felt or whether I suffered any pain. Nobody ventured to ask me to express myself because the reason was clear: nobody cared to know if I had a voice or feelings. Nobody expected me to have any feeling or the ability to express myself because, as we have come to know it clearly now, my voice was lost in the mangrove swamps.

Mangrove swamps describes a geographical landed region located in the coastal area of the Cameroons and Nigeria in West Africa. This is the coastal territory of the Gulf of Guinea. The remote swampy areas are characterized by its ultra-wild environment covered by hard woods and other plants. The swampy areas of the Atlantic coastal regions are populated mostly by wildlife, including monkeys, gorillas, apes, snakes, and various birds. Only very few sections of these swampy areas are suitable for human habitation; yet these are the same remote areas in which Nigerian fishermen spend the better part of their life in pursuit of livelihood. Its wild riches are also sought after by timber traders, and other fortune hunters, including crude oil and mineral explorers. This is the inevitable theatre of my youthful struggles and suffering under the watch of my forebears. These were the geographical areas that I found myself working as a young member of my father's fishing crew.

This book is a direct result of my strong desire to share traumatic experiences of my early life, with emphasis on how I discovered and made use of my voice from the isolation of mangrove swamps. No one would consider his or her life completely fulfilled until he or she could establish how to fully utilize what is, perhaps, the single most important human quality, the power of vocal expression. Without vocal power, no one can express or articulate feelings. If there was one thing I did not have as a result of my early life experiences, it was an opportunity for me to express myself.

The situation I am writing about was made up of repeated fishing trips on the high seas, walking in the mud to fetch supplies, cutting and lifting woods in the mangrove swamps, and attending to my father's fishing business, including net-mending. In a way of expression, this was my own "period of decadence." All that was required of me was intense physical labor. There was no room for any other child development activities. Those who go through their own periods of growth and development with the full benefit of education, training, and self-expression should consider themselves blessed or lucky indeed. Unless one actually experiences the first fifteen years of life in a vacuum, it would be impossible to understand and appreciate the pain.

The main purpose of writing this book is to narrate how I lived, as a youngster, through all of the phenomena described above and still survived to be the person I am today both as a child of God almighty and as a world citizen. I personally believe finding my voice and dignity out of a total state of isolation and obscurity was nothing short of a miracle, as is fully described in sections of the book. After starting life at the lowest point of civilization, working with my mother on the farm in one season and working with my father as fisherman in another season, I was miraculously uprooted from the village and from the mangrove swamps to Lagos under a very contentious circumstance.

When the opportunity first presented itself for me to travel to Lagos in 1959, I was unable to outwardly express my joy, even though I was inwardly overtaken with it. Of course, I did not have a voice, had no such right—and was never in any position—to express it. I could not express the joy because of my fear. Although my mother steadfastly maintained her trust in God to protect me, as she escorted me to join the lorry to Lagos, I was scared to death and afraid of the unknown and what to expect in Lagos. I had never previously traveled across Nigeria by lorry to such a metropolis. For some phenomenal reason, however, after making the first successful trip to Lagos and lived and survived the rat-race there for many years, my fears dissipated.

My arrival in Lagos marked the beginning of the process of my personal rescue or redemption. It primarily set the stage for me to seriously work toward pulling myself up with my bootstraps. For a person who had no boot or even knew what a boot was during my arrival in Lagos in 1959, the task of pulling myself up with my bootstraps was a job that would occupy my entire life in Lagos and, later, in the USA. This book is meant to help explain how I did it.

The nature of my physical activities in Lagos took me through the dimensions of serving as apprentice photographer, as a young owner of a photographic workshop, still another as eligible bachelor with a touch of romance, and, finally, as a potential foreign student traveling to the USA. Again, when the golden opportunity presented itself for me to leave Lagos for the USA in 1969, I could not help but utilize my innate courage, similar to what I had mustered from my first experience of leaving my hometown for a new and unfamiliar Lagos. I needed an even greater courage because, unlike my trip by lorry from my village to Lagos in 1959, traveling to America was going to be more expensive and scarier. It would take more than courage to complete the entire process. More specifically, leaving Nigeria for America involved undergoing expensive medical tests, paying for a travel passport, depositing to the Nigerian government an equivalent of the cost of a one way ticket to guarantee against possible deportation from the USA, obtaining foreign exchange approval from the Central Bank of Nigeria, and arranging for a careful transition of BEPCO's management during my absence.

Although my departure from Lagos, Nigeria, to the USA was yet another joyous moment that was filled with hidden fears and uncertainties, it was nothing short of a miracle, in the sense that this was not one of those ordinary trips. It was a trip to the so-called "overseas," as the Nigerians usually referred to such events. Indeed, it was a trip to the new world, as I would later find out after learning something about American history.

Having arrived in Washington, DC, it was time to start afresh on the road to facing new and lasting challenges in the classrooms, in the work place, and in the social arena. I came to learn, understand, and practice the popular game of 24/7 roulette. There is no doubt that Washington, DC, was a near perfect setting for me to undertake the task of attending an adult education center for my General Education Development (GED), while working at minimum wage jobs to meet my financial needs.

Just as I would love to attribute my success in Washington, DC, to my Lagos exposure and preparation, Washington, DC, effectively served as a socialization training ground to prepare me for my next major move to Albany, New York, which came immediately after I received my first college degree from American University and married Elizabeth Okon Bassey, who was then studying at UAlbany—State University of New York. Moving from Washington, DC, to Albany continues to be significant in my life, as it represents the last of my three major moves, which first took place from my village to Lagos in 1959 and from Lagos to Washington, DC, in 1969.

In many cases, my accomplishments in Albany make Albany very memorable as well. Not only have I settled here with my family for more than thirty years, it was in Albany that I obtained my Master of Science (MS) and my Doctor of Education (Ed.D.) degrees from UAlbany—State University of New York.

Obviously, having to move from one continent to another, undergo various kinds of changes along the way, and finally having to settle in one spot can never be described as a piece of cake by anybody; however, it is my belief that these various movements from place to place within and outside of Nigeria directly resulted from my personal needs and desires. Except for those reasons, none of these phenomenal moves and actions could have been undertaken. I can now conclude they came about for my own good.

Indeed, writing this personal memoir, with highlights of various episodes, encounters and experiences, involved introspections, soul-searching, and difficult recall of personal anecdotes. The writing evoked in me memories of nearly all of my early childhood pleasant and unpleasant experiences that were not even written down. Most of what you are about to read is the result of oral history transposed into print. I want to thank the Good Lord Jesus Christ for giving me the enduring brains, in the face of the enduring pains, that could remember so much for so long and for enabling this memory to be coordinated with sensitive keyboard fingers. Again, to describe the whole phenomenon of piecing the episodes together as a miracle can only qualify as another understatement.

The story in this book is told in four major segments: the village segment, the Mangrove Swamps segment, the Lagos scene, and the new world (USA) segment. The village scene covers the early days of my life in the village, including birth history, upbringing details, and parental chores working on the farmland. The Mangrove Swamps segment covers my repeated trips to fishing ports in the Mangrove Swamps and my fishing work on the Gulf section of the Atlantic Ocean, in the company of my father. This entire period runs from the late 1940s to 1960.

The Lagos scene represents an intermediary, or a buffer, between my village and fishing life experiences and my eventual transition to a new life in Lagos metropolis. It will cover a series of occupational and family events and activities leading to the lonely trip from the village to eventual arrival and settlement in Lagos, and all subsequent struggles and survival as adult-child professional photographer. It paved the way for my subsequent departure for the USA. The Lagos scene covers the period of Nigeria's independence in 1960 to the Civil War of 1967, 1968 and 1969.

The new world (USA) segment runs from the period of 1970 to the present time. This should qualify as the stage of awakening, or renaissance or self-discovery stage. The new world scene covers the subject of my formal education struggles, beginning in Washington, DC, and continuing to Albany, New York. It addresses the joy and agony of starting and maintaining a family through the period of the children's education.

Finally, I strongly believe that, despite the loneliness of my struggles, the physical and intellectual battles I had to encounter along the way were either necessary or inevitable in order for me to appreciate the value of positive change in my life, a change of attaining some level of education, the ultimate goal of my struggle. How else could I have done it, considering the road blocks that I had to overcome before learning the alphabet? I consider the outcome of my struggles, therefore, to be my subsequent educational achievement and a legacy of my family life, signified largely by my children's academic achievements across the board. This is my heralded triumph in life. These positive outcomes could not have been possible without my miraculous coming to America. Indeed, it is now my turn to join all of the patriotic Americans in saying' "God bless America!" I also wish to join all patriotic Nigerians in saying, "Long live Nigeria."

CHAPTER 2

THE EARLY DAYS

I prefer to characterize the early days of my life as my bitter and sweet days for the following reasons: They were bitter in the sense of all the traumatic and related incidents which occurred in my life in those days—as have been narrated in this book. Indeed, my early days were also sweet days when one considers the fact that those were the days of my overall growth from childhood to adolescence, without which I would not have made it to this point in time. It is for these reasons that I want to devote this section to the full description of those days in order to lay a firm groundwork for the reader's understanding of my story. To accomplish this aim, I will discuss my birthplace, the period of my growth and socialization, my encounter with the Night Owls, and a deep look back into my irregular learning activities.

In discussing my birthplace, I will describe its geographical area as well as the political administration of my original home state and country. In the growing up and socializing section, I will provide a full narrative of my childhood activities both in the farms and in the fishing ports. Most certainly, my presentation of the episode of encountering the Night Owls is meant to offer the reader a glimpse of the many dangers that I had to face at an early age.

Finally, in the section dealing with my early learning, I have narrated how every bit of my activity unconsciously became my learning tools and objectives, all without a plan and without any particular facilitator. Again, welcome to my early days, the days of my life in Nigeria.

MY BIRTHPLACE

As I embark upon the discussion of my birthplace, I am reminded of the three fundamental principles that govern individual history and self esteem—our names, dates of birth, and places of birth. As an example, a person who has no name, date, and place of birth, is probably nonexistent. That is why the name, Bassey Edet Essien, is so important to me, because it tells the world something about my origin and who I am. Knowing that I have a name and place of birth is also the reason why I am pleased to share my story with the world, because I am contributing to the education of people, places, and their values. Whereas our names almost always automatically give us our individual family identities and cultural history, our dates of birth inevitably get us started in the growth and maturation process. Just so as not to be outdone, whether we like it or not, our places of birth basically serve as the foundation tickets to our countries' legal rights and all the privileges thereto appertaining. It is with the understanding of these three fundamental principles that I feel so honored and excited to present a narrative of my birthplace to my readers.

Based on all of the information that I received from close relatives who were either present at my birth or had intimate knowledge thereof, I was born on May 30, 1945, in the village of Ifa Ikot Idang, Etoi, Uyo, Akwa Ibom State of Nigeria. A back check of this date in the world calendar shows the day was Wednesday—exactly the same date as Wednesday May 30th in the year 2007, the sixty-second year of my life. An interesting thing to add here in memory of my mother is that I was in her womb when the Second World War (WWII) was in progress. I recall her telling me she used to go and line up to receive a supply of rationed salt and food items, as the war was raging in Europe. Luckily for me, the war was winding down, followed by the formation of the United Nations Organization (UNO), by the time I was delivered of my mother. How I wish mother had a picture of her waiting in line for salt with me inside her belly! Sorry, but there was no such picture as it would have been a very interesting one to see.

Apparently, the end of WWII and the formation of the UNO were not the only important world events that took place in 1945. Considering the irony of my birth into an environment that was totally devoid of medical services, significant world events in the area of medical science were also taking place in the same year of my birth. They were the joint award of Nobel prizes in physiology or medicine to three recipients: (1) Sir Alexander Flemming of London University, (2) Ernst Boris Chain of Oxford University, and (3) Sir Howard Walter Florey of Oxford University—all of England. The fourth award recipient in the same medical field was Artturi Ilmari Virtanen of the University of Helsinki, Finland. His award was in chemistry.

I have referenced these four medical scientists to emphasize the point that one would have considered it a blessing to be born at the time that such medical progress was being made; however, here I am struggling to tell how isolated and difficult it was with my parents to care for me during my birth, even as these men were being recognized for their medical scientific achievements. One wonders if this was by design or simply an accident. I am convinced that it was by design, especially since Colonial Nigeria contributed manpower toward the war. How isolated could the country have been? The point is that, under colonialism, our people were considered good enough to serve but not good enough to be offered medical care and much needed educational opportunities.

I also want to add that being born in isolation, without the benefit of medical care and childhood education, did not mean that the world was isolated or without educational opportunities. It could have been the result of poor distribution of resources, since it appears that the best of the world's resources go to those who are well placed rather than those who need them most. I wonder why my birthplace would have been so isolated, even in the face of Nigeria's participation in WWII? Could it have been deliberate neglect by the powers that be? Perhaps it was due to the fact that I was born into a minority tribe in a British colony where only members of dominant tribes, namely the Igbo, the Hausa, and the Yoruba tribes were deserving of certain government benefits. How I wish that this situation had changed or significantly improved. Unfortunately, in the year 2010, long after this part of Nigeria (now known as Akwa Ibom State) has become one of the country's thirty-six states, the childbirth and health care situations have not improved in any significant way. Many women are still having children at home and without the benefit of prenatal care.

I am the third of my mother's five children, ranked in the family as *Udo*, or the second male child. Her first son (or *Akpan*) was Offiong Edet Essien, born June 30, 1939. The second child

(*Adiagha* or the first born daughter) was the late Iquo Edet Essien, born March 4, 1943. The next two children are Effionwan Edet Essien born on September 13, 1950, and the last born is Effiong (David) Edet Essien (born May 10, 1952). Following the death of our parents, Akpan became the presumptive mantle holder of the family.

Because my father married three wives, I have five step sisters and a young step brother whose family positions I can only give by explaining the marital ranks of their mothers relative to my mother's. My mother, Arit Effiong Udoh of Ifa Ikot Idang, was my father's first or senior wife. The other two were Mma Alice of Ifa Ikot Okpon, the second wife, and Mma Ekpenwan Otu of Mbak Etoi village, the third wife. My step sisters Nkoyo Edet Essien and Mary Edet Essien were brought to this world by the late Mma Alice Edet Inyang of Ifa Ikot Okpon (about three miles from Ifa Atai). My other three step sisters, Nyong Edet Essien, Akon Edet Essien (Mma Ini), Affiong Edet Essien (Mma Nurse), and my step brother Aniedi Edet Essien (Andy), were brought to this earth by Mma Ekpenwan Otu of Mbak Ikot Ebo (about two miles from Ifa Atai). Mma Ekpenwan was, therefore, the third wife to my father. Mma Ini was born on September 28, 1968, and Andy was born on February 5, 1973.

As you may recall from the onset of this section, I attributed my birth information to the relatives who witnessed my birth or could testify to veracity of the date. The reason for that is important: At the time of my birth, and in many cases perhaps to this day, childbirth was not officially recorded. Any record that could have been kept would most likely not be an official record. Over the last few years, the Nigerian federal government has set up what it calls the National Population Commission, with offices or centers in each state capital for the purpose of assisting unregistered citizens in completing age declaration and to register new births. That means that the average Nigerian citizen born today stands a much better chance of having his or her birth registered.

This is an example of why we have grown to use and rely on "oral tradition" as a tool for transmitting knowledge and understanding the early days of my life in the village. It is noteworthy that this writing will rely heavily on the memory that grew out of primarily oral description and preservation of history. The truth is that we had absolutely no choice in the matter. One of the unfortunate legacies of British rule in Nigeria has been perpetual isolation and neglect of the populace. Lack of a government office for birth registration was just one of the many examples of governmental failure to fulfill its basic functions and services to its citizenry in the Colony of Nigeria under Great Britain. Fortunately, however, lack of official registration of births did not seem to affect the day-to-day activities of the people in the village. The people of the villages just did not care about it—or they did not know enough to care about it.

My birthplace, the village of Ifa Ikot Idang, is a small section of the town of Ifa Atai, Uyo Local Government Area (LGA). The City of Uyo and its surrounding areas, including Ifa Atai, were once known as Uyo Province, within what was known as the Eastern Region of Nigeria. The Eastern Region of Nigeria was one of the three main regions of Nigeria which included the Western and Northern regions, from the colonial era through independence in 1960 and up to Nigeria's civil war in 1967. Nigeria obtained independence from Great Britain in 1960, enjoyed a short period of relative peace, and then plunged into a civil war which lasted from 1967 to 1970. It was just before the civil war began in 1967 that the regional makeup of the country was changed to the state system. Consequently, the Cross River (Calabar) section of the Eastern Region of Nigeria was named the Southeastern State of Nigeria.

The break-up of the country into states resulted directly from the political disputes between the Eastern Region and the federal government; however, the action did little to avert the civil war. It was just a few years following the civil war when the Southeastern State of Nigeria was renamed Cross River State (literally named after the Cross River, a tributary of the Atlantic Ocean, with the capital in Calabar). By 1988, the Cross River State of Nigeria was subdivided into two smaller states: the Cross River State (headquartered in Calabar) and the Akwa Ibom State (my current home state) on the mainland, with Uyo as its headquarters.

Geographically, Akwa Ibom State is located in the southeastern part of Nigeria as already indicated, about fifteen minutes from the equator or the Greenwich Meridian. The state is about four hundred miles southeast of Lagos, the former Nigerian capital city, and about three hundred miles south of Abuja, the present Nigerian capital city. The state is surrounded by the Rivers State (Port-Harcourt) on the south-west, Abia State (Aba) on the west, and Cross River (Calabar) on the north-east. In fact, my birthplace is situated only about thirty miles from the Atlantic Ocean on the south—stretching from east to west on the Bight of Biafra—over the Gulf of Guinea. In the subsequent chapters of the book, the direct impact of the Atlantic Gulf of Guinea on my life will become quite prominent.

Bight of Biafra or the Gulf of Guinea is also the main area that provides the natural resources of crude oil production from Nigeria to the rest of the world, including the USA. This region is also the geographical location of the seaport of Port Harcourt in the Rivers State—already mentioned above. Port Harcourt is the seat of many petroleum companies producing crude oil in Nigeria. Of course, both the City of Calabar, on the north end of Cross River's coast, and the City of Oron, on the south end of Cross River's coast, are also seaports. However, the two seaports are in dire need of development for the purposes of attracting shipping business and creating employment opportunities for the indigenous people of the region.

As the headquarters of Akwa Ibom State, Uyo is also the administrative headquarters of the Local Government Area governing my birth place of Ifa Ikot Idang village which is located on the southeast side of the capital city. We are, therefore, used to referring to my village as Ifa Ikot Idang, Etoi Clan, in Uyo Local Government Area (LGA). Uyo was previously known as Uyo Province of Eastern Nigeria during Colonial rule and the now Akwa Ibom State was part of Eastern Nigeria. In other parts of this chapter, I will endeavor to illustrate more details of the position of my birthplace in relation to the entire State of Akwa Ibom in particular and Nigeria as a whole, with reference to the Civil War which began in 1967 and ended in 1970.

My home town of Ifa Atai Township consists of nine villages, including Ifa Ikot Idang. Among them and their current titular heads are (1) Ifa Ikot Abia Mkpo, headed by Chief (Eteidung) Asuquo Etim Akpan; (2) Ifa Ikot Abia Ntuen, headed by Chief (Eteidung) Peter E. Essien; (3) Ifa Ikot Akpabio, headed by Chief

(Eteidung) Etim Bassey Usuk; (4) Ifa Ikot Akpan, headed by Chief (Eteidung) Etebom Effiong Akpan; (5) Ifa Ikot Idang—my hometown—headed by Mr. Ita Etim Ekpenyong; (6) Ifa Ikot Obong, headed by Chief (Eteidung) Edem Effiong Ayara; and (7) Ifa Atai Anwa, (8) Ifa Ikot O'Nsu, and (9) Ifa Uya Etoi, all headed by Chief (Eteidung) Okokon Effiong Udo-Nwa. I want to mention here very briefly that the names of heads of Ifa Atai villages that I have given above are strictly for the sole purpose of identifying these villages. In very realistic cases, some of the individuals whose names are stated here may not be alive at the time this information is in print. All that I can say is to pray and wish that the souls of those departed may rest in eternal peace, in the name of the Lord!

It is important to bear in mind that the people living in these villages do not always traditionally address each other by pronouncing all three words descriptive of their village. They most usually casually use only the last two words of the village names, such as Ikot Obong or Ikot Idang. Nearly all of the villagers in Ifa Atai depended then, as they still do, on labor-intensive farming and fishing for their livelihood. Farming is done mostly by the women, assisted by men who do the wood cutting or wood/land clearing and burning down of the tree leaves for the women to start planting. Most certainly, in our villages preparing the land for planting calls for serious machete clearing of the bushes and trimming down of the leaves, followed by burning up of the leaves to ashes. To the best of my knowledge, the practice continues to this day. Fishing is primarily the men's occupation. Other mostly mundane occupations in the villages include being a school teacher, a government public work employee, a clerk, or a tax collector. The most important tax agents, of course, were the heads of each of the villages as listed in this chapter.

Up to this point I have done my best to present a true picture of my birthplace, my home state of Akwa Ibom in relationship to the Nigerian federation. I now wish to return to the discussion of the inside, the locale, and the entire home environment where I was born. Without this additional piece, the story of my birthplace can never be complete. Again, in contemplation of doing this write-up, I cannot help but be reminded of the biblical story of Jesus Christ who was born in a manger. Scripture has it that the place was both unsightly and isolated. Notwithstanding that condition, however, it was the same Jesus Christ who grew up and overcame all odds to become the savior of the world. I am not citing this story as an attempt to compare myself to Jesus; however, I wanted to inform the reader that I always reflect on the condition of baby Jesus' birthplace as a source of strength and consolation, whenever I remember the circumstances and how I came into this world.

Having said that, I want to begin by stating, once again, that I was told by my mother and those who witnessed my birth that I was born in *Itie-Ebot* in my mother's home—not too far from *Iteneh* or the firewood kitchen. *Itie-Ebot* in the Ibibio language of Southeastern Nigeria literally means "goat's place." That is to say the place where the animals we call goats are raised, similar to a barn or a stable—but with no real resemblance. As used here in my story from my past experience, *Itie Ebot* describes the smallest available space in my mother's house that was shared by the family and the goats. From time to time, mother had the need to raise fowls as well and they very often shared the space closer to the *Itie Ebot*. This was also the case in similar households in the village in those days. There is little or no evidence to support any claim that the situation has significantly changed in my village to this date.

The goat represents, perhaps, the most popular breed of domesticated animals commonly owned by families in my village. Other domesticated animals that are also commonly owned include dogs, cats, and fowl. My mother used to raise goats, as did many other families that I knew in the village, first for sale to augment the family's financial needs and, second, to use for the purpose of slaughtering for meat during very important family occasions, such as marriages and funeral ceremonies. The latter of these occasions were very rarely the case in my experience. So it is fair to say that we raised our goats mostly for sale in open markets to raise much needed funds for the family's economic sustenance. As much as I can recall what was the common practice in my village and my mother's household, those who had money enjoyed buying goats for the purposes of slaughtering them for meat. Others bought them for offering to meet prescribed sacrificial rites—during either family crisis or celebration. The greatest beneficiaries were the primary goat and fowl herders who sold them to make money to meet their families' basic financial needs—primarily food and housing. None of the other domesticated animals received as much attention in the village.

I grew up in my mother's mud house with my brothers and sisters sharing the same roof with the goats. The total room sizes were usually not more than six hundred square feet, including the living areas, the cooking areas, and the goats' and fowls' corners. It was not the normal routine to cook indoors as this was more usually done on the porch or the corridor or the yard during normal weather conditions. The principal place of sleeping was a mud bed—basically a mixture of muddy substance constituted to the size of about two feet wide by two feet high by seven feet long and allowed to solidify and become a permanent part of the room corner. The locally-knitted mats were the usual bedspreads used on the mud beds as well as on the floor for sleeping.

One of my main house chores was taking care of the goats by providing them with food. Having fowls in the house presented no serious problems, as they would routinely walk around the neighborhood on their own feeding at random. However, the process of obtaining food for goats usually involved much more physical work. That means that I usually had to walk to the bushes with a machete to identify certain leaves, cut and tie them into bunches, and physically carry the bunches on my head back to the house for the goats to feed. This was one of my usual obligations to my mother, and there were other chores as you will see in other sections of this book, especially in Chapter 3. It was just as important for my mother to raise goats as it was for her to raise me and my siblings. In Ifa Atai in those days, particularly in my village of Ifa Ikot Idang, women or families that had goats and were able to nurture them and watch them multiply, like my mother did, were considered to be "well-to-do" women or families. In our case, my mother needed to raise goats so that she could sell them from time to time to make some money to meet some of the family needs.

From the viewpoint of an objective observer, it was considered to be perfectly normal for families, such as our's, to have goats in the household, as it was evidence of progress in those days. I am reminded of an incident that came to light following mother's death in 1989. It was revealed by one of our siblings that one of our cousins by the name of Mbekke owed a debt to mother which was the cost of a goat she had purchased and for which she had never paid. Well, that debt was not, and may never be, paid. Our God-fearing mother, in her gracious heart, probably did not consider it to be a debt in the first place. By the standards of those who could not afford goats like my mother did in those days, mother might have been thought of as being well-blessed. However, we the children never considered it a pleasant story to tell or to be told that you were born in "goat's place," at least until this writing. Some of the reasons for resenting the story were due to unsanitary conditions of those places and the lack of medical supervision to prevent diseases. The mere mention of having been born in such a place was considered a curse, reminiscent of poverty and the agony of destitution and hunger.

The question, now, therefore, is how did I manage to survive the unsanitary conditions, the poverty, and the lack of medical attention. The search for right answers to such questions is one of the compelling reasons for writing this book. Although I may not be able to provide complete answers to all of the questions from all imaginable angles, I will do my very best to pick my brains to the bare bones in an attempt to satisfy everyone's curiosity and thirst. I am convinced that what I have presented will shed a considerable amount of light on the totality of my story. Let us brace ourselves for the best that is yet to come.

GROWING UP AND SOCIALIZING

The concept of growing up and socializing in my place of birth is something that should bring a memory full of joy to me, under normal circumstances. However, that is not the case with me in this instance, as you will see in the narrative that I am presenting here. Growing up and socializing in the village of Ifa Ikot Idang was not the easiest thing to do. In the first place, I am not even sure I knew what it meant to grow up and socialize, in terms of my relationship with my immediate environment and the rest of the world. I can only acknowledge, however, that it was my consistent physical growth and maturity level that guaranteed my survival as a child from day to day. We are talking about the period of growth and up-bringing—a process by which a child is born, bred and raised, nurtured and taught, and initiated into adulthood as he or she assumes the role of a family provider or a community leader or world citizen. The world in which I grew up at the time I did was such a different world as far as I am concerned.

I consider it an enormous responsibility to embark upon explaining my growth and socialization in the village. That is because I do not even know how the two physical and conceptual phenomena (growing and socializing) came together to make me a person who survived to be alive to the day I am writing this on paper. Trying to recall some of the experiences that made me who I was—and which brought me to where I am now—is as painful and agonizing as it is exciting and promising. On the one hand, the unpleasant memories brought to mind are simply unbearable. On the other hand, the demands of writing and composing from memory is physically and intellectually agonizing and stressful. However, the excitement comes from the opportunity to do something historically important, and the promise rests in the hope that this effort will be appreciated by the Bassey Essien family, the community, and the entire world.

Without any doubt, the environment in which I grew up and socialized was a microcosm of the Nigerian economic, social, and political system. This is another way of saying that the overall atmosphere of my village could not have been so different from most other similar villages or towns in the country. During the short years of my growing up, Nigeria as a country was still under British rule. The country as a whole was made up of the Northern Region, the Western Region, and the Eastern Region. Each region had its own House of Assembly, including the Eastern House of Assembly in Enugu, where laws were made.

Lagos was then the capital of Nigeria, until the period of the Nigerian-Biafran Civil War (1967 to 1970) after which Abuja became Nigeria's capital city. As mentioned before, the present Uyo Local Government Area (LGA) of Akwa Ibom State was a small part of what was known as Uyo Province. The village of Ifa Ikot Idang, as an integral part of Uyo Province in those days, derived or was supposed to derive, its social and economic influence from the city of Uyo. Unfortunately, however, the city of Uyo itself was struggling for recognition from the Eastern Nigerian Government, one of the three Nigerian regions ruled by the British Colonial Administration.

Most friends of my parents were farmers and fishermen just like my parents. Not too many children my age were supposed to go to school in those days. Sending children to school in those days used to be such a major decision for parents, including my parents and especially my father. It might have been a miracle that my older brother, Offiong, was sent to school starting at the Methodist Central School for elementary and middle school and ending at the

West African People's Institute (WAPI) in Calabar, Cross River State. (Mention needs to be made here that Calabar, as a major seaport, occupied a strategic position in Nigerian history, from Colonialism to becoming the capital of the former Southeastern State, then the Cross River State). To the best of my knowledge, my village had not one indigenous son or daughter with a college degree, much less a master's degree. Even those who were lucky enough to go to school never really completed a college degree.

My older sister, late Iquo Edet Essien, was not sent to school. But my younger sister, Effionwan Edet Essien, was enrolled by mother at the Apostolic Church Elementary School in Ifa Ikot Okpon, four miles from our village. Mother's reason for taking Effionwan to a school at this distance was primarily to keep her identity with the Apostolic faith. It is not clear why mother failed to send Iquo or me to the same school or any other school, such as the Methodist Central School which was at least two miles nearer home than the school at Ifa Ikot Okpon. However, it became clear from my observation that mother was still more interested in our education than our father was, except that she failed to fight harder to ensure we were all enrolled in school. Notwithstanding these gray areas, mother's interest in the children's education could have been the result of her increased awareness of the importance of education and the impending changes in the world. It is fair to conclude that, though mother selected Effionwan only to attend the Apostolic Church Elementary School, instead of the Methodist Central School, her decision was not just in honor of her Apostolic faith, but to get her children started in the process of education.

I wish I could boldly cite father's role in this exercise, but father showed absolutely no interest in sending any of us to school, and, I would assume, he did not care about what mother did in that regard. Sister Effionwan used to walk a total of eight miles a day to and from that school in Ifa Ikot Okpon. I used to worry so much about her survival, even though I did nothing about it, except to think that she was lucky to go to school. As mentioned, I used to worry about Effionwan's survival walking to and from the school at Ifa Ikot Okpon because I just could not imagine in those days how one could be expected to make such long trips by foot and without shoes five days a week. I was particularly concerned about her safety as she used to walk the two-mile stretch along the dangerous foot paths of the Trunk A Road between Ifa Ikot Idang exit and Ifa Ikot Okpon exit. As a young child, I recall witnessing fatal motor accidents involving innocent pedestrians on that section of the highway. In fact, one of the Trunk A accident victims was the son of our church elder, Mr. Etim Akpan, and a personal friend of mine whose memory remains with me to this day. Although I was happy for my sister Effionwan to have an opportunity to attend school, I was silently preoccupied by her risky traveling situation, while inwardly hoping that perhaps her educational achievements would one day impact me positively.

The fact that sister Effionwan used to walk to and from school did not mean she was doing something terribly strange from the norm of the day. In the absence of a bicycle on which to travel around, active foot trekking was the most common option for many people who needed to get to and from their respective destinations. The situation was even worse when one had a heavy load to carry on the head. I do not recall ever seeing anyone in my immediate community utilizing a horse or camel for local luggage transportation, as is the case in parts of Northern Nigeria and in places like Egypt. Apparently, we were made aware of the existence of bicycles as an upscale means of transportation. Hence a bicycle owner in those days in my village was king. Not too many people could afford to buy bicycles.

After completing elementary school, sister Effionwan did not have any additional opportunity to enter a secondary school and she had no job for quite some years. As I had not yet even started attending my own formal classroom, and was not working on any plan to start one in those days, there was nothing that I could do to help Effionwan, even when I was very concerned. This was a very lonely and dark period of my life educationally, despite the fact that I ended up in Lagos. The change in Effionwan's educational status came in early 1970s, long after I had left Nigeria and had miraculously become a student in Washington, DC, and I was able to arrange for Effionwan to return to school. It all began with a talk that I had with a dear friend, the late Asuquo Johnny Umoh (may his soul rest in peace), whose recommendation led to Effionwan being given a late admission into the Teachers Training College at Itak, in Ikono Local Government Area, near Uyo. Sister Effionwan successfully completed that training program, took the prescribed government examination, and passed and has since become a certified elementary school teacher. Having been married to Mr. Sunday Udoh ever since, sister Effionwan is now working as an elementary education teacher and a deputy principal at Government Primary School in Ibiaku Issiet, near Ifa Atai, Akwa Ibom State of Nigeria.

Sister Effionwan's success as an educator was just a drop in the bucket or a sprinkle into the stream of Idim-Ewa in the village of Ifa Ikot Idang. Her success represented a historic achievement for the family, considering what was portended as inevitable failure. As a girl, she was on the border of falling into the trap of being considered by her culture as undeserving of an education. It would have erroneously justified the social expectations of the unsuccessful outcome of girls' education in the village, a situation engendered by ignorance and poverty. For example, most families in those days usually thought it was a waste of time and money to send girls to school because of the likelihood of girls getting pregnant or getting married. Well, sister Effionwan proved them all wrong, as she diligently completed her teacher training program long before getting married.

The fear of girls getting pregnant or getting married was very much at the root of parental reluctance to sponsor girls' schooling in our village and, possibly, the country. Apparently, there was a covert or unarticulated reason for this practice as well—poverty. Girls becoming pregnant was usually considered to be an embarrassment to the family. On the other hand, girls getting married was considered to be a loss to the parents who spent money to sponsor their education. In all cases, the unfounded fears and ignorance only amounted to an educational deterrents for girls. As crazy and weird as these practices might sound, however, it was not necessarily unique to my people, from what I have discovered.

Considering how bad the situation of girls' education was in my village during my growing up years, it makes little or no sense for me to cite an example of how women were treated or viewed in colonial America. However, I feel compelled to mention the historic fact that the early part of American educational history reveals that, although American women were sought after as teachers because of their caring and nurturing qualities, they were paid next to nothing for their work in those days. Moreover, American women teachers were not allowed to get married because of the fear that they might become pregnant and have children. Getting married and having children were considered to be a serious hindrance to teaching in the classroom. The women who insisted on getting married were asked to leave teaching. Of course, this sort of practice is no longer the case in America. By the same token, the situation of women education in my home country has significantly improved today.

By briefly reflecting, therefore, on the historical situation in colonial America as shown above and seeing the progress that my sister Effionwan made by becoming a certified teacher in the period described, one could conclude she belonged in the lucky minority of Nigerian women. I personally consider her blessed and special for making good use of the educational opportunities presented to her. I probably could have done as well or better if I had a similar chance. The irony of this story is that I was the male child of the family and was not enrolled in school; she was a female child and was enrolled in school, in supposedly a male-dominated colonial Nigeria.

Since I was not a female in the family, a different set of explanations of the irony may be necessary: I like to suggest that my parents defied the social norm and failed to send me to school largely because they needed an extra hand to get things done, especially since my oldest brother, Offiong, was already in school, and his schooling brought about financial hardship to the family. Overall, I must emphasize the fact that my explanations of my parents' or my people's educational avoidance in those days are purely my own conjecture based on the nuances of the time in question. Neither of my parents nor any other community member ever told me why they did not and would not enroll me and so many other children in formal educational programs. With particular reference to my parents, I think they did not wish to send me to school because they considered me to be their "right hand son," when it came to working on mother's farmland and in father's fishing business.

My initial conscription into my mother's farm and father's fishing work activities actually began from being home during the day when my sister Effionwan and other lucky youngsters would be in school. For example, as I have illustrated in appropriate sections of the book, I started learning to weave fishing nets for my neighbors to make a few pennies and shillings in those days. Eventually, as I got better weaving nets for neighbors on short contracts, it became the focal point of my service to my father. The actual contract weaving process involved signing up with the fishermen to weave several hundred yards of very thin threads into sets of long fishing net.

I started learning the net-weaving craft by watching the adult villagers weave until I began practicing and eventually became comfortable with doing it by myself. Being comfortable meant that I was able to increase both the speed and accuracy of my weaving. The amount of money that a contract weaver could earn would depend on the ability to produce a reasonable length of fishing net. Of course, I was not paid for weaving for my father, and it was customary to complete my father's assignments before I was able to participate in the contract weaving. For that reason, my main socialization centered around church events, interacting with mostly adult fishermen in the fishing ports, and traveling with father to and from the fishing ports off the Atlantic coast. Was my situation necessarily different from or worse than that of other young men or women in the village? The answer is no. This was a typical time in our family history when education of children was not a priority of most families. Only a select few families managed to enroll their children in school in those days. So, getting started with the process of learning to read and write was as difficult as trying to identify the "Star of Africa" in the sky.

I remember usually having to play with school children and others in the village and going to church with mother. In some ways, the church exposure created an appetite for learning to read the Bible. There was pressure from the church authorities to pass on the mantle of shepherdship to me. Without being told directly by any adult, you could see in the eyes of the church elders and pastors and from the body language of parents the pressure to come up for some form of recognition in the church. I still recall the many times I observed one of my contemporaries speaking in tongues just to prove he was eligible to be called. He later left the Apostolic Church to set up his own prayer house. It was expected that, as a child of God, you had to be "spiritual" and know how to "speak in tongues." For some reason, that used to scare me dearly, but I could not tell my mother for fear of being scolded.

It is interesting to note that nearly all of my village life experiences and other growing up activities centered around basic survival and the economic self-sufficiency of the family. Of course, whether this phenomenal concept of work-to-grow and work-to-learn was due to chance alone or predetermined by the almighty God, this will doubtless represent the dominant theme of this book. As an example, at least two such work activities were almost becoming full-time occupations of mine and major sources of economic survival for me and my family members. I am referring to the traditional hand craft work of *Nsiim* (or bamboo rind fish trap production) and the "wet-wood expedition" in search of mushrooms.

The term *Nsiim* refers to a traditional twenty-inch, locally handmade circular fish trap made of refined bamboo rind strings hand-stitched together in three interval sections with bamboo straw ropes (known as *Iditt*). The refined rind strings are knitted closely together, allowing no more than .25-inch of space between the rinds to prevent small fish from escaping after being trapped. Bamboo straw ropes are used to stitch the thinly-shaped bamboo rind strings together one inch from the head/mouth of the trap, then at two six-inch intervals—leaving the remaining seven or more inches of the bamboo rind strings unstitched at the tail-ends. This tail-end can be wrapped and fastened together to form a trap for the small fish when set under water and can be untied to open and empty out the catch. *Nsiim* trap construction is completed by wrapping the stitched bamboo rind strings around three wooden rings of approximately ten-inches, eight-inches, and six-inches in diameter to form a basket cone-shape. The ten-inch diameter wooden ring is then placed at the head/mouth or opening of the trap around the stitched surround to leave a wider opening for baby fish entry. The eight-inch diameter ring is set next around the second six-inch interval of stitched bamboo straw rope opening. And the six-inch diameter ring is placed at the second six-inch interval of string surround to assure the final cone-shape of the trap.

The seven or more-inch tail-end section of the bamboo rind

strings is designed basically as a free-play section meant to be wrapped together and tied into a cone bunch. The purpose of tying the tail ends is to form a trap and prevent the passage of a catch. It is also the section that is routinely opened to empty out all baby fish catches. The completed trap of *Nsiim* must have at least two internal housing pieces of mini-*Nsiim*. This refers to two small *Nsiim* pieces that are installed inside of the main housing to form a trap against any small or baby fish that would eventually travel into the *Nsiim* housing when set in the busy stream. The first *Nsiim* insert is placed against the eight-inch diameter internal wooden ring housing of the trap. The second insert is placed at the head/mouth of the trap's opening against the ten-inch diameter wooden ring. Taken together, the two internal housing pieces assure effective trapping of any small fish.

To trap fish, a set of two, three or four *Nsiim* traps is buried under the local streams with the mouth or front of the trap facing the direction of the water current. As a rule, baby fish and other stream creatures love to travel in the opposite direction of the water current. Swimming against the water current enables the small fish and other water creatures to build energy that they need for their physical mobility. Normally the energy they exert tends to be greater than the velocity of the water current, thus allowing them to push themselves into the *Nsiim* traps. On a perfect and lucky day, that would amount to much needed catch for my labor.

In the days of my work with *Nsiim* fish traps, it was a normal routine for me to line the traps in the stream for twenty-four-hour periods before going to empty the catch. The catch usually consisted of *Ntok Iyak* (baby fish), *Mbe*, or *Mkpakwong* (tadpole), and *Isobo* (or crabs). It was usually such a joyous occasion for me to come home with so much catch of the morning, as it usually guaranteed the family would have enough small fish for their meal of the day. The amount of a day's catch usually depended on how many *Nsiim* traps I was able to set at a particular time.

I learned the technique of *Nsiim* fish trap construction and fishing methods from my mother's older brother, my uncle, the late Mr. Asuquo Effiong Uwah, who was always so good with using his hands. He used to also be so good at producing many different small hand instruments, including xylophones, sporting bows and arrows, and metalwork. Of particular interest to me were the musical xylophones that my uncle made using strings of bamboo rinds similar to those I employed in constructing *Nsiim* fish trap. It is so exciting trying to remember and write about something I used to do so many years ago without even thinking of its importance or impact on my life history. Like several of the experiences I have had to remember and recount, this has been one of the most difficult ones to articulate to the world. I thank my older sister Iquo Edet Essien very much for helping me to recall some of the names I had long ago cast away from my memory out of ignorance.

"Wet wood expedition" was another one of my usual work day activities in the village. Again, this was not a form of recreational activity whatsoever. The purpose of this wet wood expedition was to search the wet bushes for both ground- and wood-grown mushrooms or truffles to be used for food. During the wet wood expedition trips, it was the practice to spread out into different sections of the woods, competing with each other to see who would be the first person to find or discover the mushrooms or truffles. The one who would find and pick the largest amount of mushrooms would be crowned the hero or heroine of the day and become the pride of the family.

There were three types of natural mushrooms and truffles we used to pick during the expedition trips. They are *Udip* (umbrella-shaped ground-grown mushrooms), *Mkpi-Ifia* (also ground-grown thin sized and dryer mushrooms or truffles) and *Anwai* (primarily wood-grown smaller forms of truffles). *Anwai* grows on wet woods after the woods might have been bombarded by rain and left to soak extensively over a period of time. It is fair to say that most of the types of mushrooms and truffles described here may no longer be growing in the bushes around my village of Ifa Ikot Idang, due to the fact that the better parts of the woods have now been cleared for new buildings in the name of progress. I can now speculate that even my people may very well be buying expensive mushrooms or truffles from distant places where they are mass-grown on farms. The bottom line is that we were depending on mother nature to grow these food products for us, and this may no longer be occurring. Even my people, out of necessity, must now learn the techniques of growing mushrooms and truffles, something that used to be left to mother nature.

This particular activity of wet wood expedition usually involved going with a group of friends who made it a point of duty to wake up early in the morning to trek into the bushes in search of mushrooms. Like most of my wood activities, wet-wood survival was not a favorite of mine, mainly because it was never a direct and focused activity. You needed to function as an investigator when navigating the bushes just to be able to go home with something in your hands. Sorry, but we never engaged the services of smart dogs. Knowing what I know now, it might have been a smart and helpful idea to employ smart dogs as the local hunters usually did to help them in tracking down animals.

Finding mushrooms and truffles that grew on soft woods or fertile ground was a very difficult thing to do as far as I was concerned. Not only was I not usually lucky enough to spot these food products in their natural habitat on the ground, it was a very tiring task, and it was risky for me as well. The risks came from the fact that my bare feet in those days, after being exposed to wet soil, mildew, and bushes with dangerous leaves, usually developed infectious boils and other wounds weeks or months later. Those painful, infectious blisters usually took weeks to heal. Of course, there were no formal approaches adopted to treat them, as usual, but it did not seem to matter to the villagers. The other thing was the lack of knowledge as to whether the picked mushrooms and truffles were safe for human consumption. Of course, nobody ever raised such a question then as no one would have been able to provide an answer. Fortunately for me, I did not fall victim to any unknown disease caused by mushrooms. Thank God I am here to write about it, after more than fifty years.

I also used to spend my home time helping my mother in the farms and doing nearly everything around the compound, including constructing the fence. It was quite common to work in small groups with my friends on small home projects like fixing the fence. As this story develops, you will have a much better feeling for how many different chores and activities I used to carry out during a given day. For example, there were days that I was preoccupied by net-weaving for my father or a neighbor. At other times it could be going to the farm to complete some work for mother.

There was simply no letting go of whatsoever I could lay my hands on in the name of chores. Even my net-weaving and farming activities became more intense, leading to other physical activities, including church-related activities. In regard to church-related activities, it was usually an unwritten rule that some of the church members had to learn to read the Efik/Ibibio language Bible, although there were no organized efforts to teach illiterate members how to read. Those who were able to read the Efik/Ibibio language Bible were expected to advance from there to take on more official responsibilities in the church. For better or for worse, and I think mostly for better, the King James Version of the Bible was probably the first English language Bible to be translated into the Efik language. Efik is the language of the Efik people; by the same token, Ibibio language is the language of Ibibio people. The two groups basically speak the same dialects and can understand each other perfectly well. That is why the two groups can read Efik language (or Efik/Ibibio) language Bible. The presence of the Efik Bible in the Apostolic church might have single-handedly forced some of the church members to learn how to read and write, even in the absence of any structure within the church to formally teach people to read and write. The very lack of any formal structure allowed many church members to avoid the often embarrassing tasks of learning to read and write at an older age. So, you can imagine how much of a "survival of the fittest" situation it must have been for many, including myself.

In the course of completing this story for publication, I was lucky to meet and discuss this subject of educational neglect within the Apostolic Church with one of the church officials who was visiting the United States of America. It was his opinion that the church did not overtly encourage children's education in those days largely because of ignorance and unarticulated fears that educated members of the church tend to challenge the elite church leaders. He stated that the Apostolic Church in the Akwa Ibom State of Nigeria has suffered greatly as a result of this problem, adding strongly that our people needed to be educated to the highest level possible if they were to play more meaningful roles in running the church and in evangelization activities.

Of course, I know well not to blame the church alone for what I went through. From the family point of view, knowing how to read and write was not a priority of my father, who preferred to take me fishing with him on the Atlantic ocean than send me to school inland. It was also not a priority of my mother, who was getting her own share of my services through the farm work that I used to perform for her. Certainly, teaching me to read and write was not a priority of the church, either; however, if I could read the Bible, then I would be "called to order," and my mother in particular would be very proud of me. It is, ironically, interesting to note that the history of Nigerian education cannot be complete without mentioning the role of churches. It was the church that first opened schools in different parts of colonial Nigeria. It was the church that first started the spiraling process of educating Nigerian children long before the government thought it necessary to set up schools for its citizens. It was many years after Nigerian independence in 1960, after running government-operated schools side by side with church schools, that the Nigerian military government issued an edict in the mid-1980s that there should be no more church-run schools in the country.

The so-called government takeover of schools in Nigeria was

one of the profound acts of the Nigerian military government during the middle of the 1980s. The question that follows the government action is whether the government takeover and running of church schools has had any positive impact on Nigerian education. I am sure there will be different opinions on that issue. It can be argued that, based on recently reported practices and the current state of educational progress in Nigeria, there are no reliable examples of educational achievements for which the government should be commended. On the contrary, a true statement would be to say that high-achieving Nigerian students learn more through their self-motivation rather than through the direct influence of the country's infrastructure or the school system.

The Nigerian government takeover of church-run schools occurred several years after I was already in the USA. For that reason, one might wonder why this action should be relevant to my story. The relevance of the takeover action is derived from the prominent role the church played in educating Nigerian children during the early colonial and postcolonial periods. It would appear as if the church's function in educating Nigerian children has been overshadowed by recent events and the fact that the Nigerian government tried and succeeded in playing down the church's direct contributions to the development of the Nigerian educational system. It is, therefore, clear that role conflicts between the church and the state eventually resulted in the government take-over of the schools. In fact, when referring to church-run schools, we are really talking about the Catholic Church in Nigeria, followed by other churches such as the Anglican, Methodist, and the Apostolic churches.

The irony of church versus government educational approaches comes from the fact that, though churches were taking the lead in children's basic education during my time in Nigeria, I was not one of the lucky ones to share in the cake, even though I was a church-going child. It was only certain individuals who usually talked to me or to my parents about school. It was a struggle of a different kind for me and those around me, being a faithful member of the Apostolic Church and resisting being blindly drafted into "shepherdship," as was always the case in those days. Of course I am not trying to blame any single entity that might have accounted for my fateful beginnings. I am only trying to describe those entities, including my parents and the church, who remained in their respective comfort zones while children like myself grew and suffered in the stream of illiteracy. It has now become clear I was a young person growing up in an environment in which the adults were only concerned with advancing their own causes—be they religion, fishing, or farming. In the environment that I am describing here, the fate and the future of the children's education were in God's hands. Although I was so young, I do not recall any official of the church making the case for parents to send their children to school. By the same token, I do not remember hearing an official of the government or of the town calling on parents to enroll their children in school. Parents who might have been told to do so were afraid of the high cost of supplies and fees they could not afford. In those days I can imagine the cost would not exceed five dollars, which they did not have.

ENCOUNTER WITH THE NIGHT OWLS

This story of my encounter with the Night Owls dates back to the early days of my growing up and socializing in the village of Ifa Ikot Idang in Eastern Nigeria, more than fifty years ago. In those days, children's minds, including my mind, were routinely imbedded or saturated with many horror stories and anecdotes, stories of ghosts, devils, witchcraft, and other abnormal practices and occurrences that were meant to induce fear and scare in children, especially whenever they misbehaved. Indeed, the horror story was more horrifying and frightening when the story of the Night Owls manifested itself to me, at about the age of thirteen, and I came face-to-face with it in a real, traumatic way. This was the one frightening incident I have decided to describe as "Encounter with the Night Owls." This has become one of the many traumatic episodes of my life that continues to remain so prominent among many others in my mind. The episode of encountering the Night Owls was the scariest one to me due to the fact that the Night Owls were considered so powerful as they ruled the nights with their demonic humming sounds all over the villages. Children were usually told by the adults that Night Owls could capture and kill those who crossed their paths. Hence, no one dared to go outside at certain hours of the night when the owls were making their rounds.

Although I was aware of these many scary stories in the village as a youngster, I was never prepared to come across the actual nocturnal bodies face to face in my lifetime. After all, it was never explained to me that some of these nocturnal scary activities were actually carried out by human beings. It was on that fateful night, at about the age of thirteen, that I was out there with my brother-in-law, Mr. Edet Ekpo Udoh, who was then most likely in his late twenties, when the incident occurred.

The entire incident marked a critically high point halfway to the end of an expedition that began unceremoniously early in the day in the village of Ifa Ikot Idang, Etoi, Uyo, Nigeria. Being an obedient young man, and in keeping with unwritten rule of those days, no one expected me to question the intent of or resent an order to participate in a family-related project no matter the potential risks. It was simply the way it used to be. My brother-in-law and I had started out in the early hours of the morning trekking bare footed a distance of approximately five miles down to the undeveloped port of Nna-Enin. Although it was damp and cool that spring morning, we did not have to worry about the tropical weather condition as the average temperature could not fall below seventy degrees Fahrenheit. Upon arrival at the location, we carefully but rapidly descended the steep, dangerous, and merciless Nna-Enin hill down to the shore where canoes were anchored. We then rented a tiny paddle canoe about fifteen feet long, four feet wide, and three feet deep. We then set sail on the narrow creek. At my age, I did not really know much about the techniques of canoe navigation on narrow creeks, so I deferred to my brother-in-law Edet Ekpo Udoh.

We paddled the tiny canoe through the creeks into the woody and mangrove/raffia swamps on a family supply mission, with the goal of obtaining palm raffia leaf thatching materials to be used for roofing and roof repair back in the village. Due to its tendency to leak during heavy rainfalls, thatched-roofing presented an insurmountable problem to home owners in my village, requiring more routine repairs or replacement. Unfortunately however, obtaining the roofing materials for either repair or replacement purposes always presented enormous problems to poor family home owners and builders. Little wonder why thatched roofing is now being faced-out in many villages and towns in Nigeria.

We might have spent as much time rowing the canoe to the swampy worksite as it took us to trek from home to the undeveloped port. We probably spent not less than three hours in the swampy woods cutting the raffia and bamboo materials, trimming and gathering them into bunches for eventual transportation home. We were really cutting it close to the end of the day, even though we were considerably removed from any inland contact with other human beings. With all probability, we might have seen and listened to the growls of more wild animals on this trip than anyone could ever imagine. We ended up returning to the shore late in the evening.

One would conclude we had suffered enough after starting out on the arduous tasks of paddling the tiny canoe via the deep creeks to the swampy worksite. The canoe in question measured approximately fifteen feet long, four feet wide, and three feet deep. One would have seriously assessed the futility and the ramifications of taking on so many risky tasks in one day and the wrong time. Indeed, in normal circumstances, one would have, or should have, called the activities to a halt as the night was fast approaching, however, this was not a normal event occurring in a normal circumstance. Calling off the event for the reason cited was not an option.

We had worked all day trampling the muddy swamps, cutting and collecting the raffia palm leaves with our bare hands, tying them each into large bunches of about eighteen inches in diameter (each bunch weighing about fifteen pounds), loading about four of the bunches back on the tiny canoe, and rowing back to the shore with the utmost care that the canoe did not take on water or capsize.

Instead of ending the activities after arriving back to the shore, we embarked on the task of unloading and storing the raffia bunches on the highland above the shore in preparation to trek home in the dark. Without any doubt, this would present a series of very daunting challenges to us. Of course, these were the challenges we had to face head-on without regard to the possible consequences. We had to face and overcome the challenges because as we were unloading the bunches of our bamboo raffia thatching material we did not have any plan to camp out there on the Nna-Enin shore and most likely share the environment with some animals, including the most friendly rabbit and, perhaps, the most unfriendly tiger, not to speak of snakes. We did not even have any food with us. This is the reason why the decision to trek back home in the middle of the night superseded any other consideration. The need to get back home could never have been stronger, no matter what might happen on the way—which of course we could not predict.

The daunting task of unloading our supplies and starting the trek home was related to the topography of the Nna-Enin shore. The shore of the Nna-Enin creek lay at the bottom of the steep Nna-Enin hills with a series of unpaved and very rough layers of steps. This was one of the reasons why many local fishermen would avoid setting sails by way of Nna-Enin shores. They would rather travel the longer distances to the ports of Ifiayong in the north or port of Ishiet in the south. Compared, however, to the very risky canoe travel to the mangrove swamps that we undertook over the crocodile-infested creek waters and the constant attacks by ticks and other blood-sucking insects, taking the bold steps to walk home, even in the dead of the night, could not be any worse, at least perceptually and practically. Without a doubt, however, walking upland out of the valley of Nna-Enin shore would eventually present an untold amount of hurdles that would involve a more physically laborious climbing of the high hills and their accompanying ridges, with their very delicate natural steps. I sometimes wonder how strong the forces were that broke open the earth to create these natural ridges and crummy hills.

As I am now recounting the episode of this fateful night, it occurs to me after these many years that we had it over our head to engage in such a high risk venture. However, I recall also that it was the urgent desire to get home and rest our body that became extremely paramount in our mind as we embarked on walking home that night. It was, certainly, a dangerous decision that would eventually drive us to the brink of our demise. Oh yes, it was not so much the fear of the risky physical invasion of the mangrove swamps and climbing of the hills that mattered so much or which might have forced us to postpone the risky venture on that 1958 night of unpredictable destiny. Indeed, this was not the time to worry about the powers of nature or the powers of evil. It was the motivation and the high need to return home to rest our bodies that drove our determination to embark on the late night trek home. Of course, it was the end of a day's work that left us tired and worn out. We had no choice but to trek home for good, and trek home we had to, even with all the uncertainties as we would later find out. Safety on the way home was not to be guaranteed. By its very design, or the lack of it, the decision to trek home at night was ill-conceived and could have become fatal due to the unforeseen encounter with the Night Owls who controlled the woody trails of the villages and their surroundings.

The encounter was preceded by a series of screams from at least two members of the group of men assembled on the village square as my brother in-law and I were approaching from opposite side of the road. We could hear the loud screams in Ibibio language trying to find out who we were. The shouting voices (in Ibibio language) took the following form: "Afo Nie? Afo-Nie? Afo-Nie"? Who are you? Who are you? Who are you? "Se-mi! Se-mi! Semi! Look-here! Look-here! Look-hear!

These words were the shouting and screaming voices of the Night Owls (in their Ibibio native tongues) alarmingly crying out and howling at what was most likely an appearance of victims falling into their nightly dragnets. The apparent potential victims having been two innocent and exhausted passers-by on what was supposedly a public strip of road deep in the Village of Ekim-Enen near the Village of Ikot Otonyie, barely ten miles from the Cross River basin off the Atlantic Ocean gulf coast of Eastern Nigeria. As you can tell from the screaming sounds, directed with broken utterances at a very high pitch, we, the two innocent passers-by, were about to tip-toe or stumble into a dangerously unfamiliar territory, an assembly of secret group of village night operators gathered on a village square surrounded by bushy savannah and ghost-harboring trees to plot their evil operational activities. Unfortunately and unknowingly, we may have been innocently risking our lives, even though we believed that we were merely walking through a village roadway as we were anxious to get home that night.

Trying to recall an incident that took place more than fifty years ago is a very painful and difficult task to me as it was full of horror on that near-fateful night. To the extent that we thought we were safe and secure in our bodies on the road, this safety and security momentarily disappeared from us as we heard the loud voices and howls of *"Afo-nie, Afo-nie, Afo-nie"* ordering us to stop and identify ourselves in the middle of the night. My brother in-law, Edet Ekpo Udoh, and I came face to face with the Night Owls and we knew not what would happen next.

As you could tell from their screams and howling after they spotted us walking down the roadway to pass through their meeting place, these nocturnal men who parade the villages to carry out their evil deeds were so angry we had interrupted their assembly. They were about six in the group, and we could not clearly see their faces as it was dark. They had to decide whether to kill or not to kill us. What a question! What a decision! We thought we would never see light of day again!

Luckily for us, and in the precious name of Jesus as my brother-in-law pronounced it in the face of apparent terror, having confronted us and threatened us with death, having deliberated our fate among themselves by addressing the question "to kill or not to kill the intruders," and having verified from us that we were total strangers from another village, the Night Owls quickly bestowed mercy on us. They decided to let us go, but with an instruction that we should not tell anybody about what had happened that night. They told us sternly to proceed to our village destination and never, never, look behind to see them, and also, upon our arrival back in our village, never to tell any body about the incident. Of course, we proceeded to our village without turning to look behind us as instructed, except for one thing: the story of this incident was meant to be told sooner or later.

This incident took place in the middle of the night when the villagers were well in their homes sleeping, or at least should have been well into their night sleep and dreaming. The actual time of the incident could have been ten PM, eleven PM, or midnight, but no one knew or cared to know, because knowing the time of day or night in those days was not routinely expected and did not really matter. Personally I was too young to give a damn, too young and too weak to even assert any measure of self defense if it were necessary. Some might even say I was too naïve to get their "grip." Indeed, I must have been too exhausted and upset that I was not on my mother's mudbed sleeping at this time of night as children my age would and should have been expected to do. Of course, why should knowing the time of night matter? After all, what really mattered was the fact that it was dark—very dark and scary. The environment and the location were just ripe and perfect for the operation of the Night Owls. The opportunity for them to execute their wrath, maybe even to kill or maim, was never to be challenged by anyone, especially anyone who was not a member of the secret club or gangsters, here referred to as the Night Owls. For the uninitiated and innocent night trekkers passing through what could have been a gang or witchcraft-reinforced village square, what mattered most was not the late night with its trembles and formidable scare. What mattered was the urgent need to trek home after a long day's labor in the swamps of Nna-Enin creeks—creeks stretching several miles, criss-crossing the swampy woods of most wilderness into the great horizon and the tributaries of the Cross River of Eastern Nigeria.

A few weeks after we had been back to our village, I personally returned to the Village of Ekim Enen in daylight, somewhat in defiance of their order but more so to fulfill my curiosity. I did not think they would even know who I was other than the fact that I could have been an ordinary guest from the next village. So, I went and told a friend in that same village of Ekim-Enen about the frightening experience. I wanted him to tell me what was going on there. I had known this friend sometime during a fishing trip with my father, and I trusted him to know what was going on in his village. This friend then attempted to inquire around to determine if such an active group existed there. He came up with nothing to satisfy my curiosity. I was not given any explanation except to be told we should avoid making such late night trips through the area in the future. How different were these lines from those of the Night Owls? Probably not much different. I would love to say nothing in this experience surprised me, but I would also add there were many things in the environment of the village in which I grew up that I did not fully understand.

Based on the nuances and beliefs of the local villagers, the Night Owls are gravely feared by everybody, especially the village women, due to the Night Owls perceived ability to travel in the invisible world of the village and penetrate homes and take advantage of helpless and innocent women. If this sounds to you like a fairy tale, then you are probably not a Nigerian or an African who knows this to be true. The rumor has it the Night Owls possess imaginary powers to invade women's privacies without the women knowing who they are. In the local villages it was, and may still be, common to hear women use the word "*Uben*" to describe what can only be characterized here as psychological rape of these women by the evil men of the Night Owls. I describe it as "psychological rape" due to the lack of verifiable physical evidence of the act and since no victim would agree to testify in public. *"Uben"* is the most common word used by the village women who suspect that they have been raped or violated by men they do not know—most probably the Night Owls. These allegations are usually referred to as "truth without believers" because of the fact that most of the neighbors would rather ridicule these women for publicly speaking about incidents that are supposed to be kept secret. For this reason, no one would demand proof. One thing that is for sure, however, is the Night Owls are not known for being afraid to kill, if and when they are confronted by their enemies or people who are likely to identify them in public. It does not matter how the killing takes place. It could be done physically by direct confrontation or through the power of the spirit carried out in the invisible world. In either case, there may not be any sustainable proof of the act in the context of the village.

Knowing what we know now, no one would have any right to demand evidence or the truth of what the Night Owls could have done to me and my brother in-law on that near-fateful night. In the event that we were killed, it would have been the end of the story for us and our families. Thank God almighty that all that I now have to prove is a full description of the incident—how it happened and how it ended—to the best of my memory nearly fifty years later. I must admit, however, that having to be alive to complete a narrative of the experience of encountering the Night Owls surely feels like I have been awakened from death, as the incident was so scary and hopeless.

Coming face to face with them as they met to work out their strategies for invading the villages was to them an unlawful act on our part, mostly due to the fear and the possibility of identifying them to the public. Confronting these evil men, however, and even trying to identify them in the public may be considered a suicidal act and are not things that anyone would wish to undertake, especially if you are in your right mental condition. This group of village men can be brutal in their act. The Night Owls are also feared by the villagers for their invisible powers to fly or hop around from place to place—from one thatched roof to another thatched roof—inflicting punishment on their perceived enemies and those who they would love to suppress or see dead. Because of their constant screeching and humming sounds that were meant to intimidate innocent villagers as they travel around at night, the Night Owls are usually identified by their characteristic embodiment of the bat during the day. Yes, the bat seen in the day is an omen conceptually representing a bad luck or impending disaster—especially if they fly into your space—because of its perceived close association with the Night Owls or evil spirits, which are usually not visible due to their generally perceived and accepted supernatural powers.

These are but partial descriptions of the Night Owls. By their nature and character, the Night Owls can only be compared to the lion in search of food (a victim) in the wilds, and its food or victim is always another animal. Unfortunately, the Night Owls share the same space as every one else in the village, and that is where the danger lies. How do we know who is who among the villagers? During my early days children were bombarded with horror stories of the reign of witchcraft in the nooks and crannies of the villages.

Up to the present time, it is not uncommon to come across stories of blood sucking juju and psychological mutilation being circulated around by words of mouth from one to another in most villages and towns occupied by the black race, stretching from Africa to the Caribbean. The horror stories manifest themselves from time to time, similar to episode of the encounter with the Night Owls. The situation gets worst because of long-lasting belief systems and anticipation of evil things. Even fatal motor accidents that might have been caused by careless or drunken drivers have been blamed on witchcraft. In my hometown there were also stories of those who possess imaginary powers to invoke energies from the people with whom they either quarreled or wished to use for sacrifice on behalf of group members such as the Night Owls. As they progress, these horror stories normally take a life of their own, especially in areas where poverty and ignorance are rampant. As a result, one may not know whom to believe and there is no need to dispute their claims, since you may never win.

Suffice it to say, however, that this group of evil doers, whom I have described as Night Owls, are among those low lifers who have contributed little or nothing to the development of our homelands. This group of people is generally suspected for practicing questionable behavior and terrorizing neighborhoods during the nighttime when others are sleeping. They derive their energies from the fear they have engendered among the people who in turn help to spread the horror stories that make them feel more invincible. Villagers wishing to stand up against them or tackle their growing terrorizing of innocent villagers needed to adopt one or two forms of antidotes: The first was deploying the power of the native doctor who knows all the tricks employed by the Night Owls to terrorize their victims. The second antidote was having a very strong spiritual power to drive them away in the name of God.

Unfortunately, either of the two antidotes have their inherent pit-falls. First of all, seeking the services of native doctors can be very risky in terms of its costs as well as rampant deception. Second, some proclaimed spiritual powers can be quite self-fulfilling if care is not taken.

My experience with some ordained church ministers and evangelists, including the Apostolic Church I attended, revealed some confusion at best, and disappointment in the worse cases. Apparently, some of our ordained church ministers believe our local community is dominated by individuals who practice witchcraft and possess imaginary powers to take lives at will. Theoretically, therefore, an ordained minister must develop spiritual power that can equal or supersede the witchcraft. In the opinion of these ordained ministers, nothing else—not even an accident — can cause death other than the evil doers in the community or the family. This sort of belief system continues to dominate the philosophical make-up of these ordained ministers resulting in serious conflicts with some of the church ministers at home and abroad. Most of my people, to this day, still believe that before any serious family or personal disaster occurs to you, there must be an underlying cause related to witchcraft or enemies. Usually these persistent belief systems justify doing all kinds of unusual rituals to fight against perceived enemies. From what I have heard and seen so far in my lifetime, this is the dominant belief of my people at home and in the Diaspora.

Due to the difficulty of explaining the function of evil doers, I must admit my brief reflection of our belief system here probably does not shed sufficient light into our understanding of how the Night Owls operate. However, I want my reader to understand that it is not the so-called imaginary power that the Night Owls possess that strengthens them; it is their plans and practices that make the people afraid and, therefore, weaken their minds and make them live in fear. Evil doers like the Night Owls secretly inflict physical harm on people and then claim to have done it through imaginary powers. In the case of our encounter with the Night Owls, as I have narrated, the important thing for us to rejoice about is that we were not killed, or I would not be writing this story now. In retrospect, despite the extreme danger of traveling on a tiny canoe measuring fifteen feet long by four feet wide by three feet deep on a danger-ous narrow creek, and despite undertaking the difficult trekking home which nearly ended our lives, this trip would turn out to be the most memorable experience I would have had with my first brother in-law, Mr. Edet Ekpo Udoh, who died just about eighteen years following the incident of our encounter with the Night Owls. May his soul continue to rest in perfect peace.

As the then husband of my older sister, Iquo Edet Essien, Edet Ekpo Udoh was such a nice family and religious person who would never leave any stone unturned in getting things done for the fami-ly and his church, the Apostolic Church. At his death he left three handsome boys, Ita, John, and Samuel (Ubon) Edet Ekpo, and one beautiful daughter, Mercy Ekpo Essien, all of whom have grown up to be their own successful family people. In fact, it is hard to recall any subsequent memorable interaction between me and Edet Ekpo Udoh after the episode of encounter with the Night Owls which took place in my formative and very innocent years. I actually left the village of Ifa Ikot Idang for Lagos just about one year follow-ing the incident. Finally, the encounter with the Night Owls episode will remain as one of the many narrow escape stories of my life for which I remain forever grateful to God.

REFLECTING ON MY EARLY LEARNING

I consider the task of describing my irregular learning processes to be an awesome—as well as rewarding—responsibility. It is a rewarding responsibility in the sense that I am overjoyed in the opportunity to articulate the distance over which I have traveled in the one-man race of my self-education. This process, however, which I would also characterize as learning by curiosity, is at the heart of my learning foundation during my early days of growing up in the village. It is, therefore, very important for me to present it in the clearest possible way. I want to begin by describing the arduous and very informal processes that became my learning routines in those early days. Again, it is more appropriate to begin defining what I mean by learning by curiosity. Learning by curiosity is my way of describing the type of informal learning that typically took place in my early life day in and day out whenever I was involved in activities of daily living, including recreation and house chores. This sort of learning, it seems to me, takes place sometimes consciously and sometimes unconsciously, without any formal instruction from any source to the child. Learning by curiosity is not a phenomenon that is almost always instantly visible or observable; however, it is always present mentally or otherwise with the exposure of the child to different experiences and different settings, whether or not the exposure is negative or positive.

The manifestation of learning by curiosity is inherently at work when the child (or any individual) is physically and mentally struggling to learn new concepts, ideas, or techniques, while trying to adjust to new and sometimes hostile conditions. This is what I believe could have happened to me throughout my childhood growing up in the village. I am also quite convinced (now) that this is what happened to me during most of my growing up. I have considered it an obligation for me to reflect on this subject covering both the village and the mangrove swamps, reserving the right to speculate only to the best of my ability and what my memory allows.

I remember how often I used to be curious and would grapple with new concepts and new ideas that, in some cases, nearly drove me insane. There were many things that made no sense to me whatsoever, and no one was there to explain them to me. The children of my age group in the village were usually my sounding board of sorts, but they were not usually as helpful as I would have liked. Sometimes they would use certain English words in my presence and I would feel ashamed to ask them what the words meant. By interacting with them, however, I would eventually figure out the meanings. The same was the case with learning the English alphabet (A to Z). Where help or support was non-existent, it was natural to turn to my internal stimuli and rote response. When all is said and done, the question remains unanswered: What was this all about, what went on here, and why?

During my growing up years, I came in contact with many things or experiences, some of which I could not fully understand but I still had to deal with them the best way I could and move on. I am certain that this is how I might have propelled or wrangle-up my learning faculty in preparation for my social growth and development, although I still have the nagging question to ask: Could growth and development be separated from learning? I think I have the answer, without regard to what the psychologists think. I do not believe that growth, development, and learning are separate phenomena, whether learning is formal or informal. I want to conclude that my level of maturity had a significant impact on my learning processes. More importantly, and on a very positive note, my curiosity to learn grew with my age and my cognitive mapping ability. These learning curiosity and cognitive mapping faculty combined to prepare me for further learning in my later life.

I find myself in need of an authority to support my contention that there is no such thing as the period of growing up that can be completely separate from the period of learning. Personally, I see the two phenomena as going or existing side by side, whether psychologists agree with me or not. According to Piaget's theory, a child's growth and development occur through a gradual process whereby the child experiences his or her environment by reflecting on the cognitive structures or cognitive maps. It appears each stage represents pieces of the maps and they are all interrelated. These maps or structures undergo expansion whenever the child encounters a new experience, also known as "alteration of cognitive structures." This is the phenomenon educators generally describe as learning, using other explanatory concepts such as stimulus response, behavior modification, or operant conditioning.

Again, from this brief description of Piaget's theory, it appears that exposure plays a critical role in children's learning processes since their brains tend to magnetize and store whatever comes in contact with their developing brains. For this reason, it is extremely important that children be exposed to a properly structured environment, or they might end up learning the wrong things as they grow up. But what happens in family settings where the environmental structure is lacking? The answer is obvious.

I am referring to Piaget's theory of intellectual development, strictly, to support my very strong belief that growing up and learning go hand-in-hand, at least when the learning environment is well-structured for the benefit of the child. Of course it is imperative that children learn something as they grow up. The real question is "exactly what are they learning?" What are the subject matters that come in contact with their cognitive structures or maps and force them to expand, to follow Piaget's logic? We need to understand that it is the ingredients of these "subject matters" that would create lasting impressions on the children's brains or "cognitive structures" to cause them to behave one way or the other. For example, time and time again, it has been shown that children who grow up in an environment of abuse, hate, and torture, will inevitably exhibit similar behaviors in later life. Those who grow up learning to read and write eventually end up demonstrating the ability to read and write effectively. This ability might even translate into effective reasoning and problem-solving abilities as children progress through different stages of their lives. Still, those children who grow up listening to religious stories and observing personal and community development stories, in addition to being exposed to random acts of godly behavior, may also grow up learning and practicing such behaviors. I hope these many examples of children's learning help in explaining my own learning process, except that I have to do more to illustrate my own very irregular learning while growing up in Nigeria.

Indeed, my story of combating, or facing the challenge of, the curiosity to learn is completely different from all of the above-narrated circumstances that impact children's learning. I hate to describe my learning process, after fifty-five years, as not necessarily "combating curiosity" but as a process of "mortal combat" or battle to the finish. This is because, although the pedagogical expectations of civilized societies are for children to grow up learning to read and write, this was not the case in my growing up period in the village of Ifa Ikot Idang. The only available opportunity for me was limited to that of my learning how to weave and mend fishing nets for my father and be the support to my mother in clearing farmlands for her to plant crops. Those were the skills I was supposed to learn. There is no doubt I learned those skills and used them well, too.

Now that I am in a position to write about these experiences, I feel really thrilled about it. It thrills me in the sense that I feel like I am writing an observation of a typical situation of a family in need of redirection and assistance. It thrills me because as I am writing these things, I am sometimes amused, even though there was nothing amusing about the type of work activity in which I was routinely involved. As described here, even when a little sense of humor might be necessary to enable me to more effectively tolerate the stress and pains of the memories, even the angels would not be laughing. I am attempting to sketch a picture or a story of a very tragic, traumatic, and very painful experience for me.

For whatever reason, I do not even know why I grew up with the curiosity and zeal to learn and to be educated. Of course these could have all been a matter of happenstance and not necessarily of any miracles. But I will leave you, the reader, to make that determination as to whether it was a miracle or otherwise. One thing is for sure: my curiosity to learn—and the almighty God—

saw me through.

To begin with, the environment for my learning was not there, although my older brother, Offiong Edet Essien, had to create it for me somewhat unknowingly. Secondly, the resources for my learning or education were not there, especially where resources would refer to learning materials, equipment, and a support system. Again, for some reason, these resources had to be improvised. By using my recently acquired knowledge of curriculum development, I can now comfortably describe those improvised resources to include the support and encouragement of people around me who cared and showed interest in my "perceived home schooling." I use the term "perceived home schooling" simply to distinguish my experience from the type of home schooling that is structured.

With reference to informal support system that became my "learning objective," I remember many times when some well-meaning villagers such as teachers would stop me and quiz me on some academic subject they thought I knew. In turn, they would talk about the other kids in the village who showed no interest in learning the alphabet, usually pointing to me as the example of what those neighborhood kids should be like. Of particular significance in the village was my most respected role model, an educated man we used to call Ette Sam Akpan. Ette Sam was one person in the village who made it his duty to remind me to learn the alphabet. He did not succeed in getting my parents to take me to school, but he was so devoted in recognizing my learning curiosity and potential. I used to feel so good about that.

Ette Sam was a well respected man who used to repair the roads in the village. He had several children of his own that he sent to school and many of them completed high school—known as college then in Colonial Nigeria. Among his children who went to school were the late Mr. Bassey Sam Akpan, a former school principal; the late Mr. Ita Sam Akpan, a former Controller of Nigeria's Central Bank; the late Mma Arit Sam Akpan, a former school principal; the late Mandu Sam Akpan, a former seamstress; Mr. William Sam Akpan, and the late Okon Sam Akpan, a former school teacher. Those of Ette Sam's kids who did not attend school include Mr. Edem Sam Akpan and the late Mr. Effiong Sam Akpan. Ette Sam Akpan, died in the late 1980s at about the age of seventy. May his soul and those of his precious children mentioned above rest in perfect peace!

Among other people in and around the village who played a role directly or indirectly in my irregular learning was my brother-in-law, the late Mr. Edet Ekpo Udoh, who married my older sister Iquo Edet Essien around 1956 and from then became my closest friend and mentor. Although he had a minimal education, he was able to read and write and, therefore, usually encouraged me to do the same, especially in the Apostolic Church where he was an Elder while my sister functioned as *Eka Iban* (or Church Matron). My association with my brother-in-law, Edet Ekpo Udoh, will not be easily forgotten. Edet Ekpo, as we used to call him, was a very hard working and positive family man who would do whatever it took to help the family and his church community. As alluded to before, not only did he have a very strong influence on my desire to learn how to read and write, mainly as a result of having to watch him read and write the Efik/Ibibio language both at home and in the church, he usually engaged me in carrying out important family work activities. Mr. Edet Ekpo Udoh died in 1975, long after I came to the

USA. May his soul rest in perfect peace. More details of my association with Edet Ekpo Udoh are covered in a previous section dealing with "Encounter with the Night Owls."

Other significant people in the village who were part of my support system included the late Mr. Edem Okon Inyang, a former Methodist Church pastor who used to write letters for my mother—and greatly influenced my writing style as I usually try to write exactly like he did; the school boys of the village who usually shared their daily class lessons with me—as I became fond of imitating them during our social interactions; and several perfect strangers in various fishing ports who took it upon themselves to confront father and tried to convince him to take me back home and send me to school. I did not know the true meaning of the phrase, "guardian angels," until now that I am recounting these stories. These people were my guardian angels, as they were unrelenting in reminding my father to send me to school, without ever getting father to respond accordingly.

These perfect strangers were usually Kalabaris and Ogonies of the Rivers State who were themselves fishermen just like my father was, but they always interrupted their activities just to have a few words with my father regarding the need to send me to school at home. My father never heeded any of their suggestions, leaving a more wider room for me to battle with my curiosity or cognitive schemata. This was purely a combat with and by myself, since I did not even have anybody with whom to battle or share my frustration.

Just to put things in perspective, I have a great deal of difficulty remembering the age at which my father started teaching me how to mend fishing nets or when he started taking me to the fishing ports. I would imagine I was ten years of age, but I remember these events vividly to my utter dismay. Suffice it to say, however, that extreme curiosity or "cognitive combat" became an ongoing battle for me both on and offshore. Throughout this period of my growing up and being bumped around from all angles, I cannot recall any formally organized effort to help me receive formal educational instruction or anything that would have been directed toward helping me grow intellectually, with the exception of those times that my older brother began teaching me the alphabet. He taught me the basics of combining these letters to spell Efik/Ibibio words. I was on my own the rest of the way. I remember so many periods of battles and struggles, most of which were frustrating and hopeless, but I always tried to build upon prior successes. I was always looking forward to the next challenge.

Now that I have the opportunity to write about these experiences, I am wondering exactly what it was that enabled me to keep my eyes on the goal line, an imaginary place of knowledge that is pursued by many but arrived at by a few lucky ones on earth. In many cases, even my effort to learn to read and write, among my peers in the village, was nothing really to be taken seriously. In some cases, I might have felt like impersonating a few of the smart students and teachers I knew, even though there was no realistic way to identify what it would take for me to truly demonstrate, in the interim, the observable outcome of my curiosity and internal desire to learn. Indeed, the grounds and the distances that I covered along the way of my irregular learning process are, perhaps, the only tools available for use by the inquiring minds' assessment and analysis. My own learning curiosity was one that simply had no plans, no navigational tools, no time frames, no schedules, no commitment, no methods, and no support. This has been a very phenomenal journey for me, one that combined with many other factors to make me a whole human being. My curiosity and my maturation laid a strong foundation for my subsequent intellectual development and accomplishment.

CHAPTER 3

FARMING, FISHING, AND THE GOAL

The King James Version of the book of Matthew 19:19, states: "Honour thy father and thy mother, and Thou shalt love thy neighbor as thyself." As a person who strongly believes in and practiced this biblical tenet, I have chosen to devote this chapter to the detailed description of all of the farming and fishing work activities which I carried out as a youngster on behalf of my parents. In my early days, I always considered it to be an obligation to serve my parents as they demanded of me, more often than not, as a sign of ultimate respect for them. The first part of my discussions will deal with my work on mother's farm. After fully discussing that, I will continue on to narrate my fishing work activities on behalf of my dear father. That will be followed by a personal trip into the unwritten and unspecified goal that became my guiding light toward self-discovery. May the souls of my parents continue to rest in perfect peace, as they are all gone to their eternal rest, leaving me and my siblings with more questions than answers. Indeed, despite how readers would perceive or interpret my stories reflecting my relationship with mother and father, I have nothing but the deepest love and respect for them. This is because they brought me into this world; without them, I would not have been here in the first place.

My parents deserve all the honors from me, and I know they could vouch for me on the subject of respect, if they were alive today. After all, I am the only son who used to prepare my father's meals in the remote fishing port during our usual fishing trips. It was from him that I learned, early on, that it is important to prepare all food items in the most careful and hygienic way. I grew up to emulate him on his insistence on being served proper (balanced) food always, even though I would not join him to attend the Methodist Church of Ifa Atai. By the same token, I have always had problems skirting my mother's religious devotions at the Apostolic Church of Ifa Ikot Idang, even though I carefully avoided placing myself in a position to be groomed and called to ordination as a pastor, something she would have loved dearly. The work of serving my parents might have been hard many times, but I could not have done it without the benefit of their love and care. May their souls rest in peace!

My village work experiences should more appropriately be described as the initiation into parental youth service, simply due to the age at which I began engaging in those services and by the amount and nature of work involved. Of course this sort of characterization of the overall experience is designed primarily to drive the story's focus to the reader. In other words, this is strictly an attempt to probe into and discuss the heretofore unexplored and unchartered aspect of my cultural milieu.

I said "heretofore unexplored and uncharted" because no one in my family or extended family network has ever attempted to articulate any such family history that sought to investigate, unravel, or explain the roles or actions of our parents in our individual upbringing within the village. This does not mean, however, that there is any written rule of conduct prohibiting anyone from openly discussing such issues; it is simply the fact that no one expected this to be done, especially when it comes to discussing parental actions and behaviors. In keeping with our own tradition and respect, I hereby appeal for the indulgence of my ancestors, my peers, and other group members who are likely to disapprove of my actions in this writing.

In our God-given tradition, we were brought up to respect our parents and follow the Ten Commandment principle to "honor your father and your mother." The effect of this has been the tendency to obscure the importance of helping children understand roles that our parents played in our lives, especially in children's early lives such as mine and those of my siblings. To the best of my recollection of the prevailing cultural practices of my village and the surroundings, the biblical concept of "honor your father and mother" was used as parental entitlement and dominion over children and there was no quid pro quo or give and take. This meant children were not entitled to a reasonable portion of the "meat" or the "salmon" at supper time, until the adults were done eating and were fully satisfied. It also meant that if a child disobeyed any adult, including the parents, the child had to be punished for the behavior, and that was the end of that.

In many ways, my parents were not the "whip-happy" types. This is to say they were not in the business of physically punishing their children for misbehavior. I can still recall, after these many years, how my parents struggled so hard to avoid becoming caught up in what used to be the behavior patterns of the community elites.

They each had their own needs and would devise different approaches to meet those needs, be they in the farm or at the fishing port. I feel the responsibility now to deal with this and other family nuances in a very critical and delicate way so that I have to ask for the support of my people and beg the indulgence of my friends as I undertake this very unpleasant task. My obligation here is to try to shed some light onto my parents' collective and individual roles in my growing up and socialization.

In completing this narrative, I will describe my role as the principal farm worker for my mother's family farming projects in the village and my adaptation to fishing at an early age under the guidance and directorship of my father. As the story unfolds, it will become obvious that I was the single most important instrument of family economy to my parents, even when they both hardly saw eye to eye in those days. Another angle of interest in the story will be a narrative of my unspoken ability to suppress the pressure generated from all forms of parent-induced obligatory work activities in order to tackle my childhood's irregular learning needs—a phenomenon which I have characterized as "cognitive battle" in another chapter of the book.

Finally, in view of all of the obstacles along the way of my growth and development, especially the lack of structure, the constant struggles to physically adjust to the conditions of working on the farmlands and in the fishing port, I have always wondered how it could have been possible for me to keep my eyes on the goal. That is to say that it had to be something other than my physical energy and my sub-consciousness that enabled me to maintain my very undiminished desire to learn to read and write, in addition to having to search for my individual identity and self dignity. This is the phenomenon of keeping my eyes on the goal, in the face of a near total state of hopelessness and despair.

One thing to keep in mind is the fact that what I have described in this book about my learning is not a function of any formal goal plan, even though it might appear as if I were following a written plan to arrive at a designated goal line. Quite on the contrary, this was a situation of which I was never aware or conscious. For example, even when I might not have loved what was going on with me while working either with mother in the village or with father in the fishing port, I was not in any position to clearly express my desires or my needs, except having certain feelings from time to time, feelings that might be engendered by certain impulses that I could not even express. Not even the patterns of my experiences could be explained by anyone.

So the question, therefore, is what were the indicators of my intellectual focus and what happened with all that pain, suffering, ignorance and idiosyncrasy? Did anybody even care about what was going on with the young Bassey Essien then? Did anybody even know something was going on? Why or why not? These are important questions, and I will do my best along the way to address them and tell the story as openly and fully as I can remember.

WORKING ON MOTHER'S FARM

I must appeal to the reader once again to please bear with me as I will not, and may not, be able to cite specific dates or years when certain activities started. Suffice it to say, though, the activities being cited here took place anywhere between 1953 and 1959. I can also state that these activities totally shaped my childhood and

Author's mother, Madam Arit Effiong Udoh

would most likely lead me to the promised land, if I may describe it as such. In fairness to myself, these could very well have been the "denied" rather than the "promised" lands, but I will leave you to judge them for yourself. I will start with a short reflection of my farming experience.

The age-old statement that "experience is the best teacher" is, perhaps, the greatest truth that ties this story together. In fact, one could argue that some experiences teach better than others. The basic difference might be whether the experiences were negative or positive, and the question then might have to do with the type of tools that were deployed in the processes of gaining the experiences. On that note, let me ask this question: Would the experience of using a machete or paddling a canoe allow one to acquire any knowledge? The answer, of course, is yes, and why not? Canoe paddling and active use of machetes to cut trees and clear farmlands were some of the major work activities which called for skills development and which I learned and became competent at a very young age.

In the mangrove swamps, it was also a normal routine to deploy an axe to chop the hard mangrove woods either for construction work or for firewood in the remote muddy huts in which we lived. In fact, I remember usually wondering why the mangrove trees would burn so quickly since it was usually the main firewood that was used to make the fire for drying fish. Indeed, mangrove trees burn as they do because these trees grow on the swamps that are full of natural crude oil deposits which have been, and continue to be, explored by oil companies in West Africa. Even though the experiences I obtained by using machetes, axes, and other local tools were more physical than they were academic in nature, they combined to make me mentally and emotionally stronger and determined to hang in there and do what I had to do to survive.

It is fair to say that many times I did not really know what I was doing at my age, whether I was just surviving or enduring stress. In any case, what a pain would it have been if I had ever known what to expect in my future life. I might have totally lost control, especially when time would seem to go nowhere, days and nights would seem to be the longest, and the end was nowhere near. Of course I will provide more details about canoe paddling in the section describing my fishing work. In this section I want to concentrate more on the use of machetes to clear bushes for my mother for planting and to generally obtain all forms of family supplies, including fire wood, fencing trees, and the feeds for the goats.

It is not possible for me to describe the principal manufacturer or supplier of machetes or axes in Colonial Nigeria. I can say some were locally made and most of them were imported from England and Germany. However, these are work tools you would have no problem buying in the local market stalls. It is important to know that these hand tools are made of steel and have very sharp edges that are designed to cut through woods when inflicted with a force. That is what makes their use extremely dangerous, especially when used by inexperienced personnel or young children. As far as I can remember, there were no organized safety instructions for using these tools. Once you had one in your possession, you were left to devise your own technique for using it and no more questions were asked.

There is at least one other important farming tool I need to describe here for the benefit of the reader: It is the hand hoe, normally used by women in clearing weeds and digging the holes for planting crops, especially cassava and cocoyam. From time immemorial, the people of my village have deployed machetes, hand axes, and hand hoes in all of their farm work. As far as I know, this situation remains the same to this day. In using the hand hoe for their work, the women usually form their own alliances or work groups (*Ewana*) to carry on their weeding and planting work, similar to the way that the boys would do. My older sister, Iquo Essien, used to organize her own farm club with her girlfriends for the purpose of clearing weeds on our mother's farms. The usual mode of day-end feasting remained the same as that of the boys.

Unlike the men who would religiously retreat from the farm to return to the fishing ports after the seasonal clearing of the farmlands, the women usually bore the brunt of the farm work from the planting time to harvest. Generally, the entire process of completing the farm work in my village was not significantly different from one family to another.

The process of my involvement in working on mother's farmland was as primitive and physical as anyone could imagine. For that reason presenting a detailed description of the experience is not the most comfortable and joyful exercise to me. However, this was the way the job was done, since no one could clear the land without using a machete. This was indeed my life and the story must now be told to the world. It took the use of a "sharpened" machete in those days for the job to be done. By the same token, it is now taking the use of a "sharpened" pencil, a regular pen and a computer keyboard, to make the strokes that describe a machete for the story to be told. With my sharpened machete—usually at the onset of the farming season, I would go into the section of the woods, clearly identified as belonging to my mother, to start my work of farmland clearing. I would make it a point of duty to join with two or three of my friends to assist me in clearing the farmland. In turn I would join these friends to clear their own parents' farmlands. Although I knew nothing of the seven principles of Kwanzaa in those days, it has now become clear to me that what I was doing with my young friends to help my mother was our own way of practicing two of the seven principles: Ujamaa (creative work and responsibility) and Ujima (cooperative economics).

For convenience of description and reference, I can now use the term "farm club" (or *ewana*) to refer to this form of association that we used to put together as young boys. The routine usually involved getting together in small groups, usually three or four boys, starting early in the morning. Sometimes there could be one, two, or three acres of farmland to be cleared. It might take one, two, or three days to complete the initial clearing work. The level of clearing difficulty would usually depend on the age of the bushes and the sizes of the woods to be cut and trimmed down along the way.

During the process of wood clearing, we were not only facing the arduous task of cutting down several woods; we were also facing a very high risk of sustaining serious injuries from misused machetes, from falling trees, or from missing steps while climbing on the trees to trim down the branches. In addition to these risk factors, there were wild snakes in those woods waiting to prey on our flesh the moment we interfered with their habitat. My own injuries were always accidental machete cuts. Those injuries used to come to me frequently that I sometimes thought the end of my world had come.

In many cases when our wood clearing assignments were completed and the injuries kept to a minimum, it was the tradition of the families involved to make a feast for farm club members by having mothers prepare elaborate foods, usually fufu and meat or fish soup, so that we would eat jointly at the end of the day's hard work. Fufu is probably the most popular among Nigerian, if not Africa's, staple foods. It is made of gari (or cassava), yamflower, riceflower, semolina cream of wheat, or cornmeal. To prepare fufu, approximately one pound of the preferred powder is poured into twenty-four ounces of boiling water and stirred repeatedly until a dough is formed. Actual consumption of fufu is carried out by scooping little portions of the fufu into sizable balls and dipping the balls in a very spicy soup before swallowing as needed or until one feels satisfied. From what I have described above there is no doubt regarding the fact that parents were pleased with us after the day's work, and they usually tried to show their pleasure by providing the best and most elaborate food for consumption at the end the day. Such treatment goes to show parents' appreciation for the work of the farm club members.

At other times, when I was not clearing a farmland, I would take my machete and go into the woods to cut assorted kinds of leaves into fodder for the goats to feed. It is nearly impossible for me to give the specific English names of the tropical leaves used for goat feeding; but our goats used to love no less than ten different types of leaves, known locally in the Efik and Ibibio languages as *Ikim Ebot* or the "goats' feeding." Among the most popular names of *Ikim Ebot* I used to cut were *Mbit Item, Ntabit, Edemedong, Ekon-Ikon, Akpap, Mboom, Ata-Obom-Okpo, and Ata-Aman-Uman.* Our goats also usually enjoyed helping themselves as often as possible to those food items that are the favorites of humans. Such food items include spinach, fluted pumpkin leaves *(Ikong Ubong)*, plantain plant leaves

(Mfang Ukom), palm tree leaves *(Ndak Eyop)*, and the cassava leaves (*Mfanglwa*). The problem came when humans would not generously share these favorite leaves with the animals; consequently, the animals would usually find their way to make use of these leaves when the humans were not paying attention.

Whenever I am not on farmland clearing or goat-feed gathering, I usually took my machete into the woods to cut small trees into six to eight feet long by one to one and a half inches in diameter for the purpose of building fences around my mother's house. Building or repairing fences around the house was one of the most common routine duties of mine in the village, but these activities came with a heavy price on my part. Not only was I overworking my childhood at this time, I was also routinely sustaining serious physical injuries and pains. I can now acknowledge the fact that the machete was not a user-friendly tool as far as I was concerned. And yet, we in the farm club used to compete against each other by seeking to show who had the best and sharpest machete in the village. I do not recall anytime anyone of us bragged about who knew the best and safest ways to use the tool. In many cases, the best machete was most likely the sharpest machete, and it usually would be the most likely one to inflict the worst injuries on its owner, when misused. With a machete, the user could sustain a cut either through careless use or by accident.

When it comes to the danger of using a machete as a tool for clearing the bushes, my experience was, perhaps, one of the worst that I would long live to remember. Sustaining machete cuts actually became a routine occurrence with me in the village over the years, For example, I sustained serious machete cuts to various parts of my body, including my head, hands, legs, and toes, as a result of carelessness or improper use of the tool. As far as I can remember, I was never attended to by a doctor or a qualified nurse. Instead, my mother usually employed hot water to clean me up and apply locally prescribed folk medicines. Mother also used to pray a lot, placing God as her first order physician. My machete cuts usually occurred while I was in the process of cutting and trimming trees to clear the woods and bushy lands for my mother to start planting. My wounds were usually bad and painful as I often bled profusely, and would take long to heal. Just the fact that I am writing this from direct personal experience makes me feel somewhat funny and stupid that I suffered through this sort of dangerous injury without receiving any medical intervention. But that is the way it was in those days.

I used to injure myself often so badly and without any particular medical attention. Instead of seeking medical care and helping me to learn prevention exercises or first aid, the villagers would engage in wild speculations as to the causes of my constant self-injuries with the machete. In fact, at the height of my self-injuries, close friends and relatives began to advise my mother to prepare for sacrificial rites for me as a way of curing me of whatever demons might have taken over my body leading me to destruction. As luck would have it, my mother refused to go along with the idea while praying to God for help. Believe it or not, wild speculations in my place of birth continue to this day. As far as my people are concerned, there is no way an accident can happen as a result of carelessness. There must be an invisible hand in control. You dare not argue this point.

As far as I was concerned, no one could put a finger on what exactly my problem was, but all the activities in which I got involved and the nature of my injuries only helped those who believed that I was possessed by the devil. Take, for example, another incident that could very well have been my final bout with life-threatening dangers in the village. I believe this particular incident occurred either in late 1958 or early 1959—not long before I finally left the village for Lagos. It was during one of those survival runs I made into an old section of our family farms that we used to call *Ndo-ohn* in the Ibibio language. *Ndo-ohn* is a term with a very deep meaning that describes acres of a family farm that are no longer being planted but to which you can pay a visit to obtain certain personal needs, such as fruits, vegetables and leaves. The closest word to describe *Ndo-ohn* is homestead.

On this final act, I went to *Ndo-ohn* and climbed a 50-foot tall coconut tree to pluck some coconuts for family consumption. Upon reaching the top and getting set to begin shaking down individual coconuts from their bunches, I met with a group of bee hives. Immediately, at about a count of three, the bees began attacking and stinging me profusely. In an attempt to escape from the danger, boy oh boy, I quickly found my way back down the coconut tree's trunk by sliding down at a very high speed. Upon landing on the ground, it became obvious that I had scraped my chest area so badly and the scratch wounds were bleeding. In addition, I was feeling severe pains from the bee stings. I was so happy I did not fall from that tall coconut tree to my death. The pains of the bee stings subsided after a week or two. It took a little longer for my scraped chest to heal as well. By our own standard of thinking and judgment, this was just one of those incidents that we did not expect to cause an alarm in the village. I personally received no medical attention whatsoever.

Sadly enough, those youths who die of similar incidents are quickly forgotten because life goes on, and perhaps no one knew what to do. One such youth, Akpan Aseri, as we used to call him, was Sarah's first son and my very close friend. He and I were climbing up a plum tree in the village to pluck the plum fruits. As we were climbing, we were both trying to show how low we could go down the tree branches together to demonstrate our weightlessness, with little or no concern about the danger involved. Unfortunately, the main tree branch on which we rested was not strong enough to hold both of us safely; it broke and instantly sent us to the ground where we belonged. Luckily for me, I was only slightly injured. My friend suffered a dislocated lower back, and we were taken to the nearest stream, *Idim Enang-Onwong,* where we were immersed in the stream for many minutes as first aid. Akpan Aseri eventually died a couple of years later. Of course, I was never told the cause of death. May his soul rest in perfect peace.

Again, it is the type of incidents that I have described here which tended to provide strong evidence to the villagers to support their wild speculations about reasons and causes of injuries. Unfortunately, because their established reasons were based on speculations rather than logical investigations, they usually failed to institute the best and reliable approaches needed to ensure personal safety in the future. As far as they were concerned, these were not ordinary occurrences; there had to be some invisible force that possessed or controlled me, thus leading to these dangers. One thing that has baffled me about my people in my life history has been their ability to identify the alleged evil root causes of people's problems, especially disasters, instead of assessing real causes and effects to arrive at a workable solution. As I have already mentioned, the reasoning behind my mother's shaky decision to seek the attention of a native doctor to perform a sacrificial rite for me actually began with rumors that there were some evil hands involved in my self-injurious behavior. Eventually, the rumors became direct "hush, hush, hush" exchanges of words among villagers. Finally, before we knew it, a native doctor was called in to prescribe things to buy for the ceremonial rites. In my village in those days, rumors usually wasted no time before taking a life of their own, especially when they were carefully generated by those who claimed to be friends of my family or significant others who thought that they had the answers to my problems. It appears this was, at least, the only way that I could be "loved to death" by my people. Unfortunately, however, I managed to survive not only the pains and suffering from my constant injuries but also the pressure of the villagers to deliver me to the whims of the native doctors.

In my place of birth it was, and may still be, traditionally more convenient to seek imaginary solutions to personal or physical problems than to realistically confront the problem and apply the obvious scientific or workable solutions. The usual solutions to problems in the village in those days, and perhaps to this day, was to perform certain traditional rites to the ghosts or the demons that were allegedly causing me these physical problems. Such rites usually involved having a native doctor or a herbalist prescribe things, such as goats, fowls, local palm wine, local "hot" drinks (spirits), black pepper, kolanut, and other food items to be used for sacrifice. Do not ask me why so many spicy food items are always associated with the traditional rites; it must be due to their tastes. Apparently, evil ghosts love tasty and spicy food items. In any case, upon receiving these items, the herbalist or "native doctor" would then prepare the material for the final ceremony to the "gods." In the end, the child for whom the ceremony was performed was given certain rules of conduct to observe and the "bizarre" behaviors and self-injuries were supposed to subside. This used to be the customary way families in my village and surrounding areas were expected to respond to the problems of their children in those days, and it might still be the same way to this day.

In my case, while sympathizing with my parents for the pressure they endured from the villagers, I am pleased and grateful to my mother who did not allow this ceremony to be performed on me, thanks to her religious faith. Although she allowed the invisible hand theory and belief to dominate the village discussions about me for quite sometime, as a member of the Apostolic Church who had a very strong faith in God, my mother was not completely convinced that performing the prescribed rites could cure the problems of my self injuries. My self-injuries continued until I left the village for Lagos in 1959. I still have many scars on different parts of my body, a living reminder of my rough childhood working for mother on the farm.

WORKING AS FATHER'S
FISHING CREW

As alluded to at the beginning of this chapter, I want to admit right off the bat that most of what I have written in this memoir about my parents have probably portrayed them in more negative light than they have been positive. However, whatever is the tone of my story regarding my childhood experiences should not take away the respect and high regards that I have had for my parents. This

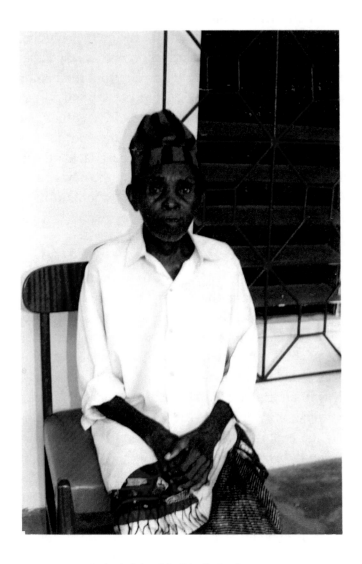

Author's father, Mr. Edet Essien Asuquo

is fundamentally due to those values we learned by observation and imitation. We observed in our villages, in the churches, and in the fishing port environment that a child had to respect and honor his or her parents. That is the way it was from the beginning and continues to be to the end of time. The other point I like to make is that I have always been extremely considerate of my parents. As a result, I have never rejoiced in taking any shot at them in the sense of trying to blame them for my past lack of educational opportunity or anything of the sort. Indeed, the news could not get any better in this regard; I do not recall ever committing any serious infraction or violation deserving of my parents serious spanking or suspension.

For better or for worse, there appeared to have existed between me and my parents an unwritten code of trust, even awe. You could smell these phenomena in the air; you could see them on the land; certainly, you could feel them on the sea. This sort of phenomenal parent/child relationship could have been due to the fact that I was an obedient child. Of course, they were loving parents as well, except they found themselves struggling to understand and identify themselves in an era that left no room for such self-understanding and identification. These are the reasons why this self-imposed writing assignment is very painful and agonizing to me. I know that having said all this, you are then wondering why I have written all that I have written about my experiences serving my mother on the farm and serving my father as a fisherman, navigating the mangrove swamps and canoe-paddling on the Atlantic Ocean. My explanation or contention is that my parents knew not what they were doing and, therefore, they should not be blamed, considering the times and the environment in which they lived.

If they ever knew what they were doing or should have done, they could not afford it, considering what their priorities of the day might have been. In fact, if anything is to be said about their actions after these many years, my parents should be praised for their good deeds by their love and care for me and all my brothers and sisters. And yes, there are those of us in the family who may never forgive my parents for what they perceived to have been our parental faults, but I am not one of them. My role and tasks right now are to tell the story—and the story must be told both for posterity and for the benefit of future generations.

Just as I have stated in other sections of the book, it is not quite clear what year my father started me out in his fishing business. I would estimate somewhere around 1955 when I must have been ten years old. You might be amused to note that, in this particular sphere of experiences from where I am drawing my memories to write this story, it was not considered important to know what year or month of year it was as I was growing up. If such knowledge and awareness were important I did not know, since I was never told. The important thing to do to please father was for me to do, simply, as I was told and provide a service in support of his dreams. It was not even important that I met some of my personal needs such as having some clothing or shoes to wear.

With specific reference to clothing, the favorite types for kids my age, including myself, in those days were open-armed cotton undershirts, locally called "singlet" but known in the USA as "tank-top" for the body and "loincloths" for wrapping from the waist down. Youngsters my age who were ever given these clothing items by their parents were usually as happy as typical youngsters today who are taken by their parents to visit a fast food restaurant or a video game store. Sorry, but I was never one of the lucky ones to be treated in like manner. Needless to say I did not demand ordinary underwear as that could have been a luxury item. I do not remember ever wearing shoes, until around the time that I had to join my brother Offiong in Lagos and that was in 1959. I can not even recall what brand my first pair of shoes was. I grew up to know of only Bata Shoes in Lagos. In my village, the nearest things to shoes that I knew were only those play slippers we used to manufacture using the raw materials *Owong Okokok*, fetched from bamboo palm branches. When properly constructed, the handmade native slippers could last a few days to one week. This was my world, the world of building and molding things that I needed to sustain my life.

It is hard to imagine how my strength and ability to perform rigorous tasks were assessed before I was drafted into the fishing profession. I guess someone looked at me and determined that I exhibited some ability to work on the farm for my mother. This inevitably led to the "logical" conclusion that I was also strong enough to work as a fisherman. Consideration of my mental strength and psychological development was not part of the equation. The story of my fishing experiences with my father, and the theatres of these experiences, constitute the title plot for this book. This is due to the risk levels involved in the execution of the principal functions of the jobs in which I was involved. For example, as dangerous as my farm work activities were, my fishing experiences might have been the most risky for my age. Consider the danger of exploring the wild mangrove swamps and plowing the deep creeks, rivers, and the giant Atlantic Ocean. I was thrown into these activities without any form of protective gear or life jacket. Wearing something like life jackets was not a thing of concern for our fishermen, and no one talked about it. The same was the case with learning to swim. Despite spending so much time on the great seas and rivers, I was never seriously taught how to swim in case I was thrown overboard or the canoe either capsized or engulfed by high waves. There is no doubt I am grateful to God that none of that happened. The one time I tried learning to swim in the deep creek of Inua Abasi, I was so afraid I never tried again, and neither my father nor anyone else ever again tried to get me to learn to swim or show me he could swim himself.

From time to time I usually observed some brave fishermen practicing how to swim in the creeks during rising tides, but this was never done seriously as a safety precaution. The same was the case with regards to maintenance of the wooden huts in which the fishermen resided, especially in the swampy areas. Inua Abasi and Inneh Mbak were quite vulnerable to the rising sea tides of the Atlantic. The situation used to be more dangerous during periods of heavy rain falls and storm winds and might even have resulted in the loss of lives. During extreme weather conditions, the wooden structures usually could not withstand the pressures from winds and rip currents. This meant that some of the wooden cottage structures could only be useful for a few years as the occupants would have to move inland and set up new wooden huts, but it was never my experience that the fishermen who occupied the huts of these Atlantic coastal swamps were terribly bothered about their safety for any reason.

When it comes to my father, I grew up to finally learn the meaning of the phrase "tunnel vision," the art of making sure that you see only the things that you wish to see and nothing else. That is the kind of ability my father had as he focused his attention only on those things I could do to enhance his financial gains through the fishing business. We never had time to practice swimming, anyway, which is another way of saying we did not even have time to die, even if our boat were to capsize or fill with water, as it usually happens during bad storms.

My fishing experiences with my father were very risky because fishing usually took place on canoes rowed over creeks and the Atlantic Ocean. At the onset of the fishing trip, the crew would row or paddle the canoe on the creek to the wild, remote, mangrove swamps, carefully secure the canoe onto a strong tree on the bank of the river, and descend bare-foot into the muddy swamps. The aim of this swampy mangrove invasion was to gather supplies to be used at the fishing port of temporary settlement. The specific material supplies gathered included firewood for cooking and drying of the fish, raffia palm thatches for building the cottages where the fishermen would reside, and various forms of natural fiber ropes for use by the fishermen onsite. On many occasions, I can remember some of the wood logs I was required to carry on my shoulder and walk the mud to the canoe loading dock on the creek. These were routine tasks that were to be performed. In most cases, the mangrove swamps lacked adequate foot paths for walking and, many times, it was necessary to improvise temporary footpaths for the day, usually by employing tree logs. Foot injuries were quite common and workers were on their own if they ever got injured because there was no formal treatment or medicine. Routine knife, machete, and broken-bottle cuts were considered to be normal parts of the job.

Because I was just so young, my father started me out by having me spend time mending fishing nets or weaving new ones to supplement those he would buy from the inland stores. The bulk of the nets, especially the longest machine-woven line of nets that were named "Yoruba," could only be purchased from the stores in Oron (Akwa Ibom State) or Aba (Abia State). During fishing expeditions, those nets were notorious for getting entangled with dangerous items on the Atlantic Ocean, such as fishing poles abandoned by other fishermen, floating timbers, rocks and sunken boats. When that happened, you would either lose the whole line of nets or you would have to engage in major mending work that could take weeks to complete. In such cases, a group of net- menders who were mostly canoe-boys (crewmembers) would be deployed to do the job. In very isolated cases, the job might be subcontracted to outside net-menders for a fee. Net- mending involved running the cotton threads through carved tiny wooden hand tools and repeatedly directing these hand tools through angles of the nets and stitching the nets in an effort to return them to the original shapes. Both at home and in the fisheries, I was widely acclaimed as child net repairer or net mender for my father. I worked on nets for the first one or two years, until I was transitioned into a full-fledged *Eyen Ubom*, literally meaning "canoe boy" or servant of the boat.

My activities of mending the net and assisting in the canoe during fishing expeditions on the Atlantic did not in any way interfere with another one of my fundamental functions on behalf of my father while we were in the fishing ports. This was the job of cooking for him. During fishing trips that would last three to four months, one of my jobs was cooking for my father. The basic tasks involved two main steps. The first was preparing soup, usually using fresh fish, palm oil, and many other food preparation ingredients. The second step was fixing the fufu made of either gari or the cassava dough that might have been brought from home on the trip. The process of eating fufu involves first making small balls of the dough and dipping them into a specially made soup and swallowing until full. The soup is made of fish or meat with a variety of good tasting condiments and vegetables.

I like to briefly explain that food preparation was, and may still remain, a principal part of caring for the heads or owners of the fishing teams during fishing trips. In situations in which a typical fishing team owner had neither a son nor a wife on board, he would normally designate a trusted crew member to handle his food preparation. Throughout the years that I traveled with my father on those trips, he never took along any of his three wives as did some of his friends I knew. It never occurred to me to ask him why. One thing I also remember vividly about my father, in connection with his eating habits, was that he was very particular about the way his food was prepared and served to him. He very much cared about food handling and the way the food was presented to him. It had to be neat and appetizing or he would not eat it. He was a very proud man when it came to his food, and I remain grateful to him for the lessons I learned from serving him in this aspect.

As stated before, my father started taking me to the fishing port of *Inua Abasi*, just beside *Inneh Mbak* off the coast of Nigeria, a short distance to the Cameroons on the Gulf of Guinea (see the map). The year could have been either 1954 or 1955. A few years after repeated trips to Inua Abasi we migrated to the coast of Uben-Ekang, which is part of the Cameroons. The reason why we migrat-

 ed to Uben-Ekang was because father upgraded his choice of fishing net to the one known as Yoruba. I will discuss that in detail later in this chapter. Whereas Uben-Ekang was sandy and dry and was pleasantly occupied by many Cameroonian and Nigerian petty traders as well as fishermen, Inua Abasi and Inneh Mbak were the most muddy fishing ports, and had no petty traders residing there-in for extended periods of time. They were no where near comparison with Uben-Ekang where the bamboo thatched cottages were in much better conditions than they were in Inneh Mbak and Inua Abasi. Inneh Mbak, particularly, was more exposed to the coastal winds and ocean waves, whereas Innua Abasi had a small creek that somewhat enclosed it from the coastal winds and ocean waves. Cottages in Inneh Mbak and Innua Abasi were mostly made of wooden structures reinforced with bamboo ropes, locally called *Iditt*, and roofed with bamboo thatch obtained from bamboo and palm trees of the swampy mangrove creek areas. Again, I will provide more details of Uben-Ekang later in this chapter when I am discussing the operation of the Yoruba fishing nets. When all is said and done, you will find that Uben-Ekang could very well qualify as the center of fishermen's renaissance or rebirth.

I am now going to make the effort of describing the different groups of fishermen. There were mainly four types of fishermen who occupied Inua Abasi and Inneh Mbak. Their specializations were usually determined by the design of their nets or fishing equipment. Included among them were the group using the net called *Eworiwo,* which specialized in catching bunga fish (scads). This is the fish with the two-sided flat body shells and sharp-edged stomach. The other one was the group using the *Umia Mmong* fishing net, which specialized in catching mainly the catfish and a host of other types of fish. Still, the other was the group that uses *Uwam* (anglers), which concentrated on catching catfish (locally called *Akpakot* and *Inaha*) and many other kinds of fish as well. The last, not the least, of the four groups was the Ibeno group who employed an extended net hoist to trap crayfish, as will be described in later part of this section.

There was a fifth group of fishermen whose specialization was determined by the design of their net as well as the location of their fishing port. This group was known as the *Yoruba* group, made famous by their ability to employ the longest line of nets for trapping the largest number of scads, referred to by the local fishermen as bunga fish or *Ibat*. The Yoruba fishing groups could only set up their operational centers in Uben-Ekang, because of land and space accessibility. For their respective fishing expeditions, each of the different groups basically explored the gulf section of the Atlantic Ocean (see map of Gulf of Guinea), even though each group lived on different coastal areas of the gulf. Each of them employed different method to cast its nets into the sea for maximum catch possible. For example, the *Eworiwo* group would go after the bunga fish, *Ibat,* The fishermen usually cast their nets into the Atlantic Ocean or the tributaries and waited in the canoe for an extended period of time, between two and three hours, before recovering or pulling in the nets with the day's or night's catch.

Immediately as the canoe with the nets and the catch had landed on the shore, the next task was for the group of canoe boys to individually free the bunga fish from the nets before the fish would be scooped inland to be prepared for final drying or smoking. This could be done either as a professional with speed and accuracy, or as a learner in which case you had to learn the technique with great care. From my experience, freeing individual bunga fish from the net was particularly risky. I can recall sustaining numerous cuts to my palms on many occasions just trying to squeeze the flat and very sharp stomach of the bunga fish out of the nets. You definitely need not sympathize with the fish when squeezing them out of the tangled nets. As you can imagine, whenever I messed up and cut my palm, and then I mistakenly complained about it, the adults next to me would just scream at me and curse me out for being weak, timid, and stupid and would command me to continue working or I would find myself in the deep sea. This was a setting that demanded that one acts like a soldier, mature at all times, no matter what your age!

The *Umia Mmong* fishing group, by design and interest, would go after catfish, locally referred to as *Akpakot* or *Inagha.* This fish family has no shells in its body but has either a somewhat pointed mouth with hard-shelled head, with sharp spines on their upper backs and the lower left and right sides. *Akpakot* and *Inagha* constitute the most popular fish family sought after by the Umia Mmong group of fishermen. Traditionally, to prepare the fish for smoke-drying, about five of them are stitched to a hardwood stick, obtained from mangrove roots, and then two of the stitched bunches are tied together to make ten fish in each bunch. In order to dry them, about ten of the bunches are set up on the hardwood racks above heavy fire fueled by mangrove woods. It takes about six to twelve hours for the fish to be completely smoked dry before they are removed and stored at the top level of the racks, waiting to be shipped inland for eventual sale on a later date. Eventually they are shipped inland for sale to the local distributors who buy them and later sell to petty traders. Other fish usually caught by *Umia Mmong* fishermen include herrings, tilapia, blue fish, trout, salmon, mackerel, tiger fish, and corker fish. These are not always caught in large numbers as Umia Mmong fishing nets were not designed for them.

The *Umia Mmong* fishermen also caught shineer fish, yellow corker fish, sea bass, and saltwater sheaphead fish. *Umia Mmong* fishing involved repetitive casting of the nets into the sea and then conducting rigorous physical rumblings of the ocean around the net in the hope the noise level caused by the water rumblings would excite or wake-up the fish to swim against the sea currents in the direction of the net where they would eventually get caught.

Uwam fishermen also practiced casting their baited hooks onto the sea and waiting for hours before hauling their line into the canoe with whatever kind of fish was caught. This group of fishermen sometimes caught the biggest fish, such as the giant swordfish, or even whales. Whenever this happened they would choose either to drag the fish to the shore or cut-off the angle hooks line and let the fish go because of the danger it posed to the crew in the small, light canoe. This could be a life and death situation for the crewmen.

The Ibeno fishermen employed a fishing method that can be described simply as "crayfish scooping" or a fishing method using a very creatively designed oversized strainer in the form of a heavy duty net constructed or weaved with raffia fiber materials. The way it works is the operators would first build a set of heavy duty nets each in the shape of approximately a forty-gallon bag. The net is knitted with very tiny holes to prevent crayfish from escaping when trapped. The baggy-shaped crayfish scooper is then treaded into a wooden ring that measures approximately thirty-six inches in diameter to form a circular housing. The ring-shaped net is then attached to the thirty-six-inch section from the base of the hard wood pole (about two and a half to three inches in diameter and seventy feet long) obtained from the mangrove forest. This is now the fishing pole with the crayfish scooping basket.

For the purpose of going fishing, the operators would load twenty or more of the fishing poles on their canoe and physically paddle the boat carrying the poles to a strategic section of the Atlantic Ocean or its tributaries. As soon as the location of the sea is chosen, the fishing poles are individually lifted and installed in streamlines, making sure the opening side of the circular net is adjacent to (not directly facing) the direction of the sea currents. At the end of this process, a decision would have to be made either to wait a few hours for the catch or leave the poles overnight to return to shore and come back the next day to collect the catch. Like many of the fishing methods described here, this particular brand of fishing is very much involved and requires a lot of energy on the part of the crews. I do not have any direct knowledge as to the end result of all these fishing operations, in terms of their gains and losses. However, the basic method of gathering crayfish from the bottom of the sea and bringing the product inland for human consumption has not changed to this date, as far as I know.

The *Yoruba* groups were dubiously considered the "Kings And Rulers Of The Sea" when their fishing method was first introduced because of the sheer size and fish-trapping power of their nets. These nets were so long and expansive it usually took a group of no less than ten canoe boys to load the nets onto the canoe as well as to unload them. It normally would take just one captain standing up on the canoe to roll the extended` net into the sea while the rest of the crew members paddled the canoe around the ocean waves.

To complete the casting, the fishing net was laid in a circle of about one thousand yards in diameter to enclose the barn of bunga fish. This was immediately followed by rowing the canoe around the inside of the dragnet circle and then rumbling the middle sections of the sea repeatedly in an attempt to drive the fish to the net. The final step was hauling the *Yoruba* net back into the canoe. The hauling process involved all of the crewmen who had to work hand in hand pulling the heavy nets into the canoe from the sea. This became an arduous task, especially when the nets were full of fish and the sea was rough due to severe winds. Rough seas caused by storms have been known to present serious danger to the fishermen, who usually lacked ocean water emergency readiness, including routine swimming knowledge. One of the behavioral patterns of the fishermen of my time had been their whole sale lack of concern for safety and emergency preparedness.

The carefree attitudes of the fishermen and poor conditions of the living cottages came close to causing my death by a machete accident that nearly took my life during one of my fishing trips with my father either in the later part of 1957 or early part of 1958. The said accident was a rude awakening to me, judging from the depth and seriousness of the machete cut, which occurred in a makeshift wooden huts in which we lived after we migrated to the place at the tip of the Atlantic Gulf called Inneh

Edem Abasi or simply Edem Abasi. This spot is geographically located off the Atlantic coast—about sixty nautical miles west of Inua Abasi. I want to take a few minutes to describe the incident, to the best of what my memory will permit.

It was just a few weeks after father's fishing team settled in the fishing port of Inua Abasi to start fishing. It became obvious that the atmospheric outlook of Inua Abasi did not convince my father that we were going to have the amount of catch that would guarantee success at the end of the wet season fishing trip. For the purpose of clarity, "atmospheric outlook" refers to the routine calculations of the wind condition, the strength of water current, including even the texture of the ocean, and the estimated distances separating the fishing ports from the fish location or habitat at sea. With all probability, father could have also overheard some of his friends proclaiming more catch in places other than Inua Abasi. Being a very calculating fisherman that he was, father decided to implement his "Plan B" which was that of moving the team from Inua Abasi to a new and, supposedly, more viable location which was Inneh Edem Abasi.

Moving to Inneh Edem Abasi was an adventure that my father came up with in the hope of realizing his fishing dreams, except that he never anticipated the danger that was awaiting us there. To implement father's plan, we loaded the canoe with our belongings and set sail across the gulf to Inneh Edem Abasi, a place situated on mangrove wetlands covered by mangrove trees. We arrived at Inneh Edem Abasi and unloaded our belongings to stay in a makeshift hut that father rented from another fisherman. About two weeks after our arrival there, on that fateful day, the morning began just like one of those "normal" days of endless activities of getting up early in the morning from a sleeping situation that was usually more of a battle with mosquitoes and other dangerous insects from the swamps than actual restful sleep. We had prepared the fishing net bright and early as usual and set sail to the Atlantic Gulf of Guinea to start *Umia Mmong* fishing operation. The fishing activities at sea lasted approximately three hours and it was well into the early night when we landed back on the muddy shore of Inneh Edem Abasi with whatever was our catch of the day. It was another typically exhausting and tiring day and night which would have ended peacefully for me if only we were lodged in a safer cottage. But there was not going to be peace for me.

The temporary cottage in which we resided had a kind of sub-flooring that was made of unfinished woods, each piece of which measured approximately six to eight feet long and three to four inches in diameter. The wooden pieces were not properly secured or tightened to the pillars and crossbars. It was there, in the beginning of the night, right after we were back from the fishing expedition and I was extremely exhausted, that I accidentally slipped off the unsecured wooden hollow subflooring, directly brushing my right leg against a machete that was unintentionally left below the wobbling wooden floor. As a result, I sustained a bad cut the size of about two by three inches near the veins and bones by the left side of my right knee and I was bleeding so profusely with unbearable pain.

The only treatment I received from the people who were there was that they tied my right knee with some available rags in an attempt to stop the bleeding. I didn't receive any formal medical treatment as such care was not available in the first place. I am actually reluctant to use the word "tourniquet" to describe the procedure used in tying my right knee because I do not know if anyone in that group and place knew anything about such an emergency procedure. I personally knew nothing about tourniquets at that time of my life. Only a few years ago while in the USA that I came to learn about tourniquets in a first-aid class as a procedure that can be used to stop severe bleeding. As would be expected, I have not been able to stop myself from having flashbacks to the time of my severe cut and comparing my treatment to a tourniquet procedure. However, the important thing is that my wound had since healed, notwithstanding the very unconventional treatment that I received after returning home to my mother.

The cut I sustained to my right knee was so deep and painful I was no longer able to function independently. As a result, for the next two weeks or so, I was cared for by the wife of my father's friend from Ibeno, Mrs. Okon. I never asked or remember what her first name was. The wound was so deep such that many people were saying I could have bled to death if the main arteries adjoining my knees were severed. Also, knowing what I know now, I wonder how I survived the wound since I was never vaccinated against the deadly tetanus, a known infection that kills so many of my people even to this day.

Eventually, my father decided to take me back home after two weeks of unsuccessful treatment and after realizing I was no longer useful in doing my job in Inneh Edem Abasi. The trip across the Atlantic Gulf of Guinea took about twenty hours. Upon our arrival at Oron seaport, father put me on a lorry on the westward drive home. On the way, we stopped at the Methodist Hospital, Ituk Mbang, where I was taken out of the lorry and admitted for treatment, and my father continued on home to Ifa Ikot Idang to inform my mother about my accident. Until father actually had me admitted to the hospital while he continued home to inform my mother about my accident, neither my mother nor any other relative back home knew that I was seriously injured. This was due to a lack of means of faster communication in those days—and being in the mangrove swamps was as remote and as isolated as anyone could imagine.

Upon learning of my accident, mother was extremely upset. Consequently, she hired a bicyclist to transport her a distance of about five miles to come and see me at the hospital. It was obvious that her anger and sadness were overwhelming to her and myself as she sighted me in the hospital ward. Mother did not waste time deciding on the next action to take. Mother quickly set up to take me back home with her that evening by hiring one bicyclist for herself and another for me. To this day, I still cannot imagine what Mother said to the doctor or the staff of the Methodist Hospital to let them release me to her care that quickly that night. For one thing, my mother trusted God so much that, I am sure, she knew that God was going to heal the wound. That is how much my mother trusted the almighty God.

As a result of taking me home to Ifa Ikot Idang from the hospital, my mother assumed the sole responsibility of treating my wound by herself. She made it a point of duty to treat the wound with hot water every morning. Usually after using hot water to clean the open wound, she would then apply a natural substance, such as lime, to the wound's surface. Mother followed her procedures very carefully for a period of about one to two months until the wound eventually healed itself. Mother's treatment, having been administered with love and whatever substance she was able to obtain and apply to the wound, was all that I needed at that time.

I might also have needed to get away from the hostile environment of Inneh Edem Abasi.

When the wound healed, it left a three and a half by two inch scar on the lower left side of my right knee. This scar is still very much visible to this day; it remains another one of my notorious body marks or scars. Another old wound mark is located just about three inches above my right knee on the left side. This "V" shaped scar was caused by a burn that, I am told, I suffered from some hot tobacco pipe dust dropped on my right thigh by a pipe-smoking grandmother while I was crawling as a baby. Tobacco pipe or Eki-Ikong smoking was one of the unfortunate deadly habits of the elderly men and women of my village that I can recall. Sadly for me as a baby, I became a recipient of its unanticipated wrath and have to live with a permanent scar on my thigh. There are several other scars on different parts of my body, including my head, my arms, and my feet. Most of the wounds that left the scars on me came from machete cuts in the village, but there were those I sustained in Lagos from different incidents about which you can read in the chapter dealing with my Lagos experiences.

Although I did not benefit from any medical treatment from the Methodist Hospital at Ituk Mbang, I believe that father made the right decision to have me admitted there. This was the nearest hospital south of Ifa Ikot Idang on the way to Oron. The next hospital could have been St. Luke's Hospital which is located at Annua in Uyo City, about eight miles farther away than Methodist. I recall vaguely during my admission that there was no medical equipment at the Methodist Hospital and the buildings were in very poor shape. In fact, during my short visit to the hospital in the year 2007,

I observed that the hospital's physical condition remains the same to this day as it was 50 years ago. I would hope that, at some point, the Government of Akwa Ibom State of Nigeria will consider making positive improvements to the hospital for the benefit of the citizens of the state. The hospital could be a great asset to the people, especially since a new airport is being built within a few miles of the hospital.

The fact that I sustained a severe machete cut to the lower part of my right knee and suffered through the pain and fear of dying was not a sufficient reason, as would have been expected, for my father to stop taking me to the fishing ports. Even after all of the battles to keep me alive as a result of the accident in Inneh Edem Abasi, I was back on the canoe to the mangrove swamps again with father's canoe boys the very next season. By this time father had upgraded his fishing nets from *Eworiwo* to *Yoruba*, the so-called king of the fishing nets. This type of fishing nets was supposed to be the best in terms of its bunga fish catching power. For my father, this great expectation never materialized.

Again, due to demands of work space and convenience, the *Yoruba* fishing groups could only reside in Uben-Ekang, a peninsular fishing port which also functioned as a trading post located on the Atlantic coastal section of Cameroon. Unlike most other muddy mangrove swamps that I have already fully described, Uben-Ekang was the only sandy fishing port that could allow father's crew to handle and manipulate the very long *Yoruba* nets. So we had to load up the canoe, once again, with all our belongings and set sail to Uben-Ekang to set up for the brand new fishing challenge. Recall that it was the same father of mine who had the fishing team moved from Inua Abasi to Inneh Edem Abasi, a location where I nearly lost my life in a machete accident. With the move to Uben-Ekang which involved a total change of the line of fishing nets, I could not help but ask the question whether this new adventure into new territories was going to improve my father's lot in the fishing profession. Was there a room for him to come out at the top? The answer is flatly no. It was not good for my father, and it was not good for me, the son.

Moving to Uben-Ekang and starting out with a new line of fishing nets was indeed a great challenge because my father was never familiar with the technique of using this sort of fishing net before. He did not even have the personnel to do the job. Before departing for Uben-Ekang, he had to travel to different parts of the state, including the entire Ibibio land, Opobo, Eket, and Oron, to recruit for a captain to run the new fishing operation. Recruiting for canoe boys used to be a major part of the pre-fishing trip preparation. On the average, it was usually necessary to acquire no fewer than six canoe boys. For the giant *Yoruba* nets, it was better to have eight men on board in order to ensure adequate canoe rowing power and net handling. It was customary to make down payments to those men just to be assured of having enough canoe boys on board.

As a rule, upon returning home at the end of the fishing trip lasting three to four months, the canoe boys would have to be paid again, based on the profits made from selling the fish. If there were no significant gains, my father was not obligated to pay the canoe boys any additional money, and the canoe boys would not be very happy. If they were not happy, they would not be likely to make a repeat trip with father. My father used to suffer this phenomenon so often that he used to spend much time recruiting each year, because it was never possible for him to maintain continuity of crew members. This was one of the reasons why he would not let go of me, even for the reason of being enrolled in school, because I was considered an asset to father's fishing empire. Any talk of father taking me home to go to school was a form of foreign language to him and did not fit into his vocabulary or the scheme of his fishing operation.

Uben-Ekang is a sandy coastland, with a long creek that clears into the Atlantic Ocean, with the interior portion of the creek leading into the rear of the fishing port without penetrating the mainland. This, therefore, leaves a good section of the land of Uben-Ekang surrounded by water. The sandy beach section of the land faces the Atlantic Ocean and is considered to be its front. The far northeastern part of the Uben-Ekang coast leads to the Cameroonian port cities of Victoria (now known as Limbe), Tiko, and Douala. On clear and bright weather days, it was possible to stand on the Cameroonian coastland of Uben-Ekang and view the landscape of Spanish Island of Equatorial Guinea on the horizon across the Atlantic Ocean.

As an international open market for different people from both Nigeria and the Cameroons, and due to its geographical position and land formation, Uben-Ekang was a very convenient operational center for smugglers and petty traders. I can still recall seeing the Nigerian liquor smugglers crossing the Atlantic Gulf to and from the island of Fernando Poe in Equatorial Guinea. The boats used by the liquor smugglers also usually carried additional human cargoes for a fee in the persons of Nigerian laborers to Fernando Poe. Presumably, the practice of ferrying Nigerian laborers to what could have amounted to labor camps in Fernando Poe might have been stopped by the mass repatriation of the poor Nigerian laborers back to Nigeria in the middle of the 1970s. It is unbelievable how human beings would volunteer themselves for slave labor in the name of survival. Of course I was not thinking of the gravity of the practice in the days I used to see it being carried out.

It was this strategic location of Uben-Ekang in the Cameroonian coast that became father's new operational center as a result of having upgraded to the long and winding fishing nets of *Yoruba*. As funny as it might sound, I had no idea in those days that there was a tribe in Nigeria known as Yoruba. I still do not know why the long winding fishing nets were so named. After being exposed to a few of Nigerian cultures, however, and having lived in Lagos with Yoruba people for many years, I believe that the Yoruba net was so named because of its length, as our fishermen thought the Yoruba tribe was made up of taller men. I also suspected our fishermen learned the long fishing net was introduced by a Yoruba company. I must say I could stand corrected here by those who might come up with the best explanations of the name of the Yoruba fishing net. I hope my Yoruba friends reading this book will help me find the final answers.

My overall experiences working as fisherman in the sandy port of Uben-Ekang were not too different from those of the muddy Inua Abasi or Edem Abasi already described. The main differences in Uben-Ekang were the dry sands, mobility, and availability of petty traders. Physiologically, the lay-out of the area made it possible to walk around from one spot to another and buy things from the Nigerian and Cameroonian petty traders. As a matter of fact, I recall usually walking around retailing a handful of my personal bunga fish just to make a few shillings in those days. It was always a thing of joy for me to make even one shilling of my own, since it was never the practice of my father to pay me even one penny as part of my reward for all the work that I used to do for him during fishing trips.

As a typical tropical coastal environment, the Uben-Ekang fishing port also had its dangers. One of them was the presence of infectious insects and ticks that could live under the sands and could fly as well. Some of the insects were capable of biting and penetrating your skin, lodging and feeding themselves on one's blood and growing there until they were physically carved out. As I recall it, those blood-sucking insects looked very much like maggots in their appearance after they have lived and grown in your body for a few days. I was always so terrified of those insects each time they penetrated my feet. The cavities between the toes were the most vulnerable sections of the feet. The cavities offered instant access and refuge to the tiny insects and ticks, allowing them to hide and penetrate the body more quickly. It was usually so difficult to intercept them once they lodged themselves into the skin. The normal practice for those affected, including myself, was to allow them five to nine days to feed on the blood and grow strong enough for the victim to carve them out of the body. Imagine how long you would have to endure the pain and suffering, but this was the way of life in that neck of the woods. It was possible to walk around with several of the insects in one's feet, feeding and growing, until the individual was able to dislodge them from his feet. We were never told of the health effect of these insect infestations on human feet. Nobody cared about that sort of information—and nobody cared to search for it either. When mother and father nature are in control, you dare not question their wrath. I am sure these conditions may not have changed significantly to this day in this particular section of the world.

As far as I can remember, there were many other diseases in Uben-Ekang, as in most other coastal fishing ports. And nobody really took them too seriously. Most common were communicable diseases which made Uben-Ekang buyers' and a sellers' market for quack doctors who called themselves "chemists." Unlike the inflictions of the maggot type which were not considered worthy of medical treatment, communicable diseases victims were usually referred to the "chemists" on the street corner. The most common treatment modalities I can recall were the injection of Penicillin by the "chemist." Although the liquids used for the injections were called "Penicillin," nobody really knew what the medicines were and whether they were genuine or fake. The important thing for the individual being treated was that he got treated. In some cases, it would take two or three rounds of "injections" to cure a given disease. Of course, the rate of cure was another matter.

It was a common practice for the so-called "chemists," who wanted to make money, to travel from one fishing port to another to offer treatment to the sick. These "chemists" did not have to receive any official training or certification by any authority, either in Nigeria or in the Cameroons. All they needed was the courage to take an adventure and make some investment. Uben-Ekang became an attractive breeding ground for the chemists, mainly due to the dry sandy land which also attracted many temporary settlers and traders. Please note that in those days the "chemists" were highly respected and regarded by the people. After all, in a country where many are blind, the one-eyed person might very well be crowned king. The "chemists" fulfilled a vital community function and they were well rewarded, too.

The practice of quack medicine was, and has continued to be, a worthy profession in West Africa, as in most other developing countries. This profession primarily involved the art of using expired and completely fake medicines to treat sick people. In many cases, the medicines used for a given treatment are supposed to cure all forms of diseases, including male impotence. Of course, no such strong word as "impotence" is ever used to scare men who would never even admit to having such problems. The men are simply told that the treatment will significantly transform or increase their sexual prowess such that they would forever be respected by their women. This information ultimately help to boost sales for the chemist.

There are not too many of us alive today—African or the Nigerian people—who might not have been treated by the so-called chemists. Of course some of my friends would like to take issues with me on this; however, I am speaking from a direct experience. The procedures employed by the "chemist" cover all aspects of medical treatment, including giving injections, administering intravenous drug solutions, selling fake medical products, and, in some cases, performing surgery. It is the number one reason why so many African women die during childbirth. Pregnant women receive little or no prenatal medical care, and they die of any number of complications during delivery, because of inadequate or lack of medical care. The profession of fake medical practice in developing countries is notable by the absence of a government monitoring or oversight.

I want to be sure the reader is not surprised one bit by this real life story. Throughout sections of this book, I have attempted to narrate directly from my childhood and adolescent memory various events and situations that sound crazy, out of this world, and sometimes unbelievable. The fact is that some of these situations might have been worst than I have managed to describe them. One such situation is in the area of medical self-care or the lack of it. The best part of the story is about those individuals, including me, who might have been treated for any condition by the quack chemists and lived to remember it. The worst parts are about those who never made it out alive. This is where the ironic truth comes into play: whether the fishermen themselves directly articulated the point or not, their behavioral patterns inevitably showed that those who did not survive the poor conditions and other traumas were not to be remembered so much. They wanted to prove that life goes on; therefore, the survival of their "noble" fishing profession was to remain their primary concern.

The last part of my Uben-Ekang experiences that I can remember is the boat tour of the coast of Cameroons. Without necessarily knowing why, my father took me along with the crew on a boat tour of the coast of Cameroons. I would like to speculate that we went to sell fish and make good profit, although I personally never received a dime of any such profits. It must have been 1958 or the early part of 1959 when we traveled from Uben-Ekang to Victoria (now Limbe) and Tiko, barely missing a stop over at Douala in the French Cameroons. We actually anchored off the coast of Douala, and I recall watching and admiring the neon electric lights of Douala. I also recall being told that Douala was a city where many inhabitants spoke the French language. I was very curious about that and even felt like learning to speak French. Sorry, but we did not get to land at Douala. As we landed on the shores of Victoria (now known as Limbe) and Tiko, respectively, we were able to disembark and walk around to see the extent of work sponsored by the Cameroon

Development Corporation (CDC). I vividly recall watching trains transporting bananas and palm fruit bunches from the plantation to the ships. I can also still remember being amazed at the ability of machines to crush rocks that were used for road construction, as we observed.

At Tiko, I was so lucky to trace a friend of mine by the name of Peter whom I met a few months earlier when he stopped over in Uben-Ekang on his way to Tiko to work at CDC. We have not seen or heard from each other again since then. I hope that Peter, a native of Ibeno, is still alive and doing well in the year 2010. If he is no longer alive as is the case with many of my childhood and adolescent friends, may his soul rest in peace.

FOCUSING ON THE GOAL

On page 186 of the African American Catholic Hymnal, the author of the hymn, "His Eye Is On the Sparrow," advances three thought-provoking questions, followed by three cogent responses as well. The author states: "Why should I feel discouraged? Why should the shadows come? Why should my heart be lonely and long for heaven and home, when Jesus is my portion? My constant friend is He. His eye is on the sparrow. And I know He watches me."

There is no doubt that this is one of the most inspiring hymns that Christians throughout the world have reflected upon to restore the emptiness in their hearts and rebuild their hopes in times of distress and when searching for the guiding light. More than anything else, the theme of this song seems to more clearly explain the phenomenon of the unseen power that watched over me throughout the struggling period of my early life. It also helps to focus the mind on the invisible hands and eyes that guided and watched over me as I literally tiptoed my way to the goal line, even when there appeared to be no searchlight to guide my naked eyes.

The idea of focusing my eyes on the goal is an attempt to explain how and why I managed to maintain focus and keep my eyes and heart on the goal of learning to read and write, despite all of the obstacles and hindrances that tended me along the way. From all that I have already covered in other sections of the book, it is clear there was a very good reason for me to learn to read and write, because this was the only way for me to prepare myself for further learning, and further learning would contribute, in no small way, toward my subsequent achievement in life. These are all worthy goals, though it was not possible for me to sit down and plan them as events were unfolding in my life. Having to deal with events and unexpected occurrences in my early life, and growing up to witness the outcome of these events, has forced me to raise questions as well as seek answers to many puzzling issues. Among them are, why was I born? Were there reasons for being born into abject poverty and ignorance? Why did I have to face a large number of hurdles in such a short period of my early life? What made it possible for me to forge my way through such a mesh of obstacles to reach my goal?

On the one hand, my attempt to address these questions inevitably evokes in me a feeling of extreme sadness, because of having to recall and acknowledge, as already shown in this book, all of the missed opportunities I could have enjoyed in my childhood. On the other hand, I also feel a strong sense of excitement and reward from being alive to tell the story of my life—indeed, the story of life's miracles—despite the missed opportunities. Just like the negative and positive charges of electricity collide together to light up the world, having to feel sad and be joyful at the same time, as I have described above, has also combined to energize me to carry on as I have done thus far both in my life performance as well as in telling my story.

Just think for a moment about a youngster who enjoyed no nurturing and teaching processes to help him grow intellectually and psychologically. This youngster eventually grew up learning to read and write in unusual circumstances and even went beyond that to become a competing student, a teacher, and now a personal memoir writer. What possible reasons can I offer to explain what I consider to be truly a miracle from God? Nothing short of a miracle could have yielded such an outcome. Mine has been a life rooted in trauma, risky adventures and marked by survival. This was a case of a youngster not even being given a chance to appreciate what life was all about. It is difficult for me to return to the past just to assess how I felt about what my life was. As far as I was concerned, I had nothing to look forward to from one day to the next. Frankly speaking, serving on my father's fishing crew meant nothing to me whatsoever except in energizing my senses and psychic integrity.

Whenever opportunities present themselves for me to reflect back to the days of my struggles and how I lived through them, in terms of managing myself and maintaining my integrity from day to day, I usually wondered when all would end for me. Of course, it has been said that no condition is permanent, which is another way to say that change was inevitable under any condition. Thank God that the condition ended, but without ending my life. Thank God for the great change taking place in my life. Despite the fact that, as a youngster, I had to perform my duties as an adult, I was not appropriately compensated such that I could purchase even a common loin-cloth in those days, perhaps because I was just a kid. It was one of those situations in which time had to be used proportionately—time to serve my father on fishing trips and time to fend for myself upon return. To be able to raise funds to buy a loin-cloth or underwear for myself, I would have to walk the bushes to fetch certain natural supplies for sale in the open market on market days. The products that I usually fetched included plums, pears, and assorted leaves used by retailers to wrap market commodities for their customers.

Having reflected on all these experiences, I am left with a critical question. That is how did I manage to keep my eyes on the goal or concentrate on my future, in the wake of all the negative vibrations? The short answer to these questions is found, perhaps, in my initial quotation taken from "His Eye Is on the Sparrow" to open this section. Even when I did not know all along the way as I was struggling, Jesus was and continues to be my portion. He has been watching over me. That was really the secret key to keeping my eyes on the goal.

CHAPTER 4

PREPARING TO LEAVE THE VILLAGE

After spending the first five years of my adolescent life serving my parents by working in the farm and in the fishing ports, an unexpected miracle was about to knock on the door for me. That miracle could very well signal the end of my farming work and fishing trips. I would call it the miracle of hope. However, like every important blessing that comes to a person in a mysterious way, this one was not going to arrive my doorstep under a very welcoming atmosphere, as I will explain in this section.

What I can now describe as my preparation to leave my village was not a friendly preparation. It was made of hostilities, family feud, and more controversies engineered by my father. Having to endure all these actually brought back or reawakened my senses of traumas, the sufferings, the injuries, and the pain, that were the hallmarks of my young age. To my father it meant that my impending departure from home could deal a serious blow that could most likely result in a collapse of his fishing business. The amount of turmoil and restlessness, as described above, resulted directly from the fact that my struggles were not only reaching a point of no return and life and death; they were moving my fate up to the next level. The one problem for me was how to handle the prospect of moving to Lagos several hundred miles away, leaving my family home in disarray. Before worrying about the unfamiliarity of Lagos, however, the task at hand was first to persuade my dear father to please let me go in peace. Letting me go would take a lot of debating and persuading actions to mellow down my father just before my departure from the village would see the light of day.

MY LAST FISHING TRIP

.As I discuss my preparation to leave the village, perhaps it is appropriate to assert that the entire episode of preparing to leave the village could not be so far separated from the near disastrous outcome of my last fishing trip with my father's friend, Mr. Ifiok Ayanga. Indeed, my participation in Mr. Ayanga's fishing trip was not an accidental occurrence. It was probably the best example of my father's unending scheme and effort to use me as his main source of income, under any circumstance. One of the reasons for using me as a source of income was the fact that he did not have to spend a penny on me either for my health care or my personal appearance. In fact, while my father would be forced to make down payments to individual crew members (canoe boys) before they would sign up to join each fishing trip, my father never had to pay me anything either before going to, or after returning from, each fishing trip. It was usually my problem or my mother's problem to find other means of clothing me or caring for my needs after returning from fishing trips.

So, the question then is how did I end up taking the fishing trip with my father's friend, Ifiok Ayanga? How did this one trip become the needle that broke the camel's back? Let me try to address these questions the best way I can—and you will be able to discern how pursuit of money, self-assurance, and neglect would combine to form a dangerous and destructive alliance in some one's life. In this case, I am now convinced, more than fifty years later, that it was my father's neglect of me, combined with his friend, Mr. Ayanga's passion to make money at all costs that produced such a serious threat to my survival in the village. Ironically, however, it appears as though these were the forces that needed to actually come together to provide the evidence to force the issue in support of my desire to leave the village.

It was most likely in May, 1959, that the entire story of my departure began to develop. My father and I had returned from *Uwat Nda-Eyo,* or the dry season fishing trip, that we took to the fishing port of Uben-Ekang, off the Atlantic coast of the Cameroons. Some of the details of this and similar trips have already been given elsewhere in this book. As part of the tradition of the fishing industry, each operator had to take two fishing trips in a year. The first trip was considered to be the regular sunny season fishing trip or *Uwat Nda-Eyo.* The regular trip was taken during the dry season, described locally as *Nda-Eyo.* This season usually had very hot sunshine and what is known as harmattan dusty condition during December and January. It was traditional in the culture of the fishermen to expect that the business owner could return with the same crew to the wet or the rainy season fishing trip, but the current crew would have to be extremely happy and well paid after returning home. Otherwise, they would not be enthusiastic about returning to same owner for the next fishing trip.

In consideration of my immediate future, if I wasn't going with my father on the wet season fishing trip, I would be left idle at home for the next three months, and this would mean a financial loss to my father. It must be noted here that if, indeed, I was not going with him to the wet season fishing trip, the alternative plan was not going to be school attendance. The reason for this conclusion is clear. It was never the intention or future plan of my parents that I, their second son, Bassey Essien, deserved to be registered in school, even if I were to be left idle at home for three months. The question of going to school was never raised and it was never discussed. It was a closed case. However, my father was not done with me yet in this matter. He was about to reveal his next major decision which would have far-reaching consequences as this story unfolds.

Faced with the inevitable truth that his own wet season fishing trip plan would not come to pass, my father came up with a solution, similar to a plan B, to the issue of keeping me at home or keeping me working. He negotiated with and received three pounds sterling from his friend, Mr. Ifiok Ayanga of Ifa Ikot Akpabio. My father then ordered me to accompany Mr. Ayanga as a crew member or canoe boy for Mr. Ayanga's wet season fishing trip, *Uwat Ukwo Edim,* for the 1959 half season. Indeed, this is clearly the point at which pursuit of money and neglect on father's part, and Mr. Ayanga's self-assurance conceptually joined together to create a potent force capable of my destruction. It must have been the month of May, my birth month, or early June when I went with Ifiok Ayanga to Inua Abasi on the fishing expedition known as *Umia Mmong.* I knew nothing going with him; yet, I came back with so much in the way of suffering and bad memories.

As a young man in the village, I knew very little about my father's friend, Mr. Ifiok Ayanga of Ifa Ikot Akpabio, but I remember he was a stutterer and a very controlling and egotistic man. Like my father, he was a very aggressive fisherman who would end in being nothing less than the most successful fisherman in town. Mr. Ayanga operated primarily *Eworiwo* and *Umia Mmong* fishing nets. As far as I can remember, he did not venture into the *Yoruba* line of fishing nets as did my father. However, like my father, he might have overemphasized the need to be the most successful fisherman, to the exclusion of the welfare of his crew men, *Ndito Ubom.* Working for him left no room for relaxation or recreation. As a routine, it was impossible to separate mealtime from work time. To do so would symbolize laziness and a propensity to fail. In his push to be ahead, he could not afford to miss any one of the two fishing seasons, the dry season, *Nda Eyo,* and the wet season, *Ukwo Edim,* fishing trips. That is where I became involved in his fishing business, with my father's consent. The purpose of having me join Mr. Ayanga's workforce was to ensure that he stayed ahead of the competition in the field.

Right from the word go, embarking on fishing trip with Mr. Ayanga was going to be a difficult adventure for me. Since my father had volunteered me for the trip, it became my job to go with Mr. Ayanga and to show how strong and mature I was, even at the innocent age of fifteen. I have no clear memory of how my parents prepared and sent me away on this trip. However, my suspicion is that it was very uneventful, mainly because this was the period of my life during which I was literally treated with no respect whatsoever. I was thought of as an income-producing work horse and not as a human being who had any feelings or human dignity.

I accompanied Mr. Ayanga to the wet season fishing trip as ordered. We started, as usual, by going through the creeks and the tributaries of the Cross River and into the Atlantic coastal swamps in search of supplies. It was customary for fishermen to make initial stops along the way at the mangrove swamps to obtain supplies for the duration of the trip. The supplies we gathered included raffia thatching supplies, the rope supplies known as *Nkukip,* material obtained from extended roots of the cedar mangrove trees, to be used for tying individually stitched sticks of fish before placing them above raging fires for drying, and certain wood and material supplies—all for use at the remote fisheries in the mangrove swamps.

At the fishery, the story got even worse for me as the duties got extremely rigorous, most of the time under very heavy rain storms. There was little or no rest or sleeping time. It was time to work hard for the money my father received as a down payment for my joining the wet season fishing trip with Mr. Ayanga. With little or no sleep, I routinely collected and lined the nets of *Umia Mmong* as needed, repaired, and stored the nets in a careful manner, carried the nets to the canoe, and set up ready for casting into the sea with utmost efficiency. It was important as a crew member to be in the condition to either cast the net or to energetically row the canoe as the net was being cast into the Gulf of Guinea section of the Atlantic Ocean. After the net had been cast into the sea, the canoe must be paddled around as a designated crew member continues to bombard the sea water heavily with a hand-held stick attached to a circular wooden board about one inch thick by twelve inches in diameter. The aim of the water rumbling, theoretically, is to excite the fish so that they will swim faster underwater toward the nets and, hopefully get caught there-in. Finally, the crew member or the canoe boy must be able to assist in hauling the net with any number of fish into the canoe for the final trip back to shore.

There is no one aspect of these activities that was not hard and energy-draining for me. All of them were hard and physically stressful, especially when I had very little food to eat each day. I was being scolded and ridiculed, scurrilously and constantly by Mr. Ifiok Ayanga and his upperclass crew men. Mr. Ayanga was never satisfied with any aspect of my work, at least based on his usual remarks. Mr. Ayanga's overall relationship with canoe boys was extremely belligerent and hostile. The atmosphere both on the sea and at the fisheries was always like being in a war zone.

If I were ever to cry or complain about suffering from some pain, I risked being publicly scorned, being pushed aside, and being left to die. So I had to endure the pain day in and day out, and I could say absolutely nothing to vent my pain and frustration. If I had died as a result of the nagging pain and suffering, absolutely nothing would have happened, because no one would have done anything about it. There were, and may still be, many back then who died from similar situations. Did anybody care to find out? There was no accountability, especially since the bottom line was money—money from which I could not benefit.

It feels so very painful that I have to recall some, if not all, of my past bitter experiences working in the fishing port, with particular reference to those aspects of my services that could easily be reminiscent of slave labor. Since I was totally isolated at the time these events were taking place in my life, I had no knowledge of the issue of slavery and what was going on then in the world in the lives of oppressed people. It hurt me more when I eventually learned the history of slavery to realize I had endured conditions similar to those endured by slaves. The only difference in my situation was that I had a home to return to at the end of the ordeal. The only question was whether the home to which I was returning was going to make any significant difference to me in the short run. I am not sure what is the best way to address that question.

As I returned home from my first fishing trip away from my father at the end of the month of August of 1959, it was only natural that my short relationship with Mr. Ayanga would come to an end and that it was time to face a new hurdle. This was when the pressure for me to leave my father's fishing empire began. The push actually began subtly in 1958 with the departure of my older brother, Offiong Edet Essien, from home to Lagos to start a new job under the then colonial government of Nigeria, headed by Sir James Robertson, who was then the Governor General of Nigeria.

INVITATION, PROTEST AND COMPROMISE

Upon learning of my return home from Mr. Ayanga's fishing trip, my brother Offiong, who had lived in Lagos for only one year, wrote back home to my parents requesting that I join him. I cannot state unequivocally how my brother Offiong learned of my ordeal with the rainy season fishing expedition with Ifiok Ayanga, but he had a general idea of my suffering in the fishing port, and I am grateful he took action at the time he did, because his action made a world of difference. I am also happy to be alive and able to write about the whole nasty and traumatic experiences that few children in my situation lived to talk or write about.

Immediately after I received the letter of invitation from brother

Offiong requesting that I join him in Lagos as soon as possible, it became apparent that brother Offiong was not alone in his thinking. There were many other community members in the neighborhood who were wondering when and how I could leave my father's fishing work. This line of collective community thinking became emboldened by my poor physical health, following my return from Mr. Ayanga's fishing trip. It was obvious that my suffering was beginning to create an uproar among some villagers in my neighborhood. Nearly every well-meaning person in the village of Ifa Ikot Idang showed interest and expressed an opinion on the issue. My physical appearance was too overwhelming and disturbing for anyone to look the other way. People who saw my condition thought I might have weighed something like ninety pounds at that time.

Among those who were very upset were my mother and one of my two step mothers. Mma Ekpe-Anwan, my father's junior wife, specifically said she suspected I was poorly fed; otherwise, I would not look so thin. Just coming back home and looking so thin was all the people needed to know about the bad conditions I endured on the fishing trip with Mr. Ayanga. Indeed, there could not be anything worst than my condition to support my brother's request for me to join him. However, it was one thing to receive my brother's letter of invitation, but it was another thing to be able to honor that invitation, as you can see later in this section.

When the invitation was disclosed to my father, he was not happy with the prospect of not having me with him on his next fishing trip. As far as he was concerned, not having me as a member of his fishing crew was not going to happen. Interestingly, with all of the obvious expressions of disappointment by people over my poor physical condition after my fishing expedition with Mr.

Ayanga, I do not recall my father saying anything about my physical appearance. Father actually became very furious and angry with my mother for her role, or for being the mastermind, in trying to get me to join brother Offiong in Lagos. Without taking the law into his hands, despite his anger, father went around inviting selected members of the community to come and talk me out of going to Lagos. Among the invited guests to this meeting were the late Mr. Bassey Otu, the late Mr. Edem Okon Inyang, the late Mr. Edem Otodi, the late Mr. Effiong Umoh, the late Mr. James Udo Obot, and Mr. Bassey Umoh. There could have been others whose names I might have forgotten to add to this list.

From the way he approached the entire situation, father appeared to have two main objectives in his demands. The first was to request the condemnation of my mother for instigating my departure. The second objective was to stop my trip to Lagos. Father did his very best to present his concerns to the panel members that he had assembled, not to deliberate on the matter but to stop my eventual departure. What I can remember most about the deliberations of the "panel" was that nearly all those men responded, not according to father's wish, but by following their instincts and best judgments. They showed extreme sympathy for me and concern for my situation. For some reason, despite their low levels of education, they were praying for me to leave the village of Ifa Ikot Idang in the hope I might discover an opportunity to better myself. Obviously, these men knew that after about five years of fishing with my father, my situation was steadily going from bad to worse. As far as the panelists were concerned, there was no room for any meaningful change to take place in my life, unless I was able to leave the situation in which my father had placed me. In many ways they were right, because they had taken note of my suffering and could not predict what would happen to me if I continued under my father's rule. Indeed, it is sad to reflect on the fact that, for my people and most other Nigerians, having to leave home to seek new opportunities for self-improvement continues to be the mode of survival even to this day. We seem to perpetually invent and maintain the "survival of the fittest" type of environments that leave young people hopeless and without viable options for their lives.

DEPARTURE FROM THE VILLAGE

The panel deliberated for about two hours following intense pressure. Eventually, they collectively persuaded my father to let me leave for Lagos to join my brother Offiong. They convinced him that "Bassey was not going to forget" him and that I was going to return home at some point to make daddy proud. My father finally, reluctantly, agreed with the panelists that it was acceptable for me to go. After receiving the decision of the panelists, my mother started getting me ready for the trip to Lagos. It was on the ninth of September, 1959, that I finally left Ifa Ikot Idang, Etoi Uyo, for the then Nigerian capital of Lagos. Exactly one day before I left the village, my mother made sure I was baptized in the Apostolic Church in the local stream of Idim Ewa by Pastor I. B. I. Ita, who died just in the early 1990s. May his soul continue to rest in perfect peace.

At the time of my departure, the stream of Idim Ewa, literally "the stream of the dogs," was the nearest source of water for baptizing most Christians in Ifa Atai. This stream usually rose to its fullest during the rainy season—the months of May through August—and would dry up completely during harmattan or the dry and dusty season—between the months of November and January. Both my sudden baptism and departure were glorious moments in my life, representing the winning of my freedom from my father, at least partially, and spiritual rescue in the precious name of Jesus. I think my mother made me sign up for the baptism in Idim Ewa because she was always praying to God to protect me, and there was no other assurance of God's protection than to be baptized in His holy name.

I sincerely thank my mother again, even in her grave, for the trouble she took to escort me to the Nigerian Trunk A Road where I boarded a lorry to leave my village for Lagos. Trunk A Road is the main highway that runs between Uyo and Oron in Akwa Ibom State and continues straight to Aba in Abia State of Nigeria. A Trunk 'A' Road is the equivalent of an interstate highway system in the USA, except that the shape and build of the road has no resemblance to an interstate system. Colonial Nigeria's Trunk 'A' road systems were basically two-way roads that were practically unsafe for high speed driving. Tremendous efforts are being made by the Nigerian Federal Government to improve those road networks; however, they continue to pose serious hazards to travelers in many parts of the country. The lorry that I joined on my way to Lagos was one of the heavy duty trucks fitted with wooden benches used in those days to transport passengers over very rough roads. The journey, which began in the village of Ifa Ikot Akpan, passed through Uyo, Ikot Ekpene, Aba, Umuahia, Onitsha, Asaba, Benin City, Ijebu Ode, Ibadan, and finally Lagos. The major break on the journey took place in Onitsha in the east, where the transport owners provided us with a place to sleep until the next morning when we crossed the River Niger on a ferry boat to the town of Asaba. The River Niger was bridged during the late 1960s, and crossing it from one end to the other has been easier ever since.

My mother used the occasion of my departure to give me a little lesson right from the holy Bible. She told me that, as I was leaving the village for Lagos, it was important to remember the biblical story of Jonah, who was lost in the sea and was swallowed up by a giant fish. The same fish was eventually caught by a fisherman and taken to the shore where Jonah was recovered by the fishermen and he came back to life to serve the Lord. Although she was not able to read the Bible herself, my mother's description of this biblical story of Jonah was a very powerful influence on me, although I found the need to attach an additional explanation of the ironic twist of the story of Jonah with respect to my story. In the book of Jonah 1: 1-17, the story shows that Jonah was running away from obeying the Lord's command when he boarded a ship for refuge. Sadly for him, the spirit of the Lord caused a severe storm that forced the crew of the ship to throw Jonah overboard in order for the crew to survive the storm. The Lord was not done with Jonah just yet, however, and he was swallowed up by the fish. After three days, the fish was caught and taken to shore where Jonah was freed up from the stomach of the fish and he came back to life. The story gets more interesting as Jonah acknowledges the miracle work of the Lord in his prayer (Jonah 2: 2-10):

"He said: In my distress I called to the Lord, and he answered me. From the depths of the grave I called for help, and you listened to my cry. You hurled me into the deep, into the very heart of the seas, and the currents swirled about me; all your waves and breakers swept over me. I said, 'I have been banished from your sight;

yet I will look again toward your holy temple.' The engulfing waters threatened me, the deep surrounded me; seaweed was wrapped around my head. To the roots of the mountains I sank down; the earth beneath barred me in forever. But you brought my life up from the pit, O Lord my God. When my life was ebbing away, I remembered you, Lord, and my prayer rose to you, to your holy temple. Those who cling to worthless idols forfeit the grace that could be theirs. But I, with a song of thanksgiving, will sacrifice to you. What I have vowed I will make good. Salvation comes from the Lord. And the Lord commanded the fish, and it vomited Jonah onto dry land." (NIV)

These are the words spoken by Jonah that my dear mother never forgot, even though she only listened to others reading the words to her. It should now be clear why my mother told this story to me repeatedly. She wanted to convince me that even though I might be lost along the way, I would be found in the end as the Lord is always with me. By my own interpretation, I believe my mother was trying to reassure me not to be afraid of traveling to Lagos alone because God was watching over me, although the text of Jonah's story could be misconstrued by others, considering the fact that Jonah was running away to avoid obeying God's command. I would, however, prefer to emphasize the positive outcome of the episode in Jonah's story, his subsequent survival and triumph, instead of the beginning of the text that shows him trying to escape from the Lord's command. Whatever the case may be, I am grateful for the inspiration that I have received from Jonah's biblical story.

It was my mother's strong faith in God and some of her positive stories and prayers that helped me to muster self-confidence to keep on trying. Yes, she did not enroll me in any formal educational program, but she had the mother's instinct and the urge to push and propel me along the way to my personal salvation. My mother had a way to make me and my siblings feel like God was with us always—at home and away from home. She convinced me I would not fail. I believe that my present status in life is an indisputable proof that she was right in her faith and belief.

I believe it is appropriate to add a few more words to this narrative in her memory and honor: My mother passed away in July, 1989, just eleven months after the death of my father. Her death was a real shock to me, because she had not been ill for a long time, even though she had become weaker as she got older and still struggled to make ends meet. I received an international phone call from Dr. Charles Ukpong, the present husband of my niece, Mrs. Atim Essien-Ukpong, after he visited with mother and found her seriously ill. Dr. Ukpong then suggested that I should travel home as soon as possible. I was able to fly home within ten days of the call, only to find my mother in and out of a coma. She managed to ask about my wife and children; these were her last words to me before she passed on to eternity. Although the Apostolic Church of Ifa Ikot Idang played a leading role in her funeral service, the family was honored with a visit by the choir of the United Methodist Church of Ifa Atai, and the women organization representing the different villages of Ifa Atai. All of us in the Essien household will forever remember mother for all her care, love and sacrifices. May her soul continue to rest in perfect peace!

It was very unsettling for me to interject the story of my mother's passing into the description of what I could only consider to be a moment of triumph in my life as it was my mother who saw me off when I was leaving the village for Lagos. On that note, I also cannot help but recall another feeling that reminded me of the time of my departure from the village. It was about the absence of father as I boarded a lorry for Lagos. How I wish he was there with mother just to see me off. As I am writing this story, I still do not know what father's final feelings were about my departure and eventual success in Lagos, and later, the USA. I found it emotionally difficult to understand why father was so upset about my departure; however, it was obvious he was upset about losing me as a dependable member of his fishing crew. Thank God that my departure from the village has brought glory to his name and the entire family.

Even after visiting my village to see my father again in 1986 and 1988, following my long stay in the USA, we both never thought it fit to discuss this or other episodes or events in our life history. During the 1986 visit home from the USA, my parents and all of my siblings had a chance to finally meet with my wife, Elizabeth, and four daughters, Eno, Ime, Anniedi, and Iquo. My father was still in good health in 1986 during this family visit and was able to ride his bicycle. He had stopped fishing and was now buying fish from the fishermen and transporting them by boat to sell to the local traders. Unfortunately, during my home visit in May of 1988, his health had taken a turn for the worse, and I had to arrange medical care for him, but his condition was too far gone. He was not able to eat properly, ride his bicycle, or carry out his usual business duties. The doctor who tended him told me that my father's condition appeared to have been the result of a stroke since his normal physical activities had significantly slowed down.

Before leaving home to return to the USA, I gathered my sisters and brothers together to discuss what should be the family's course of action in the event of father's death. I also asked father to state his preference as to whether the Ekpe Society or the United Methodist Church should conduct his burial ceremony. I asked this question because, right from his middle age, father was a member of the Ekpe Society, a traditional society that wields power and influence in the village and awards specific palm fruit harvest rights to its members, following initiation. In addition to the Ekpe Society, father was also a long-term member of the United Methodist Church of Ifa Atai. In his response, father said that he preferred to be buried by the church, and he instructed the family to negotiate and settle the demands of Ekpe Society in order to get them off our back.

Ekpe Society is a group that exercises power and dominion over acres of palm fruit trees in the village and that routinely awards the right to newly initiated members to harvest and market the palm fruits for a three-month period for their own profits. One of their membership benefit functions is burial of their members. Father passed on in August of 1988, just a few months after I had visited with him and a few days after my wife and two of my children arrived home for a short visit. We did our best to adhere to father's request that we honor the entertainment demands of the Ekpe Society. It need not be over-emphasized that this has been an extremely difficult story for me to write, while struggling to reconcile my feelings.

Based on the information that I have given here, it is now clear that father's death in 1988 was not completely a surprise, but thank God that my wife arrived home from the USA a few days before he passed away. As soon as my wife called to inform me of my father's death, I contacted my brother David Essien in Connecticut, who was able to fly home to attend to the funeral arrangement with the help of my wife. It turned out that the August 1988 trip that my wife took to Nigeria with the two children was quite a historic one for me and the entire Essien family, as they witnessed the burial of my father. I loved my father dearly, and I know that he never meant to do me any harm. May his soul rest in perfect peace!

CHAPTER 5

ARRIVAL IN LAGOS

Following my turbulent and controversial departure from the village of Ifa Ikot Idang, my arrival in Lagos on September 10, 1959, brought me face to face with the reality of self-discovery and new adventures. With reference to self-discovery, coming to Lagos was the first opportunity that exposed me to the urgent need to find out what I was capable of doing in my life for myself, other than clearing farmlands for my mother or repairing fishing nets and navigating the seas and mangrove creeks for my father. It was through the process of discovering myself that I ended up venturing into new areas of endeavor that would have direct impact on my future as an individual.

The highlights of my self-discovery and adventure would begin with an informal meeting with my brother Offiong to discuss and select my future occupation; enrollment in Paramount Studios in Surulere as apprentice photographer; eventual establishment of my own photographic studio, the Bassey Essien Photo Company (BEPCO) in 1965; the battle to survive self-employment and competition as a professional photographer; and my subsequent departure from Lagos to the USA in 1969. In terms of the level of impor-

The author, Dr. Bassey E. Essien (First personal photo, Lagos, Nigeria, 1960)

tance that I have assigned to the position of Lagos among the many stages that I have passed through in my life history, Lagos ranks very high. Lagos provided a principal arena for me to gradually transition from dependency to total independence.

CHOOSING AN OCCUPATION

After my arrival to settle in with my brother Offiong at 47 Falolu Road, Surulere, Lagos, the first important action that took place was the urgent need to make my occupational choice known to my brother. Considering all of the depressing and traumatic experiences I had gone through, my brother Offiong was very concerned about my future and what I was going to be doing to become economically productive to myself, to the family, and to society. With regard to the issue of reading and writing, it was not clear from our discussion what approaches brother Offiong wanted to adopt in getting me into a school or study circle. The unfortunate point is that the subject never came up. He simply wanted me to decide on what kind of occupation I would love to learn. I imagine my brother Offiong concluded that whatever type of occupation I chose, Lagos was the best place for me to get started with it. However, the decision to choose an occupation was not the easiest thing for me to make, since I had no prior experience from which to draw and there were no straight lines to follow in making my choices.

Despite the fact that I knew little or nothing about different types of occupations and did not know how to read a crystal ball, I recall thinking about carpentry and small engine mechanics. Yet, I embraced photography as my choice. Photography was the one type of work that struck me the most from the first time I saw brother Offiong take pictures with a Brownie camera in our village in about 1956 or 1957. I happily recall how curious I used to be observing my brother take pictures then. If my memory serves me right, I might have gone with my brother Offiong to the Sunlight Studio at Uyo, near my village, where I saw a photographic shop for the first time in my life. So, after just a few days of thinking, I ended up choosing photography as an occupation, because I thought it would force me to learn how to read and write English. Of course, by the time I arrived in Lagos I knew how to read and write in the local vernacular (Efik/Ibibio) language, thanks to brother Offiong's earlier home teaching lessons. Moreover, I could understand or spell some basic English words at a very rudimentary level. All in all, I was nowhere near a level at which I could compete or do much academically.

It was my conclusion that, after all, no one in the environment from whence I came would know how to properly operate a camera or mix photographic chemicals without being able to read and understand written instructions. This idea, however, was somewhat misleading because, in reality, I was not going into remedial education by way of becoming an apprentice photographer. I was going into an apprenticeship to learn to become a photographer. If that was the case, how then was I going to merge these burning desires of mine to achieve the result I was seeking? I like to think and believe the true answer to this question was not readily available to me since I was not even equipped to formulate any theory or identify solutions. For whatever it is worth, I want to believe I was on the right track when I decided photography involved a lot of reading and writing, and it was perhaps the only known item in the mix that would open the door for me to pursue more reading lessons.

That is how I ended up choosing photography by enrolling in the apprenticeship.

Picture taking forces one to learn how to calibrate depth of field and the focal plane, set the exposure time, read the light meter, and determine appropriate film speed relative to available lighting conditions or the electronic strobe light to be used. The same general principles apply to photographic printing or processing in the darkroom. You must know how to properly mix both the developer and the fixing salt (hypo), how to select the appropriate grade of sensitized printing paper to be used, how to determine the exposure time, and how to properly calibrate the length of time that you must expose the sensitized paper to the photo image projected from the negative through the photographic enlarger. Knowing what we know now, how wrong could I be in choosing photography as an occupation? The answer is not one bit. (Of course, I have to acknowledge the revolutionary changes that have taken place today in picture taking and printing as a result of digital technology. Readers should know that it was not that easy producing photographs in those days.)

My conjecture is that my choice of photography as a means of forcing myself to learn reading and writing must have been a subconscious way of keeping my eyes on the goal, as I characterized it in a previous chapter. In practice, I believe I used the opportunity to its fullest extent. And yet, the concept of a goal was nowhere near any figment of my imagination at that time. I simply did not know what a goal was. It was not something or an idea that I could articulate in any way. The simple point is I could not have a goal if I knew nothing about the concept and if I could not possibly devise the means to get there, but I could be doing things to survive, depending on my particular circumstances and the amount of energy and determination that I could muster to put into the pursuit.

ENROLLMENT IN PARAMOUNT STUDIOS

After I shared my final choice with brother Offiong, we proceeded to complete financial arrangements and other related negotiations which culminated in the signing of training agreement between my brother and the proprietor of Paramount Studios, Mr. B. A. Olowu. It was then time for me to start my training in full swing. There was not much delay. Paramount Studios was located at 24 Ishaga Road, Surulere, about three miles from our residence at 47 Falolu Road, also of Surulere. It was also only four miles from the current location of the University of Lagos Teaching Hospital. Ishaga Road was a very busy street in Surulere. This means the studio was quite visible to street traffic, making it an attractive location for customers.

The basic mode of operation for me did not present an unusual problem, especially considering my early start in the village and in the mangrove swamps. The routines I had to follow on a daily basis involved basically walking back and forth between our residence and the studio. The schedule required me to report to the studio for work starting at 9:00 AM and return home at 2:00 PM. I was to return to the studio for the evening shift around 6:00 PM and work until 9:00 PM. Just a few months after entering this program, my brother decided to move from Falolu Road to #1 Kusanu Street, near Akobi Crescent and Mabo Street in Surulere. It was about the same walking distance to the studio; therefore, the move did not present any significant traveling problem for me. The distance between the studio and our residence was a critical factor in my training program since I had to walk back and forth between home and the studio.

With reference to how I met my training obligations, while at the same time serving my brother at home, my daily routines were such that I would wake up in the morning to prepare breakfast for my brother before he went to work. After my brother Offiong left for work, I would then leave on foot to be in the studio by 9:00 AM. While in the studio, I would perform any number of tasks as directed by Mr. Olowu, my boss. The activities ranged from mixing photographic chemicals (developers and hypo fixers), washing printed black and white pictures, drying and glazing them as necessary, to general cleaning and maintenance of the studio. I would leave the studio at two o'clock in the afternoon to return home and fix food for my brother. It was very important to my brother Offiong that his food was ready for him when he arrived home from work. I must also mention that this would be the time for me to eat and prepare myself for the rest of the busy day. The only problem was I never had time for myself. I would, as a rule, return to the studio no later than six o'clock to work until closing time at nine o'clock in the evening. Undergoing training as an apprentice photographer was, for me, an important milestone as well as an eye-opening experience. As expected, despite all the excitement, I started the training with fears and insecurity about my future success in the strange land of Lagos.

The city of Lagos, which I prefer to describe as a bastion of Nigeria's multiculturalism, was to me a very strange land even though it was the capital of Nigeria. I had traveled two days by road to get there, and many people there did not speak my native language of Efik/Ibibio. Notwithstanding the fact that it was then the capital of the nation, there was not much orientation or information available to guide newcomers like me. Being in a photographic studio did not make any difference either. I was there to learn, strictly by doing, not by receiving lectures about Lagos. Yet I needed to know how to get around the city; otherwise, I will fail in my mission.

The main modes of instruction at the studio were primarily hands-on actions, observation, and time-lapsed practices. Time-lapsed refers to a photographic concept describing the time allowed for light to affect a chemically-coated surface. The crucial idea is the time one must wait for a phenomenon to materialize. In my journey, I passed through different forms of time-lapses—hence the present story.

The skills I learned in my apprenticeship training ranged from mastering the techniques of camera operation to processing of photographs in the darkroom. It was quite important to learn by imitation, trial, and error. That was the whole point of apprenticeship. It was not so much a question of learning by listening to daily lectures as is the case in a formal school setting. It was imperative for me to succeed in this apprenticeship or I was out of luck. Not succeeding would have been devastating, considering the fact that this was my first formal training in something other than farming and fishing. The main tasks that I had to perform included washing and drying printed photographs, cleaning the studio and the darkroom, helping with picture framing, assisting with customer service, learning and helping to mix photographic developer and fixing chemicals, and doing whatever was demanded by the proprietor.

By comparison, the tasks described here simply reminded me of some of the labor-intensive tasks I used to perform for my mother on the farm and my father in the fishing port. Those tasks were always extremely physically draining and not usually broken down into manageable steps. The real difference for me was that I was not walking the mangrove swamps or paddling canoes on creeks and on the Atlantic. I was pleased with the fact that I was in Lagos getting some hands-on training away from my hometown.

In working through my apprenticeship at Paramount Studio, I did not hesitate to handle any task that was assigned to me. I handled all my functions with great delight as if my life depended on them. Walking back and forth between the studio and home became a habit for me. Photography is actually a multi-tasking profession. For example, the photographer is routinely required to perform many functions simultaneously, such as paying attention to lighting in the studio during portraiture, ensuring that the customer is properly posed for the shot, selecting the best exposure setting for the shot, and protecting the equipment and other supplies used for the shot. This is the case with regard to processing of photographs in the darkroom. In some cases, a photographer may be invited to go and cover an assignment on location. That calls for not only having a reliable means of transportation but using very reliable photographic equipment and supplies. I had neither of these during my apprenticeship or immediately after completing training, except when I managed to buy a very cheap hand camera for use in my freelancing. I also did most of my local travel either by foot or by taking the city bus whenever possible.

I do not have a vividly pleasant memory of my apprenticeship experiences, except to say they were mostly cut and dry. That means I concentrated on waking up in the morning to prepare food for my brother, taking care of myself, and then walking to the studio to get on with my tasks. By the middle of the day, I would walk back home to attend to my brother Offiong, have my own dinner, rest briefly, and then walk back to the studio to continue to the 9:00 PM closing.

My apprenticeship lasted for a little less than two years. It is difficult for me to remember any form of inspiring interaction I might have had with my trainer, the proprietor of Paramount Studio, Mr. B. A. Olowu. Mr. Olowu was a person who was very concerned with doing a good job and satisfying his customers. He did not believe in any detailed instructions, but he always wanted me to observe what he did and do it exactly the same way. He was very sensitive about catching me doing something the wrong way. For some reason, I can still remember his screams. He used to shout at me, "Stop doing that, capola" or "Get out of here, capola." I still do not, and did not care to, know the meaning of "capola." In fifty years I have not even thought about this word, until now. A similar sounding word in Spanish language, "capolar," means to kill or chop something into little pieces. This meaning does not seem to have any relevance to the situation that I have described above. I am left with nothing more than a mystery.

My relationship with Mr. Olowu and Paramount Studio ended right after my freedom, or graduation, on August 30, 1961, when Mr. Olowu signed and presented me with my first Certificate of Apprenticeship. Apparently, completing my apprenticeship meant a new problem for me. For example, right after my graduation from Paramount Studio, I became very anxious about what I was going to do or where I was going to work. Paramount did not offer to employ me as its own graduate, and I do not know if I would have accepted the offer, either. As a result, I instantly became jobless.

This meant that I had to do something to pull myself up with my bootstrap. I had to get a job as quickly as possible.

I then went to different studios to apply for employment as a journeyman. I was anxious to work at the famous studios in Lagos in order to learn a lot more about the photography profession and, therefore, position myself better to stand up against competition in the future. Among the studios to which I applied were Studioland Photographers in Yaba, Jackie Phillips Studios in Lagos Island, and the Osidele Photographic Company (OPC) Studios on Ikorodu Road. As luck would have it, I ended up being employed by OPC. Though I do not remember exactly how much money I was paid, it could not have been more than three to four pounds a month, or the equivalent of five to seven dollars a month, based on the exchange rates of the mid 1960s. It is of no use trying to compare the current rates of exchange between the two currencies due to the fact that the value of the Nigerian Naira has undergone a complete reverse when compared to the US dollar. In 1966 Nigerian currency was higher in value than the US dollar by approximately 30 percent. For example, 100 Nigerian pounds exchanged for about us$70.00. Today the dollar is much higher in value than the Nigerian Naira by more than 1000 percent. Again, as another example, in 2010 $100.00 will exchange for approximately N13,000.00 (Nigerian Naira). The important point to make about my monthly income from serving as a journeyman is that I was able to meet some of my basic needs.

As far as I was concerned, it was not how much money I was making as much as it was the kind of experiences I was acquiring and the buying power of the cash at hand. Working at OPC would have been a good opportunity for me to put my professional skills

The author, Dr. Bassey Essien, in his makeshift photo processing laboratory, assisted by Mr. A.J. Esenyie (Lagos, 1963)

to work in front of important customers and to find out if I knew what I was doing. Unfortunately, however, OPC never really allowed me to do that much, fearing that I would make an expensive mistake. Mr. Osidele, the proprietor of OPC and a German-trained camera repairer, had a commercial camera repair workshop next door to the studio, and he spent more time repairing cameras and training apprentices than he did in the studio. He made his wife the manager of the studio and the principal photographer in charge of all studio operations. I used to greatly admire her handling of the camera. Both she and her husband made sure that all my movements were under their watchful eyes and that I would not undertake any activity they did not closely supervise.

Consistent with what had become the norm for me, there is no single aspect of my experience at OPC that I can pleasantly recall, although I very much admired the organization of the studio. Every transaction was carefully recorded and numbered and filed for easy reference. Customers were treated like queens and kings, and good quality photography was job number one. I did not spend even one year working at OPC, due to the fact that there was no significant difference between working at OPC as a journeyman and working as an apprentice at Paramount Studio. The condition of work was just the same and there was no room for me to grow as a human being with dignity.

After trying to work as a journeyman to gain more experience as a professional photographer, I still found myself running in circles trying to find myself. This was really the testing time of my life, in terms of putting my maturity level to work for me. As a young man who went through a series of painful and traumatic experiences in my early years, having now completed some two years away from the village in an apprenticeship and finally actually working as a journeyman, I needed to show my maturity level, strength, and determination to survive, if not to succeed. However, my situation still left me with the feeling of helplessness. I still felt like I was treading water with no end in sight.

Although I came to Lagos two to three years earlier with the assistance of my brother Offiong, who also enrolled me in photography apprenticeship, he gently faded away from my life after I completed the training. He did not offer any meaningful guidance to me or cared to know how I was going to survive from that point on. At some point I had noticed this behavior pattern on the part of brother Offiong, however, I never allowed myself to be overwhelmed by it. I just could not help but ask some questions, such as why was it that I was always expected to perform miracles without necessarily being guided or assisted by an adult? Why was I expected to grow up so fast without having the chance to learn and grow in wisdom and strength? It was the case while I was in my village.

Except for my apprenticeship training, my Lagos experience was quickly shaping up to be the same as what happened to me in the village. While I did not quite understand the root cause of the problem, I was not going to sit there and wait for my demise. I had to concentrate on helping myself. For quite sometime, there was a near total loss of communication or interaction between me and brother Offiong. He became completely disconnected and unconcerned about how I was doing and where my apprenticeship training was taking me. The situation was worsened by the fact that, after completing my apprenticeship, I started working as a freelance photographer and working as a journeyman. I was no longer able to serve my brother the way I used to do during the first year of my residency. Hence brother Offiong began showing a very negative attitude toward me and my affairs.

Having left Paramount and joined OPC studios, I was totally on my own. Of course, brother Offiong was struggling with his work with the Nigerian Federal Government, and that was all that concerned him. As long as I went to the studio for my training and returned home to prepare food for him, that was what mattered to him. So here was another challenge confronting me in my continued struggle to become a man or to become self-sufficient. Since working at OPC was not a viable future career opportunity for me, my future appeared bleak once again. This meant it would take a lot more sleepless nights for me to restart my life and my career. It would also take a lot of prayers and resilience as I had to find a new place to live on my own and began paying my own rent.

My new place of residence was number 6 Ebun Street, Abula Oja, Yaba, Lagos. During the early 1960's, Abule Oja was one of the poorest areas of Lagos, occupied by about one thousand families, had no known paved roads, and was far removed from the commercially busy sections of Lagos. Abule-Oja was the only section of Yaba, Lagos that I was lucky enough to find a one-room apartment at the cost of about two pounds a month. The good thing about Abule Oja location for my residence was that it was situated not too far from the business section of Sabo in Yaba, Lagos. It was also possible for me to walk the short distances of about two miles to the public transportation on Herbert Macaulay Street, until I could afford to buy a used bicycle. It is fair to say that trekking by foot was my first primary mode of getting around town.

Getting my own place to live was a significant event in my quest for being independent. It marked the beginning of my adventure in working to pull myself up with my bootstrap. Unfortunately, the road ahead was not looking too rosy or promising for me. I felt like I needed more than just a physical energy to get past each day. I was almost lost and out of steam. I needed an uplift.

Indeed, for a young man who was sent away a few years earlier by a mother with lots of prayers and a very strong spiritual blessing and influence, I had stopped any active involvement in any religious activity or even prayers while in Lagos. Although I completed an apprenticeship, I did not know if the light was going to appear for me at the end of the tunnel. Consequently, as I found myself at the lowest point of life, literally walking in the valley of the shadow of death, I began to search for sources of spiritual strength and God's guidance. As I conducted my search I came across Guidance House of New York City, an organization that provided home study lessons in spiritual truth and metaphysical healing. After reading about them I became convinced that reading their lessons would be of immense benefit to me. I quickly enrolled in their lesson plans and began taking the lessons. In those days when the Nigerian currency was higher in value than the American dollar, Guidance House would advise me to send the Nigerian currency directly to save time from having to go through exchange controls. So they started sending me home study lessons. As a person who was always so eager to read something to keep my brains active, I immersed myself in reading those lessons. I am convinced now than ever before that reading those lessons and learning to meditate and pray helped to boost my confidence levels and self-esteem at a very critical point and enabled me to withstand the untold amount of stress and depression brought on me by ignorance and all that happened to me.

I do not quite remember how I found out about Mikhail Strabo of the Guidance House. I most probably read about him in a religious or self-help journal and decided to write to him. I know I have since misplaced the Guidance House reading material that used to be my daily words of wisdom, but I have to give them a tremendous amount of credit for the impact of their lesson materials on my life. I could not have learned how to be patient, directed, and self-confident without those lessons, going back to 1963 in Lagos. Perhaps the greatest thing is to thank God I was able to read the materials.

Certainly, the nature of my personal problem was multi-faceted; consequently, it called for a multifaceted solution as well. That is the reason why I needed to start by doing the most basic things first to pull myself out of the rot. I have already alluded to the spiritual lessons above, the aim of which was to rebuild and restructure my mental and spiritual capacity. For the financial solution, I had to resort to making use of the skills that I learned: the use of my hand camera as a freelance photographer in Lagos. Doing so required the application of some technical skills. For example, in my unending quest for knowledge, I improved my photography knowledge through self-instruction while still being trained at Paramount Studios. I remember ordering a book called The Boys Book of Photography from London. I was determined to do everything in my power to read and understand that book and be proud of myself.

The Boys Book of Photography was a very useful resource for me, in terms of enriching my photography knowledge. I read and enjoyed nearly every chapter of the book. I also followed nearly all the instructions, especially the direction for constructing a photographic enlarger. For example, when confronted with the urgent need to print pictures, and since I had no money to buy an enlarger for myself to process photographs, I followed the instructions in that book and constructed my first photographic enlarger, which I used in enlarging photographs taken with my own camera.

According to the book's instructions, the pieces I needed to build the photographic enlarger consisted of the baseboard or easel, the stand, the elbow, the clamp to attach the elbow to the stand, the opal glass used for spreading light in the lamb housing, the lens and lens holder, and the lamp holder with the electrical connector plug. The baseboard measured about three feet long by two feet wide by three quarters of an inch thick. The next important things I needed were time and patience to mold the elbows, install the electrical connectors, and put the pieces together. Without taking the time and exercising a lot of patience, I would not have been able to assemble the pieces and bring the enlarger building project to completion. The actual assembly of the enlarger involved attaching the three-foot high stand to the baseboard, gluing the elbow to the lamp housing, attaching the lens holder to the narrow portion of the elbow, installing the opal glass into the lamp housing, and installing the electrical connector pieces to the top of the elbow. Of course, I had a lot of time and patience, based on where and how I began my struggles. Consequently, I completed constructing my photographic enlarger, but I had no darkroom in which to work. There was no electricity or running water in the building where I lived in Abule Oja, Yaba. For that reason, I approached my friend, Akpan John Esenyie, who lived in an apartment in a building in the Shomolu

The author, Dr. Bassey E. Essien, between his father and mother

The author, Dr. Bassey E. Essien, with sisters Iquo Essien (left)
and Effionwan S. Udoh (right)

The author, Dr. Bassey E. Essien, with his father, mother, and brother
Offiong Essien (far left)

The author, Dr. Bassey E. Essien, with sister Iquo Essien (center) and brother, Attorney David Essien (far right)

The author, Dr. Bassey E. Essien, with Mrs. Mercy Umoren (right), Mrs. Edo Essien (left), and Ms. Ruth Edoho and her mother, Mrs. Mayen Edoho (far left)

The author, Dr. Bassey E. Essien, with New York State Senator Neil D. Breslin

The author, Dr. Bassey E. Essien, with Congressman Paul D. Tonko,
Representative of the 21st Congressional District of New York

Bassey and Elizabeth Essien after receiving their US citizenship in April 1995, at the Federal Courthouse in Albany, New York.

Photo shows members of Bassey and Elizabeth's family who witnessed the citizenship ceremony, April 1995 in Albany.

The author, Dr. Bassey Essien, with Dr. Molefi Kete Asante of Temple University
(picture taken at a conference in New Orleans, LA, 1989)

Dr. Bassey Essien with world-renowned Nigerian juju musician King Sunny Ade during his visit to the pital District of New York State. Sunny performed at Bassey's send off party in Lagos, October 1969.

The author, Dr. Bassey Essien (left) with friend and classmate, Dr. Peter Kitonyi (right), during a UAlbany graduation ceremony in 1981.

section of Lagos, for assistance. The building had electricity and one centrally located running water. John had been struggling in his own way working as office clerk assistant under the Federal Ministry of Communications in Lagos, while taking evening lessons in typing and shorthand writing. Mr. Esenyie offered me a corner of the room in his apartment, which measured approximately eight feet by eight feet in size, to set up and print pictures during the night.

Having now secured a spot in Mr. Esenyie's apartment, the next critical thing I needed to do was to secure proper darkness and a safe red light for handling light-sensitive photographic papers. As you can imagine, I had to improvise to meet this challenge by covering the windows to prevent outside light from shining into the room and by installing low wattage red light inside the room section that now became my darkroom. From then, I was able to utilize this makeshift photo-processing set-up to print black-and-white photographs to meet my immediate needs, the ability to produce professionally-looking pictures that would satisfy my customers in Lagos.

With the cooperation of my friend, Mr. Esenyie, it was possible for me to set up the homemade photo enlarger and three trays in the dedicated corner of the room at night for the purpose of printing pictures. One tray contained photo rinsing water, the other contained photographic developer, and the third one contained photo-fixing salt or the hypo. The rectangular-shaped trays each measured about fifteen inches long by eleven inches wide by three inches deep. I worked in this makeshift darkroom approximately two years, from early 1962 to early 1964, until I was able to move the operation from my friend's apartment to my own apartment in Abule-Oja, Yaba.

By the time I moved my operation to Abule-Oja, electricity was finally connected to the building in which I lived. The village already had a centrally-located water pump, which meant everybody in the neighborhood had to always take a short walk to fetch water from the tap in a bucket and carry it to the house. Indeed, considering my experiences in the mangrove swamps, or in my village where we used to dig holes on the ground searching for water, carrying a bucket to fetch water at a street corner was a piece of cake for me as well as a blessing.

At this instance the population of the village of Abule-Oja also increased measurably, largely due to the establishment of the University of Lagos nearby. In two short years Abule-Oja became one of the most sought-after sections of Lagos by the larger populace, after the construction of the University of Lagos between the period of 1962 and 1965. I remember taking several black-and-white pictures of the new students during their matriculation ceremony. Today Abule-Oja has become fully integrated into the wild and crazy city that is known as Lagos, the former capital of Nigeria.

THE OPENING OF BEPCO

Having successfully completed my apprenticeship at Paramount Studio, having served as a journeyman at OPC Studio, and having started life as a totally self-supporting and independent young photographer, I now considered myself qualified and able to operate a photographic studio of my own. With all these facts in mind, it became necessary and possible for me to launch a search for a location to set up my own photographic studio. Although I endured the hard times in Lagos and successfully completed an apprenticeship in photography, the one nagging doubt in my mind was whether my maturity level could withstand the pressure of being a workshop owner and operator. My answer was that I had to continue with my plan. If I did not do this for myself, nobody else would do it for me. It was imperative for me to embark on this adventure. My young age was no longer a factor about which to be concerned. Neither did I have to worry about experience or resources. In the absence of any strong reason against my decision, I opened the Bassey Essien Photo Company (BEPCO) on Herbert MaCaulay Street, Yaba, Lagos, in the year 1965.

Before the door of the studio was opened to the public, there were many things that needed to be taken care of in order to get the place ready to function as a photo studio. The actual studio had to be painted with a very bright color and the lighting system had to be installed. The darkroom had to be set up and the necessary photographic equipment needed to be purchased. In particular, the professional standing studio camera, the state-of-the art photo enlarger, the necessary workshop and showroom furniture, and all required supplies, had to be purchased. Indeed, the big sign of BEPCO had to be designed and installed in front of the building to get the attention of the public.

Just in case any one wonders how I managed to do all of the above, the answer is that I was very determined to do what I had to do to sustain my plan. In the first place, I had gained a lot of self confidence and experience during the period that I was going around Lagos from one corner to the other taking pictures with my hand camera. During that time, I was able to still get out into the

Lagos scene testing out my talent and skills as a photographer. Based on my immediate past experience in living through and surviving hard times, not only was I ready to go all out to put up a big fight for my business survival, I was also using all the available resources as parts of my individual education process and self-empowerment. I am still personally amazed at how I managed to do these things at the time I did them. Surviving the Lagos scene was one of the greatest challenges of which I will live to remember and be proud.

My mastery of the Lagos scene did not just happen by accident. It came from my original interest in freelance photography. For example, going back to my village years ago, I recall the first time I observed brother Offiong using a Brownie camera to snap pictures just before he left for Lagos. He used to go around snapping pictures for people for a fee. Though he stopped doing that after arriving in Lagos, his initial actions left a strong impression on me. Consequently, not only did I select the same occupation, I ended up going from house to house in Lagos, snapping pictures for those who needed them. I ended up making a lot of friends in the process and, in turn, I was able to create my own market and use the same as my base of operation.

The ability to take pictures and process them for people for a fee was the one work activity—and the strongest foundation block—that paved the way for me to open my own photographic studio at 251 Herbert MaCaulay Street, Yaba, Lagos. The other principles of operation that I was able to adapt to my business were honesty, service, and customer satisfaction. I rented a garage inside the building owned by Mr. A. K. Blankson but occupied by his mother. Blankson was a Ghanaian immigrant friend of Nigeria's former head of government, Dr. Nnamdi Azikiwe, who passed away only recently in the year 1996 at the age of ninety-two.

Blankson spent most of his life in politics with Azikiwe. He was also a private businessman. In nearly five years of occupying the premises on Herbert MaCaulay Street, I did not personally see Blankson more than five times. I was told he usually traveled around Nigeria with Dr. Azikiwe on political engagements. I do not recall ever seeing them together. Mr. Blankson usually visited the premises very briefly just to see his mother and leave. He preferred to leave everything to his mother and sister Amanda and never really tried to get involved in talking to me directly about any issues.

I rented the garage at the cost of five pounds a month with a one-month rent deposit. (For the reader's benefit, one pound in 1965 was equal to approximately seventy cents). I decided on the location because Herbert MaCaulay Street was a very busy and commercial street. Most people simply could not believe that I had managed to open such an elaborate and modern studio at my age. I also remember that I registered BEPCO as a business name in the Lagos business registry. I was told by the business register to change my age on the form from twenty to thirty in order to be allowed to register my name because the age of twenty was considered too young. I did so, because I did not want someone else to register BEPCO, but the game of registering a business name in Lagos was not a serious issue for me to worry about.

As far as I was concerned, the thing for me to worry about was how I was going to manage my photo studio, satisfy my customers, and make the money to pay the high cost of rent. At this point, I had to buy an eye-level camera, a standing professional studio camera, a professional photo laboratory enlarger—an upgrade from the one I had constructed and used before—and all necessary furniture, including installing a business phone with the number 46330. For the record, Bassey Essien Photo Company, with the phone number of 46330, appeared in the Lagos Telephone Directory from 1965 to 1970. Even though I considered it a great challenge for me to establish my own photographic studio in Nigeria's capital of Lagos, I was pleasantly surprised at the ease with which I was able to run the studio. The only significant problems that I had were threats to my personal safety, theft of my equipment, and how to satisfy customers who were never convinced that I was the owner and the operator of the studio.

I want to take a moment to shed some light on the three issues relating to my personal safety, theft of my equipment, and customer satisfaction, just so that the reader will know that Lagos was not the most friendly city for me, despite my heralded accomplishments there. There is no doubt that my life was seriously threatened in Lagos, even though I never spent any sleepless night to worry about it, as I was always on the forward march. I was involved in two separate motorcycle accidents. The first one occurred in the dry daylight while sitting on the back of the motorcycle driven by a friend, Dr. Aniekut Ukoh, crossing Eko Bridge from Lagos island into mainland, near Ebute Meta. It was something like a magic when the motorcycle suddenly lost traction and flipped over and we went down quickly. We wore no helmets, and to our greatest amazement and luckily for us, there was no other automobile approaching our path, and we survived with only minor injuries—without the need to go to the hospital. This accident could have occurred either in 1966 or 1967. I kept no record of it whatsoever.

The second motorcycle accident took place at night on Western Avenue on the way to Apapa. I was driving my motorcycle in a rainy weather condition going toward Apapa, when I accidentally drove into a pit full of water. Again, I wore no helmet and, unfortunately for me, I did not escape unhurt from this accident. I sustained cuts in three different parts of my legs and arms. I was able to pull myself out of the shallow pit and travel with pain to the hospital in Lagos where my wounds were stitched and I was able to return home to heal. Permit me to enter a quick note here regarding the use of helmet by motorcyclist in Nigeria: It was not required by law as far as I can remember, and the motorcyclists never went out of their ways to wear them.

The third of the incidents that I want to describe was a robbery which took place right inside the darkroom of my photographic studio in Yaba, Lagos, during the later part of either 1966 or 1967. The robbery occurred at night as I dozed off with the darkroom window open. Having spent exhausting hours hand-processing black and white photographs as I normally used to do, I became extremely tired and fell asleep without closing the window properly. It must have been somewhere between 2:00 AM and 3:00 AM as many people in the neighborhood already went to bed. It was at this time that the robber, a young man of about 20 years of age, climbed into the room through the window with a knife in his hand ready to start his operation and to inflict damage on me. As he made his move, he first took my new German-made automatic OSCO wrist watch and proceeded to take my German-made Rolleiflex professional (120 size) camera which was kept in the room a few feet from me. At this point, praise be to God, his movement quickly woke me up. As I opened my eyes, I quickly realized that something was wrong and I jumped up to grab him, not knowing he had a knife. He quickly began stabbing me by swinging the knife from left to right and right to left repeatedly, until he quickly jumped back through the window to escape with my watch leaving the camera behind, while I was bleeding. I sustained stab wounds on my left hand, my chest, and the lower left side of my left eye. It was the loud noise of my screams that woke up neighbors who came out to assist me by calling a taxi to take me to a hospital where my wounds were stitched before I went back home to heal. I must thank the good Lord for saving my life and for helping my wounds to heal as they did.

In addition to the three serious motorcycle accidents and the robbery that I have just described above, the repetitive thefts of my personal properties were particularly hard for me to fathom, especially as they came in series. I am speaking of the theft of my first bicycle, my first radio stolen right from my workshop in Yaba, and the stealing of my motorcycle parked in front of Central Bank of Nigeria on Tinubu Square, Lagos. Despite all of the untoward incidents that I have narrated here, I did not allow my spirit to be broken to the point of neglecting my customers, especially as I needed to convince some of my doubting customers that I meant to satisfy them with my work and to remain competitive as a professional photographer regardless of my young age.

Eventually, as more customers became familiar with me and were satisfied with the professional quality of my work, they began to come around and cooperate even more. There was really no reason why my customers should not be satisfied. I managed my studio with the fundamental principles of business operation, the fact that customers are always correct and that their satisfaction comes first. Because of my adherence to these principles, no customer of mine was expected to accept any photograph with which he or she was not well-pleased.

ADVANCING WITH BEPCO

The successful establishment of my own photographic workshop in Lagos, after all of the difficulties and lack of external support system, was definitely a living example of my ability to pull myself up with my bootstraps. However, actual management of the studio, in terms of meeting customer demands and satisfaction would present a challenge I was not sure I could handle. Without the day to-day application of an effective professional management principles, the actual advancement and continued success of the business could not be assured. Judging from the way everything turned-out, I am proud to say, in retrospect, that I stood up squarely against the challenge. I will use the remaining section of this chapter to explain how I was able to handle this situation.

First, I was too young and too inexperienced as I entered the cut-throat world of competition as a professional photographer in Lagos. Second, nobody could have predicted my chance of success as I lacked name recognition and adequate resources. The third item is an issue that was not unique to me alone in Lagos or anywhere else—the fact that if I could not make the money to pay my bills, then I would not be in business. This latter element was, undeniably, the real fact of life in Lagos for poorly funded business starters. It was a situation of survival of the fittest, because surviving as a professional photographer in Lagos belonged only to an exclusive group of people. It was very common to see new businesses, including photographic studios, open up and close down after just six months of operation due to the lack of customers, and lack of customers was usually a direct result of poor professional performance. To my greatest pride and joy, this did not happen to BEPCO, as will be explained later in this chapter. Whatever type of preparation I underwent for myself up to this point, it was certainly time to put it to the test. This was not as much a test as it was an attempt to operate a small business by applying the most basic common sense approaches to work. These approaches consisted of fundamental customer service, quality control, and capital management.

With regard to customer service, it was my goal to do everything within my ability to satisfy every person who came in contact with me as a photographer. My idea of customer satisfaction was that if a customer did not like his/her pictures, the pictures must be retaken or the customer did not have to pay for them. This business philosophy was too simple for me to overlook. As young as I was, I never gave my customers the impression I was too immature to know what I was doing. I had the best relationship with my customers, whether I met them on location or in my studio. When it came to pleasing my customers, they were the first priority in my own scheme of things. I also used to have new friends and customers referred to me by those who were happy with my work. As a routine, I usually went to public gatherings carrying flyers with my business phone number to advertise myself and to solicit customers. I vividly remember one of the famous lines on my flyers: "…secure your shadow ere it fades; for your snapshot tells stories best…." My customers were usually so impressed with my professionalism and they were always ready to work with me or to recommend me to their friends. I will return to discussing my customers right after a brief review of my business management approach.

The main trick or technique I used was quality control, another way to describe the fact that I paid close attention to the details of what I was doing in presenting BEPCO products and services to the public. In those days, we were limited to producing only black-and-white pictures. The quality of pictures that were presented to customers was a function of lighting to produce appropriate shades of gray. There was also something called "retouching," a technical approach whereby the professional photographer used a very sharp pencil to make light strokes to correct wrinkles over the facial section of the customer's image on the photographic negative. The aim of retouching is to restore the natural appearance of the visual image of the customer whenever it becomes necessary. In addition to doing retouching on the negative, it may sometimes become necessary to re-touch an already printed picture depending on the nature of correction needed.

Again, when it came to photography, the exposure time had to be accurate, or the picture quality would be affected. Calculating exposure time is one of the important subjects in photography that modern day armature photographers do not have to worry about, as a result of electronically regulated processes of taking and printing photographs. Finally, all delivery of pictures must, as a rule, emphasize customer satisfaction, because without that the customer would be lost—and lost for good.

With specific reference to how I managed BEPCO, while I had never received any business school training on the subject prior to opening my shop, I knew what I needed to do for the interest of upholding my business reputation. My concerns were that I had to take good care of my workshop so that it looked attractive to my customers. I was able to accomplish this by furnishing the studio attractively, by presenting the best showroom display, and by paying my bills in order to remain in business. Even the function of buying photographic supplies was not overlooked in the process. One of the common problems of some young and inexperienced photographers in Lagos was not having supplies ready for use, because they never expected to have a large number of customers at a given time. Some photographers were in the habit of delaying a customer while they ran out to buy supplies. Valuable customers would be discouraged by such actions and might never return to such shops.

The final point to make about business management is that of standing up to the competition by being generally positive and lively, whether at the shop or on location. Having proper equipment was also very helpful to me. I recall having to buy modern flash-guns that could flash whenever, or as often as, they were needed. As part of the forward-looking management and upgrade of BEPCO, I was able to expand the studio after the first two years of operation by renting the front shop of the same building and using it as the showroom and reception area. The inside of the garage studio continued to be used for picture taking and photo processing. Having a separate showroom and reception area was considered a major upgrade for BEPCO; however, I needed to devise a different work ethic to survive. Although I usually made more money when people came to have their pictures taken in the studio, I did not believe in waiting for customers to come to me in the studio; therefore, I made it a common practice to go out to events to take pictures and would often charge about half of the usual prices for such pictures, just so that I would get the customer to know the studio. The same was the case with government employees who usually invited me to their offices in Lagos to take pictures. The first tall building in Lagos, the Independence Building, was one of the government office buildings I used to visit to take pictures of the workers in their offices. As a result of their satisfaction with pictures taken of them in the office, many of the office workers would also find time, after work, to visit my shop in Yaba with their friends or families for studio portraits.

BEPCO was a favorite name among many groups and friends in Lagos over the years of my operation. Specific groups included the Igbos, the Yorubas, other eastern and midwestern Nigerians, government workers, the diplomatic corps, and the business communities. One particular group whose members became my most reliable customers was the Indian group. This group was united in its love of BEPCO based on the frequency of their invitations for BEPCO to cover birthdays, awards, and anniversary dinners. I still remember one of the favorite sites of the Indian anniversaries—the Cathay Restaurant on Broad Street, Lagos. This was one of the best international restaurants in the Nigerian capital city. In one of the most elaborate Indian anniversary parties held there, a special table was set aside for the designated photographer, known as BEPCO. That memory lives with me to this day. My friendship with the Indian community of Lagos is one thing that I will not easily forget. Immediately after my arrival in America, I recall receiving the news of the tragic death of one of my favorite Indian customers, Mr. Kalra. He was one of many who died in an air crash over

Lagos about three weeks after I arrived in Washington, DC, from Lagos. May his soul and those of others rest in peace.

A significant aspect of my relationship with my Indian customers was the level of respect I enjoyed among them. It was always so motivating and encouraging for me to hear some of them openly praising me for the way I handled myself and my photography business. My friendly relationship with my Indian customers did not only yield long-term benefits to me, it also led to my first serious emotional and romantic involvement in Lagos as well.

Perhaps the most touchy-feely of my experiences with my Indian customers was the one with an Indian family that operated an imported clothing distribution shop in Lagos. The family had three young children for whom they engaged the services of a live-in baby-sitter named Grace Udo. Of course, as the baby sitter, one of Grace's functions was to prepare the children for me to take their photographs whenever I was invited by the family to do so.

One of the things the Indians loved dearly was to have the children's photographs taken from time to time, especially on their birthdays, so that they could send them back to India to share with members of their family. Indeed, the practice of taking many pictures of children and having the families sending them home, in effect, became a major line of business for me. I cherished doing it and I miss it dearly since leaving Lagos.

In any case, as a result of my frequent visits to the Indian household for the purpose of taking the children's photos, I became familiar with Grace, who, incidentally, was also from the same Akwa Ibom State as I was. Grace was apparently isolated and unexposed to any social life outside of the Indian family residence. I was filled with certain desires and urges to establish a relationship with the opposite sex, as is typical with young men. Consequently, it was inevitable that Grace and I should start a relationship. However, it was not possible for us to meet as often as we would like. It is my belief that the very infrequent contacts between Grace and me usually precipitated some anxious moments. So I needed to take the first step to invite Grace over for a visit on her day off. It took a little courtship and persuasion for me and Grace to become emotionally involved with each other. Grace had little or no objection responding to my gestures and getting to know me, especially after finding out that we both had a lot of things in common, spoke the same Ibibio language and came from the same part of the country.

My romantic relationship with Grace, who lived with the Indian family in an affluent section of Victoria Island section of Lagos, began with an invitation for Grace to visit with me in a much less affluent section of Yaba, Lagos. This section of Lagos was mostly residential mixed with storefronts, movie theatres, schools, and banks. The *West African Pilot* newspaper, which published my first article on photography in 1965, was also situated in Yaba. The point is that I had reached the age and time to make my own choices and decisions without interference from either my parents or my brother Offiong. It did not matter whether or not I always made the best choices and decisions based on my emotional needs and urges and with due consideration of long-term consequences. But it was my duty to act as an adult and duly take responsibility for the outcome of my choices and actions, with particular reference to my relationship with Grace.

As could be expected, right after Grace and I began our sexual relationship, Grace became pregnant, and, before we knew it, she bore me a baby boy in July of 1966. Sunnyboy was born in Island Maternity Hospital, Lagos, under the ward matron who was known as Mrs. Tuyo. Having known her for years and taken pictures for her and the husband, I called her Aunty. Throughout the period of Grace's pregnancy, Mrs. Tuyo took a personal interest in caring for Grace. After the baby was born, Mrs. Tuyo carefully advised us on how to care for him and we did so for a few months. However, it was not a comfortable situation for us and the baby, especially as we had no family home. Consequently, Grace informed me that she would like to take the baby back home to the then Eastern Region of Nigeria. She had become frustrated with the unsettling situation of my life in Lagos and the fact that Nigeria was preparing for a civil war.

Grace's decision to take the baby home was emotionally difficult for me to deal with. As the baby came into our lives under a very chaotic living situation, I was unable to persuade Grace to stick around with me. First of all, we were not married, and I was not even thinking of marriage yet due to many unpredictable factors. Second, I had virtually no viable economic base, even with my photographic studio which was less than two years in operation. Third, I must admit that my maturity level as a family man at that time was much less than desirable, in spite of my professional courage working as a photographer. Finally, Nigeria was on the verge of breaking out into civil war, with labor strikes, tribal disputes, and the persistent military control of the government. For these many reasons I allowed Grace to travel home with Sunnyboy to the Eastern Region of Nigeria.

Grace went home with the baby at a time of great uncertainty surrounding our lives in Lagos, particularly, and Nigeria in general. It is fair to state that the chaos in our personal lives was made worst by the chaos that existed in the country. This was the time when the Federal Government of Nigeria was having serious disputes with the military governor of Eastern Nigeria, Col. Odumegwu Ojukwu. The dispute resulted from the massacre of Eastern Nigerians in Northern Nigeria, following the second military coup d'etat in less than a year, forcing eastern Nigerians to flee the North to the East. All effort to restore the confidence of the people of Eastern Nigeria proved abortive as the Nigerian military leader, General Yakubu Gowon, could not come to an agreement with Col. Ojukwu. With this and other uncertainties, many more people of Eastern Nigeria origin began leaving Lagos as well to return to the East. Nearly everybody was convinced of an impending civil war. Under the circumstances of the confusion, we all agreed that it was a good idea for Grace to go home with the baby.

While at home in the east with Sunnyboy, Grace lived mostly with my mother in the village while I was still in Lagos running my photography business. As fate would have it, right after Grace returned home, Nigeria plunged into a civil war which effectively cut us off from communicating with each other for nearly one year. During the Nigerian Civil War, I had no way of knowing what was going on with Grace, Sunnyboy, and my family. It was a period of severe confusion and suffering in Nigeria. Depending on whether you were on the Biafra side or the federal side of the war, you either joined the war efforts for your own survival or you remained on the run for your own safety. The choice was yours. You could either be killed by a bomb or be kidnapped by an enemy. Whether you liked it or not, the confusion was the same on both sides. Having to live through a period of civil war is not a thing to smile about. It was hell on earth. It was not something to wish on an enemy.

Right after the federal government of Nigeria was able to reopen communication lines between Lagos and Eastern Nigeria (then known as Biafra), the first letter I received from Grace reported that Sunnyboy, my son, had died. This incident probably occurred in the latter part of 1968 while the civil war was still raging. The cause of death was not given other than a description of a possible blockage in the throat area which was not noticed early enough to seek medical help. In the final analysis, it is reasonable to say that this episode, which began with my romantic involvement with Grace, will remain on the record as my own personal share of the tragedy of the Nigerian Civil War.

By the early part of 1969, Grace had decided to come back to Lagos, but at this time our relationship seemed to have died with Sunnyboy. We just could not restart anything. This experience will live in my memory as one of those incidents that had to happen to a young man whose life had been full of childhood dramas, uncertainties, missed opportunities, and severe struggles for survival. Sunnyboy would have been a grown man by now if he had survived the Nigerian Civil War, but it probably was not meant to be. Once again, may his innocent soul and many others who perished as a result of the war continue to rest in perfect peace!

PREPARING TO LEAVE LAGOS
The initial idea for me to leave Lagos for the USA started at about the beginning of 1969 when my good friend, Akpan John Esenyie, wrote to me from Washington, DC, to suggest that I join him. Mr Esenyie left Nigeria in 1968 for the USA to pursue further studies. As a reminder, this is the same Mr. Esenyie who offered me his

apartment to set up a makeshift darkroom where I deployed my home-made photographic enlarger to process pictures from 1962 to 1963. Mr. Esenyie had left for the USA through the support of friends, including myself; he was determined, from that time, that he was not going to leave me behind, in keeping with the principle of true friendship. When he first contacted me with the idea to come to the USA, I did not take him seriously. I did not see how I could obtain a visa to travel to the USA, leaving my successful photographic studio behind. However, as time went on I began carefully considering the idea up to the point of convincing myself that it was quite possible for me to put the idea into action. From that point, it did not take long before Mr. Esenyie obtained an I-20 student admission form in my name from a business school and sent it to me during the summer of 1969. After receiving the I-20 form, I had to start thinking quickly about my next action. This was a short period of uncertainty for me once again.

First of all, I was not sure I had sufficient amount of money to prepare myself for the trip. Second, I seriously did not know what was going to happen to my photo studio. Although I had one assistant and one apprentice working with me, I did not know how and whether they could manage my workshop effectively in my absence. This was a period for me to be proud, sad, and terribly conflicted at the same time. Notwithstanding this uncertain situation, I began preparing myself for the inevitable events to come my way; I started the process of obtaining a visa for my travel. Although this was one action that should have been very intimidating to me, I did not permit myself to be afraid. I thought of the fact that, over the past few years (1966 to 1969), I used to escort a few friends coming to Lagos from Akwa Ibom State to the American Embassy to help them obtain visas. With this direct exposure, I learned quickly how to prepare and present one's visa petition to the American Consul in Lagos. There was no reason, therefore, for me to be afraid of going to the American Embassy.

In order to obtain a travel visa, it was required of Nigerians to show that they had enough money to support themselves. To be able to take your money with you, however, you had to first obtain exchange control approval from the Central Bank of Nigeria. Having begun to feel frustrated with the process, I decided to go to the then Governor of Central Bank of Nigeria, Dr. Clement Isong, to request his assistance. I was surprised when Dr. Isong, an American college graduate, accepted my request to meet with him to obtain an exchange control permission. I did not realize that meeting Dr. Isong was going to become my only formal orientation to surviving in America. Not only did Dr. Isong authorize the approval of my exchange control application, he spent time explaining to me, during our brief meeting, what to expect in America as a student. My decision to meet with Dr. Isong at the time that I did was certainly one of the best moves that I made in my pursuit of American visa to travel to the USA.

Dr. Clement Nyong Isong served as governor of Central Bank of Nigeria from 1967 to 1975. During his tenure, Governor Isong introduced new organizational structures for the Central Bank which integrated the complexities and volume of the bank's operational activities into prospective expansion of the bank's branches throughout Nigeria. As an American trained economist, he was the second indigenous Nigerian to be appointed Governor of the Central Bank of Nigeria. The first one was Alhaji Aliyu Mai Bornu who served from 1963 to 1967. Immediately before Nigeria became independent, Mr. Roy Pentelow Fenton was the Central Bank Governor, having begun his service in 1958 under the colonial government and continued as governor beyond independence in 1960 to 1963. Following a brief period of retirement, Dr. Isong served as the governor of Cross River State (CRS) from 1979 to 1983 when the military took over the government of Nigeria. Dr. Isong gracefully passed away in the year 2000. The Nigerian government has memorialized him by placing his portrait on the N1,000.00 (Nigerian currency). May his soul rest in perfect peace!

After obtaining the required exchange control approval, which authorized me to take my money with me on my trip, I then went to the American consulate in Victoria Island, Lagos, to obtain my travel visa. Obtaining an American visa was such a good feeling to me since I had no big-time sponsor or government scholarship as did some lucky students. I was simply a self-supporting individual who had worked hard and who was looking forward to learning new skills. The consul who issued me the visa was Mr. Johnny Carsons, who in 2009 became the Assistant Secretary of State for Africa, Department of State, Washington, DC. In fact, I had also met Mr. Carsons a year or two earlier during my visit with a friend who had applied for an American visa.

Up to that point, I thought of Americans as very friendly people, but I also wondered why they discriminated against black people as it was being reported in the media. Unfortunately, even after studying at length and spending forty years in America, I still have the same feelings and unanswered questions. Perhaps it will take writing another book to explore the answers to those questions. One thing was certain: having obtained a visa to travel to the USA, there was not going to be any good reason not to proceed on the trip.

Despite all of my pre-departure activities and self-confidence, despite making the right contacts in my preparations, I still consider my departure to the USA as an extraordinary event—much like my departure for Lagos from my hometown of Ifa Ikot Idang in 1959. To be very candid, I do not believe I was mentally and emotionally prepared for such an adventure. However, the trip had to take place and nobody could stop it.

One of my most memorable experiences was the gathering of a segment of my customers, along with many of my personal friends, in my send-off party. The party was set at the Palace Landing Hotel on Herbert MaCaulay Street, one block from the BEPCO Studio, on the night of October 5, 1969. The music was supplied by King Sunny Ade and his then Palace Landing Band. One of my very dear friends, Mr. J. Ade Tuyo, director and owner of DeFacto Works, Ltd., served as the chair and keynote speaker of the occasion. I will always feel greatly honored by the friendship and support of the late Mr. Tuyo, who was also the president of the Nigerian Chamber of Commerce for several years. Mr. Tuyo used to engage my services to take pictures of the Lagos slums and used the photographs to petition the government in Lagos for clean-up actions. Like many of my other important friends who were at the send-off party in my honor, Mr. Tuyo used to give me meaningful pieces of advice on what it took to be a successful business entrepreneur in Lagos. I will continue to treasure the pictures taken at that send-off party, some of only very few pictures I brought with me from Lagos.

I will also continue to appreciate the support of so many friends and business customers who stood by me right from the beginning of BEPCO and even after I was gone, though it was time that one era had to end. It was time to get back on the road in search of new friends. Indeed, it was time to look across the horizon to America. Up to the time of my departure, I had minimal contacts with Americans but had tremendous knowledge of what was going on in the USA, due to the media and the resources of the United States Information Service (USIS). In fact I was one of those who visited the American Embassy on Victoria Island, Lagos, to observe America's landing of Neil Armstrong on the moon early in the same year of my departure.

I also developed a friendship with an American Reverend Father at St. Dominic's Catholic Parish in Yaba and another American professor, Ms. Mitchell, at the University of Lagos. I remember being invited to photograph Miss Mitchell's wedding to another professor whose name I do not remember. Most of my minimal contacts with Americans always made me wonder what kind of a country America was, especially considering their well-publicized poor civil rights records, the assassination of President John F. Kennedy, and the assassination of the Reverend Dr. Martin Luther King, Jr.

I still recall listening on the radio to Dr. Nnamdi Azikiwe of Nigeria speaking in condemnation of white Americans over their feeling of being superior to black people. The news used to be quite disturbing and confusing to me. Dealing with the news of my departure from Lagos was one bitter and sweet phenomenon for me and my BEPCO studio customers. The time left for me to prepare for departure was so short that many of my customers began to show up for their final poses in the studio. In some ways it was nice to feel loved by many; yet I also felt as though I was abandoning my friends and very loyal customers. Even the hurriedly arranged send-off party did not do the trick, as there were still many who felt a great sense of loss by my departure.

FINAL DEPARTURE FROM LAGOS

I flew out of the Murtala Muhammed International Airport, Ikeja, Lagos, to Washington, DC, in the morning of the ninth of October, 1969, on British Overseas Airways Corporation (BOAC), Flight BA509. BOAC (now British Airways), in conjunction with the Nigeria Airway, was inaugurating the first flight on the new DC-10 jumbo jet to London, England. As anyone would imagine, I was very excited about the opportunity to fly to the USA by way of London. I considered it to be a double-blessing and a very significant event in my life. Indeed, for a young man who only traveled by paddling canoes off the Atlantic coast of Nigeria and the Cameroons, riding on bicycles in the village; and riding to Lagos by lorry, having to fly to the USA was a great thing, if not a miracle.

It was significant that I had to leave the country by this flight at the time that the Nigerian Civil War was still raging and when fear for personal safety was the rule of the day. The flight from Ikeja, Lagos, was quite an enjoyable one, stopping over temporarily in Rome, Italy, prior to flying to London. It was my first time on European soil when we were given time to visit the Rome Airport for a short sightseeing tour. Compared to the hectic and civil war-torn environment of Nigeria immediately preceding my departure, the atmosphere of Rome was a world of difference for me. It was the first time in about two years for me to be in an environment where a person did not have to run for dear life, avoid shining street lights for fear of bombs, and incessantly mentally practice civil defense lines: "Do not sit on the fence. Join the civil defense." To the surprise of no one, my feeling of freedom at Rome Airport went a little beyond what was expected as I nearly missed re-boarding my flight to London on the way to Washington, DC. It was the Rome Airport security staff who located me and alerted me to the fact that the flight crew was looking and waiting for me to re-board the plane. Needless to say I was lucky to get back on the flight.

The flight from Rome landed in London at night and I was transported to the Kings Court Hotel for overnight accommodation and to wait for the next flight to Washington, DC. I do not remember the name of the airport at which we first landed, but I remember that we traveled the next day some distance to Heathrow Airport where we departed for Washington, DC, at about 3:00 PM. The length of the bus travel to the airport tends to convince me that we first landed at Gatwick Airport during the night and later traveled to Heathrow. During the flight from London to Washington, DC, I noticed that the sun was shining most of the day, and I kept wondering why that was the case. It appeared as if we were following the sun light as we traveled from Europe to the United States. I have now come to realize that, we were actually flying in the direction of the sun and eastern time zones. In any case, we landed at John F. Kennedy (JFK) International Airport during early evening. With a little help from the Airport Red Cap personnel, I took a taxi from JFK to Laguardia Airport, about six miles away, to join a flight to Washington, DC. Upon my arrival at the Washington National Airport, I was picked up by my friend, Mr. Akpan J. Esenyie. My heart was full of joy at the sight of my dear friend, Da Esenyie.

251 Herbert Macaulay Street,   Yaba, Lagos
6th October, 1969

My dear Parents,

I am happy in the name of God to write you. I hope I pray that you are all well with the family.

My send-off party took place yesterday Sunday October 5th. It was so great an occasion. About 150 people in Lagos attended. All people of Ifa origin were there and they did very well. I thank God for that.

I will leave Lagos on Tuesday morning October 7th, By air for London I will stay one day in London and join another plane to Washington D.C. U.S.A. (This means I will be in Washington D.C. as from Thursday 9th October. I will write you as soon as I get there. Please my parents, do not worry too much about my going to the States. Just do not worry too much - I know you will worry. Keep on praying and God will protect us all, I will pray for you as well.

Please greet everybody for me and take good care of everybody. Greet Mama, Alice, Mary, Efionwa, Adiagha and children, Edet Ekpo and others. Greet everybody.

Please do not quarrel, stay in peace with all and not in pieces. God will help you more if you maintain peace.

I have spent L1000 (one thousand pounds) to go to America. If you pray for me, God will help me to go and come back to help you more.

I have sent L10 (ten ounds) to you all. But sorry, I could not enclose everything in the same envelope. But L5 to father and L5 to mother. You must not blame me for anything. You know am doing all these things alone, except God. Remember that David is here and I am the one caring for him (maintainance and schooling) But, all the way, I cannot tell you all the things. God will protect me so that I can be able to help you all.

Please write to me in Washington as follows:-
1457, Park Road, NW@303,
Washington DC 20010, U.S.A.

Tie Sung,
Ami edima eyen mbufo,

Bassey.

Celebration of the author's departure for the USA. (1969)

Celebrating the departure of a dear friend, A.J. Esenyie (1968).

CHAPTER 6

ARRIVAL IN WASHINGTON, DC

As would be expected of any new person arriving in a strange land, I arrived in the nation's capital of Washington, DC, with all kinds of fear and anticipation of what was going to confront me. Although I knew that the city was the capital of the USA, little did I know about the civil rights demonstration which took place, as I came to find out, only a short while after my arrival. Having just left a civil war-torn nation of Nigeria where citizens literally had to dodge bombs and bullets for their safety, there was no way I could pinpoint any structural damage to the city as a result of a recent civil rights demonstration. However, it was just a few days following my arrival, when we traveled along 14th Street in the Northwest section of the city, that my friend began to mention very lightly to me that the city had just suffered serious destruction caused by civil rights demonstrators.

Even my friend's attempt to show me the damage did not have a very serious impact on me as there was a lot of construction and rebuilding work going on and I could not even tell how anybody could try to damage or burn down such a beautiful city. Moreover, it was impossible for me to tell, by looking at people's faces, whether or why anybody was unhappy in Northwest Washington, DC. The fact of the matter is that I did not understand the whole concept of civil rights or civil rights struggles. Civil rights? What about it? Although I used to hear about the divisions that existed between black and white people in the USA, I had never read a book on the subject before coming to the country. Indeed, I came to the USA, not as a person who was loaded with all kinds of knowledge about all kinds of things, including civil rights issues, but as a person looking for something to read in order to gain some new knowledge. I just was not able to tell that this was going to be one of the pieces of the new knowledge that awaited me. However, I can now proclaim that the issue has followed me anywhere I have been—from Washington, DC, to Albany, New York.

At the end of my brief orientation to the city, the first official and critically important act to follow my arrival in Washington, DC, was that of resettlement. This primarily consisted of three major activities, including making arrangement for my accommodation, taking me to the US Social Security Office to obtain my social security number, and helping me to obtain part-time employment. With regard to shelter arrangement, my friend John allowed me to stay with him and his then room mate for an indefinite period of time, with a promise on my part to contribute funds towards the monthly rents. In the case of obtaining a social security number, I did not really know what that meant; however, I remember being taken there and I was asked to show my Nigerian travel passport before a number that begins with five was issued to me. Again, little did I know that this number was going to follow me all my life in the USA.

Having obtained my social security number, the next task at hand was to start searching for a part-time employment. Before we actually got to that point, I had accompanied John to his night job just to have a feeling for what it was like to work at night in Washington, DC. Unlike when I used to sit up late into the night printing black and white photos in Lagos, this was not the same for me, especially since I was doing nothing and had to keep my eyes open. Please do not bother asking what was my inner feeling at this point, because I did not know. I can only say that I had a lot of mixed feelings. So by the next day we started a more serious job search. One of the places that we went to was a restaurant in a major hotel in Northwest Washington, DC. I applied there to work as a dishwasher at the restaurant and the manager offered me the job and asked me to start working immediately, while he sent my file to the hotel's doctor for review. The doctor called me in for an instant physical examination. Although everything else went well, the doctor said that I could not work in that restaurant doing the kind of job that I was asked to do which involved lifting heavy dish containers, because of my umbilical hernia. When the doctor first told the restaurant manager not to hire me, the manager did not think he was serious. The manager kept me working there for the next two weeks, until the doctor personally came to the restaurant to warn the manager that he would be held accountable if I dropped dead while working there. He then went ahead to refer me for immediate surgery to repair my umbilical hernia, so that I could return to work at the restaurant, since the manager wanted me so badly to work there. At this point the manager apologized to me, looked at me on the face and asked me to leave the job.

This treatment gave me my first mentally traumatic experience and shock of my early settlement in Washington, DC. Needless to say that I did not go to hospital to register for any umbilical hernia surgery, largely because I was so new in town, had no medical insurance, and was so afraid of what might happen, including death, if I should ever undergo such a procedure. Again, no such incident has ever happened to me since then. Repairing my umbilical hernia has never been requested by any employer or any school admissions office or even my personal physician. In rare occasions, my personal doctor has said that he could recommend me for the procedure, only if I requested it. As far as I am concerned, I have never requested it because my umbilical hernia has never caused me any pain or been on my way. Those who have been lucky to have a glimpse of it have always been thrilled to death.

The experience that I have just narrated above did not stop me from going somewhere else to get a job, except that I was harboring the fear of the experience repeating itself wherever I went. It just did not happen again. I will remain forever grateful for the direction and guidance I received from my friend, Mr. Esenyie, and many others, regarding provision of shelter as well as helping me quickly to secure part-time employment. Whenever the need arises for me to reflect on my arrival and settlement in Washington, DC, I am always reminded of the fact that there were the caring and God-loving hands of Mr. Esenyie. He was not just the one who urged me to come to the USA; he was the one who picked me up from what is now known as the Washington's Reagan National Airport on that night of October 10, 1969. As much as I might have been apprehensive of what to expect after my arrival, I can honestly testify that all went well with me, despite the temporarily disappointing experience with the hotel restaurant. Nothing made me happier than landing at the National Airport to see Da Esenyie, as I used to address him. The term "Da" is used in Efik/Ibibio culture to address a very close friend with whom one is co-equal. I am still extremely grateful to him for having been there for me and for making life so comfortable for me during my arrival in the nation's capital.

Although I am writing about what happened in the past, at the time of this writing Mr. Esenyie currently resides in Atlanta, Georgia, with his wife, Mrs. Nse Esenyie, and their five children: Nsikan (11-27-81), Idotenyin (12-8-83), Enobong (1-24-85), and the twins Godwin and Uduak (9-30-88). Note that Godwin is the only boy among the five children. Esenyie obtained a bachelor of architecture degree from Howard University and a master's degree in urban and regional planning from the Catholic University of America. He returned to Nigeria in 1977 to work in the Cross River State Housing Corporation, a quasi-governmental agency, until 1985 when the Nigerian Army took over the government, forcing him to resign his position. He then attempted for a while to run a private architectural drafting firm in Calabar, until he managed to return to the USA with his family in late 1986 to start a new life. After helping to resettle me in Washington, DC, in 1969, he needed no new lessons on doing the same for his family in Atlanta.

Having partially completed my resettlement process following a brief period of uncertainty and received a cursory lesson in American survival; having been guided by Da Esenyie and other friends in obtaining a social security number; and having started a part-time job working as a porter, it was now time to proceed to the second official act of my arrival, the decision regarding my future education. That decision would be crucial in charting the course of my life in

America as will be noted in subsequent sections of this book.

Like many previous decisions I had made, whether they were questions of my departure from the perils of the mangrove swamps of the Atlantic coast of West Africa, leaving my birth place of Ifa Ikot Idang to travel to Lagos in 1959, or walking away from my photographic business that I painstakingly created in Lagos, this was one decision that called for serious thinking. All the necessary ingredients I needed to make that decision were at my disposal. The greatest of them was feeling free to choose. In this case, to choose the way of education, which was heretofore mystical and elusive to me. The opportunity and ability to choose meant the doors to the promised land were beginning to open for me despite my latent fears. Washington, DC, became another arena that I needed to make up my mind. As an educationally-nurturing milieu, the city of Washington, DC, an international city, was full of diverse cultures and resources that were fully accessible to me. I could not help but simply be happy for the opportunity.

ENROLLMENT IN ARMSTRONG HIGH SCHOOL

My decision regarding where to go to school could be classified as the second official act of my Washington, DC, arrival. I want to give credit to several of my friends who encouraged me very strongly not to rush matters by going to a photography school for nine months. The rationale was that such a program would be too narrow in scope and would not offer me much needed opportunity to improve myself academically.

After a short period of soul searching and consulting with my friend, Mr. Esenyie, I decided to enroll at the Armstrong Adult

Education Center (also known as Armstrong High School), located at First and 'O' Streets in Northwest Washington, DC. Armstrong Adult Education Center was one of those educational programs funded by the District of Columbia government to help minority students gain high school diplomas or GED. The school was noted for maintaining high standards of academic programs. In addition, the professionalism of the teaching and counseling staff constituted a good example of the school's commitment to improving the educational achievement of its adult students. The school was particularly equipped to cater to new international students like myself. This is not to say that its academic programs were designed for international students. The well-rounded quality of Armstrong was just one of the many reasons that my friends urged me to enroll in their program.

I was registered for beginning arithmetic, English, social studies, civics, and American history. Without allowing my fears to overwhelm me, I started formal classroom instruction immediately after registering. Although I was happy to be registered for classes at Armstrong, this was a very frightening experience for me due largely to fear of the unknown. Remember that this was the very first time in my entire life for me to ever enroll for instruction in a formal classroom setting.

Before I started classes, there was a very well-organized counseling session conducted by the staff of Armstrong. This counseling enabled me to become very comfortable as I was beginning to take my classes, despite some of my latent lingering fears. It was important for me to learn quickly that I was in for a race of my life, the type that was going to take the next few years of my life. Without making too much noise about it, my inner self was praying and lamenting constantly for God to come down or send His spirit to guide me through the challenge and to ensure my success. Judging from the outcome, the good Lord definitely answered my prayers.

Perhaps the most memorable and cherished teachers that I had at Armstrong were Mr. Garcia (English grammar), Ms. Keys (social studies), Mr. Neusom (English composition and English literature), and Mr. Thompson (government and civics). Other teachers of record included Miss Martin in the chemistry department and Mr. Rogers, who taught black and American history. I also have fond memories of Mr. Clark, a guidance counselor, who left no stone unturned in explaining many things to me, particularly what courses were required for those who were interested in entering college. His academic advisement helped me to deal more effectively with my fears of failure and any other emotional difficulties that I might have had in the period of my adjustment and social integration.

Several teachers, such as Ms. Keys, who taught social studies, and Mr. Thompson, who taught government, routinely gave me positive feedback on assignments, to the extent of citing my work as an example to other adult students. I was highly enamored with the phenomenon of sharing common experiences with other adult students while at the same time being praised by the teaching staff. It was the positive experience I had at Armstrong that helped to alleviate some of my fears in a very big way.

In fact, after leaving Armstrong, going through different universities, and having learned different educational and teaching theories, I can now truly understand the concept of Pygmalion in the classroom which states that the more classroom teachers perceive and expect their students to achieve mastery of the subject matter being taught, the more the students ultimately achieve. I can vouch that this was the case with me at Armstrong because I was never expected to fail. At Armstrong, I could observe that a note of appreciations and recognition was always extended to each adult student who exhibited a strong potential to succeed academically.

Speaking of individual classes, the positive reinforcement and encouragement were the order of the day in Mr. Thompson's government class. Mr. Rogers, who was also a history teacher, even tried to convince me to apply for admission to Virginia Union University in Richmond, Virginia, his alma mater. I even played with the idea of enrolling at Tennessee State University in Nashville, after talking to some of my teachers. However, having already become familiar with the DC area, where I could take advantage of part-time jobs, it was impossible for me to move elsewhere to start college without any strong financial support. My most difficult classes at Armstrong were mathematics and chemistry. I continue to be grateful to those classmates and other friends of mine who helped to provide tutorial assistance that enabled me to pass my required classes. I now realize all I needed was to put in a few more days and weeks studying those science subjects; I might have gone on to more advanced classes, even in college.

SURVIVING THE TWENTY-FOUR-SEVEN GAME

Now that I have officially started classroom studies in full swing, the next challenge for me was how to face up to the demands placed on me twenty-four hours a day, seven days a week. This was not going to be easy for me to confront, despite my high level of motivation to succeed. The beginning was extremely difficult, considering the fact that I needed to spend extra time with my studies, while at the same time I had to work to support myself. I found myself totally bewildered and divided between two priorities, the priority of getting an education and the priority of making a living. It was practically a battle that I had to face head-on, twenty-four hours a day, seven days a week. Specific activities covered in this battle included going to school during the day and some evenings and working at night to earn some money to support myself. There was simply no time to lose as I knew that starting school as an adult called for me to work harder to catch up with those who were already far ahead of me.

I particularly remember the summer of 1970 when I had to register for and take summer classes in two of my required high school level subjects, while taking on additional work assignment. For a three-week period that summer, I would go to cleaning work in the mornings, summer school in the afternoon to early evenings, back home for dinner and one hour rest, and back to an overnight relief duty in the office of an apartment complex in Northwest Washington. After completing that schedule, I became very proud of myself and quickly reaffirmed the world's popular saying which states that when there is a will, there is a way.

Most of what happened in subsequent years of my studies and work schedules was not significantly different from the 1970 summer schedule; however, as I proceeded on my daily routines in Washington, DC, I needed to seek out some sources of inspiration and strength. I drew a tremendous amount of inspiration from other Africans around me who were also putting in a lot of effort to obtain college degrees while working part-time to support themselves. Another source of inspiration that enabled me to deal effectively with the pressure of twenty-four hours a day, seven days a week, came from some motivational speakers and religious broadcasters. I specifically remember those glorious nights when I used to drive a taxicab on the streets of Washington, DC, while listening to the radio broadcast of the Reverend Ikerenkoeta (Ike) of Boston, Massachusetts. He used to spread the idea that "great minds make millionaires." Whenever I remember Reverend Ike's statement, I usually feel inspired or motivated to think about great things. It is still my hope that one day I will use my mind to do great things that would benefit humanity, especially the children of Africa who are dying in refugee camps and from poor living conditions of their homes.

In addition to Reverend Ike, another religious broadcaster whose words have helped to influence my mental actions has been the Reverend Robert H. Schuller of Garden Grove, California. Although I do not recall exactly when I began watching his weekly television broadcast, I have made it a duty to emulate Schuler's popular philosophy which states that miracles do not just happen; miracles are the result of goal setting, goal implementation, determination, faith, persistence, and hard work. Up to this day, I continue to pay close attention to the inspirational statements of Dr. Schuller. Ironically for me, I did not know how to set goals prior to starting my adventures from Nigeria to the USA; however, considering Dr. Schuller's ideas, I am convinced that I have been doing the right thing by facing my struggles with positive attitude, persistence, and hard work, guided by some form of invisible goals. I believe in determination to succeed, faith in positive thinking, persistence, and hard work with self confidence. I know I did not know Dr. Schuller or hear him speak in those days when events started to unfold in my life. However, after watching and listening to him on television, I believe he speaks my mind.

This has been an attempt on my part to highlight some of the issues that I encountered and how I confronted them during the first few years following my arrival in Washington, DC. Assuming that I may not have provided the best illustrations of what a typical new-comer has to deal with after arriving in a strange land, since each person has different experiences, what I have described in this sec-tion represents purely my own direct experiences following my arrival and resettlement. By the same token, the way I have present-ed it reflects my own style.

It is fair to state that I would not have been able to handle some of the issues as best as I did in Washington, DC, without the bene-fit of my experiences prior to leaving Nigeria. Although I have given details of my past struggles and, in some cases my success-es, in earlier chapters, I want to emphasize two more important points: The first point is that what underlay my success during the beginning of my activities in Washington, DC, was my strong desire to learn, engendered by my conviction that education was a means of gaining my place as a true member of the society. With this conviction, I had no choice but to give it all my best in all my tasks, whether it was in the middle of the night or in the middle of the day. The second point is I am quite convinced that I arrived in the nation's capital at the right time when it was possible for me to adapt to that city's multicultural environment which, in my opinion, particularly stimulates learning. I believe that my maturity level and my experiences being in Lagos had prepared me one way or the other to benefit from the Washington environment.

Without all of the above-identified factors positively coming together to propel my actions, it would not have been possible for me to survive the so-called twenty-four hours a day, seven days a week, game. Just like all other pieces of my traumatic and triumphant milestones that came together to get me out of the village to Lagos and from Lagos to Washington, DC, (see earlier chapters), the twenty-four hours, seven days a week, challenge was something that I carried over to all my school activities, including college work. It is one important aspect of all challenges that I have faced and which I will long live to remember and be proud of conquering.

ENROLLMENT IN COLLEGE

It was a historic milestone for me to start attending a college exactly two years after leaving my home country of Nigeria. My initial registration at the District of Columbia Teachers College in September of 1971 was the greatest thrill of my life. Having gone through all the drills of taking the Scholastic Aptitude Test and the American College Test, it was another period of uncertainty as to whether my scores were going to be high enough for me to be admitted to any college. The academic advisors had assured me, however, that those scores were not the only items to be considered for college admission. Among the other items I was required to submit to the admissions officers were my high school transcripts, teachers' recommendations, and an essay. In my case, I had to also submit the test transcripts of my GED examination. In fact, I think college admission officials were very pleased to see the transcripts of my GED performance in addition to the high school transcripts and all of the other items. I do not quite remember how many schools I applied to for admission, but I recall I was accepted at Howard University and the DC Teachers College. While I decided to start classes at the DC Teachers, I had to pay the mandatory deposit of sixty dollars (us$60) to ensure my Howard admission would be held for me when I was ready to start.

I was accepted into the DC Teachers' College's Teacher Certification Program. According to the orientation information given to me during admission, if I successfully completed the program, I would receive a teaching certification that would enable me to teach in the public school system of the District of Columbia. The program was offered to me tuition-free as long as I maintained an acceptable grade point average. To start classes, I registered for English composition, French language, history of world civilization, remedial mathematics, and art.

As I plunged into navigating my classes, overwhelmed by heavy reading and writing, there were several problem areas that needed my immediate attention. One of them was completing class assignments on time. For one thing, I did not know how to type my class papers then, so I was always uncomfortable submitting hand-written assignments to professors. My memory does not serve me too well as to whether my good friend, Mr. Esenyie, might have assisted me in typing my class papers sometimes or whether I simply picked at the typewriter keyboard to get my papers typed. (The problem of typing my class papers was not resolved until much later in my college years when I had to register in typing class).

Eventually, as I began to overcome my anxiety and fear of failure, I slowly began to adjust to the new environment and eventually became more comfortable with my college work. Becoming comfortable with my college work simply meant I was beginning to settle in one day at a time to do my class assignments and feel like a true member of the class of 1975. However, I still walked around with latent fears. And then, there were the constant concerns over how I would pay my recurring bills, including living expenses, books, and transportation. Thankfully, at District of Columbia Teachers College there was no tuition to be paid by students who enrolled in the Teacher Certification Program.

On the other hand, however, I never considered that my financial problems and the stress of studying presented an insurmountable problem to me, especially as I did not have to worry about the tuition. Indeed, based purely on my earlier experiences in life, I knew I would overcome most of my difficulties through sheer hard work and persistence. In other words, I was inwardly convinced that any possible academic problem I might have had was remediable through extra reading and studying. What other solutions could be better than that?

Without excessively repeating myself, I want to extend more credits to those who rallied around me within the school as I struggled to ensure my success. For example, there were support services and tutorial assistance available for those who needed them. In fact, I can state here that whatever was the nature of my perceived academic difficulty was not due to my lack of understanding or lack of assistance and resources; it was due largely to the struggle to make a living while at the same time trying to nurture my intellect. The pressure to survive the twenty-four hours a day, seven days a week, game was one that manifested itself to me in just a different form. In retrospect, given the outcome of all the struggles so far described, I'm convinced that the tassel is definitely, and literally, worth the hassle. I did not quit.

I was at DC Teachers College for one year, from the fall of 1971 to spring semester of 1972, before transferring my thirty credit hours to Howard University in the fall of 1972. At the time I completed the Howard application form, I had applied to be admitted into Howard's School of Business. This was just before the new School of Communications was opened. By the time I went into the University, I requested to be placed in the School of Communications, but such a request had to be approved by the dean. In the process of getting my request approved, I was interviewed directly by the renowned communications specialist, Mr. Tony Brown—the first Dean of the School of Communications—who later became the producer of America's Black Forum. Dean Brown looked at me in the face and asked: "Do you want to be accepted into the School of Communications?" My answer was an unequivocal, "Yes." However, I later found that, despite my request to be transferred to the School of Communications, my student record at Howard remains in the School of Business to this day. This is just an interesting item of note.

My main reason for transferring to Howard was not due to any problem or lack of support from DC Teachers College. After all, I was offered a tuition-free education at Teachers, and the support system and counseling program were excellent. So why then did I transfer? There were many possible explanations for my action. One of them was the global concept of perception and image. Howard University was the institution that gave a lasting name to Pan-Africanism embodied in Africa by the late Dr. Kwame Nkrumah of Ghana and the late Dr. Nnamdi Azikiwe of Nigeria. It was, therefore, considered to be an honor to be associated with Howard University. Another reason was my life-long interest in studying communications. Since Howard had just created the new School of Communications, I needed to get into that program as soon as I possibly could. In reality, my interest in becoming a journalist or a broadcaster was crystallized in August of 1965 in Lagos, Nigeria, when I published my first newspaper article in the *West African Pilot* calling for the establishment of a photographic institute in Nigeria. It was my long-time interest and professional pursuit to merge photography with journalism as a way of telling stories more effectively.

After that first publication, I began receiving requests for more articles from local publishers, but I did not have adequate intellectual preparation and the resources to conduct more in-depth research to be able to write more articles for publication. I also could not take too much time away from my photographic duties to concentrate on writing. In fact, there was no promise of how I was going to make a living while working as a freelance writer. You can now see that it was such a great pleasure for me to step into a school of communications, which was quite an upgrade for me from being in a photographic school, as had been recommended by some friends.

Transferring to Howard was quite a bold step for me, but it was an expensive move as well. I can now happily say my action was another example of elevating student craziness and curiosity to another level. As an example of the craziness that I alluded to, whereas I was receiving my education tuition-free at Teachers, I had to start paying close to one thousand dollars tuition a semester at Howard—this was money that I did not even have. This is just the type of thing that only college students do, including even the poor students like myself. It was an ambitious mistake.

In addition to the high cost, perhaps due to the number of students at Howard, the standards of the undergraduate counseling services and support system were relatively weaker than those of the DC Teachers College. For a student like myself starting out in college with a very weak high school preparation, strong counseling support and instructional resources must be of paramount concern. This was the case at DC Teachers College, but the system into which I transferred at Howard was simply not the same as what I had left behind. As far as I was concerned, the age-old phenomenon of survival of the fittest manifested itself heavily at Howard University. It was also a lesson for me to learn.

Howard students were expected to be more independent and self-reliant. They needed to know how to set their educational goals and choose their academic areas of interest on the basis of how well they were prepared in high school. In my case, having received my most formal classroom instruction in an adult setting, followed by a short stint at DC Teachers where the counselors spent a little more time talking to the students, my initial experience at Howard was less than inviting. It was somewhat different from DC Teachers where counseling was considered job one in my opinion. The District of Columbia Teachers College was located just one traffic light away from Howard University on Georgia Avenue, in the Northwest section of Washington, DC. What a difference a traffic light can make in a person's life! In fact, Howard has since absorbed District of Columbia Teachers, and they are now one and the same institution.

But you could not tell Bassey Essien in those days that the situation at Howard was insurmountable. If you tried, you would have been wasting your time. It was my belief that whatever it was that appeared to be strange and difficult was meant to be dealt with and ultimately overcome. That was my frame of mind then. Some of the difficulties that I had at Howard were not necessarily the fault of the counselors, although it is easy for students to blame their problems on the school or the counselors. The fact of the matter was I had no financial support to pay my way and I spent the better part of my time working to make money, usually to the disadvantage of my academic work. I did not have the same financial security as other students who had enough time to study and, therefore, excelled in their academic work. With this understanding in mind, no one should be surprised with my situation.

With regards to working part-time to support myself and pay my bills, this was a normal routine of mine that does not need too much mention; however, I like to reflect briefly on the hassle of doing this, even though I already discussed the point of meeting the demands of twenty-four hours a day, seven days a week, activities. Other than working as a porter, one of the last jobs that I signed myself up for during the remaining years of my studies in Washington, DC, was taxicab driving. This job required that the driver learns and truly understand the traffic regulations and layout of the city, which is surrounded largely by Maryland and Virginia. Without this knowledge it would be impossible to pass the cab drivers examination. Studying for that exam was no different from studying for an academic examination. By the same token, most foreign students, including myself, who passed the examination considered it to be a major accomplishment as it made it possible for the student to work flexible hours, while studying full time in college. Taxicab driving became my number one source of income which enabled me to pay my fees and meet all my needs up to the final moment of moving from Washington to Albany.

A few words need to be said about driving a taxi in the nation's capital. It takes some courage, special skills, energy, and luck to drive taxicabs in Washington, DC. It is a very risky business. In addition to the safety problems, you must have a good knowledge of the layout of the city, which must be verified through an examination. Since the city is largely surrounded by Maryland and partly by Virginia, you must know all of the details of the road networks linking the two major suburban areas in order to be able to survive working as a cab driver. On a very sad note, I lost at least two friends through an armed robbery and a possible heart attack while driving in the city of Washington, DC. That is just how dangerous the job is. Unfortunately, as human beings we are always exposed to danger, whether it is our homes or the work place.

As alluded to already, the greatest benefit I enjoyed working as a cab driver was its scheduling flexibility. It was always possible to leave a class and then start working right away by picking and dropping passengers at different locations. While at Howard from 1972 to 1974, it was cab driving that helped me to meet my school financial obligations. Of course, working and attending a competitive school like Howard was not the least of my challenges; however, my academic experiences at Howard were very positive in the end. Most of Howard's professors were bent on ensuring that all students receive a well-rounded education whether they were in the sciences, humanities, communications, or mathematics. The one message I have taken with me from Howard is that in the real world, there are many challenges, and you have to be prepared to meet them all head-on. You have to start on the college campus.

Whether you like it or not, the truth of the matter is that a well-rounded education, by whatever means it can be acquired, is one way of preparing one's self to meet those challenges. I like to think that this is the basic motto for all colleges throughout the world, though I could be wrong.

Even though I later decided to transfer my credits to American University in my final year, this was not a negative reflection on Howard. It was mostly due to problems with the undergraduate counseling and guidance. Specifically, I was turned off by my adviser, who refused to tell me directly what were the remaining requirements for my graduation. I now conclude that had I been a little patient, it could have all been worked out. Another reason for my transfer from Howard was the need to satisfy my life-long curiosity for communications. I desired more practical knowledge in the field. It was my hope that American University had the resources needed to move me faster and closer to my ultimate academic and professional goals in broadcasting and journalism.

Just as in the case of my earlier transfer from DC Teachers to Howard University, transferring to American University was a very expensive venture for me. For example, whereas my tuition cost at Howard was in the neighborhood of $1600 a year, it was $3000 at American University. This move added more stress to my life in Washington, DC. However, it now gives me a good feeling that I was able to overcome the stress and I am now able to write about it.

After spending just two semesters at American University, I graduated with a bachelor of arts degree in broadcast communication in 1975. It would seem as if I were beginning to take control of my life at that point, but that was something yet to be seen. My graduation immediately catapulted me into the receiving end of three competing needs that required my immediate attention. The first was the need for me to obtain a professional employment; the second was getting married; and the third priority need was for me to obtain an admission to a graduate school. How I addressed and, eventually, resolved these competing and priority needs would, again, determine the direction of my future in the USA.

To begin with, the importance of getting a professional job as a foreign student who had just received a degree from an American school was not even a subject worth being debated. At the time I graduated from the American University, the American media were never known for integrating foreigners into their main stream employment. The fact that I needed permission from the United States Immigration and Naturalization Services (INS) did not exactly make me an attractive candidate for employment. Please note that INS has since been renamed the United States Citizenship and Immigration Services (USCIS). Even when I was given permission to obtain a job for the purpose of practical training, getting a job in the field of broadcasting and journalism was still an impossible dream for me in the USA. The American University exit counselors offered me no support whatsoever, especially since they expected me to return to Nigeria immediately and they were not going to do anything to prevent that from happening. In the end, my priority of getting a job was not resolved satisfactorily, due to several uncontrollable factors. I can group these factors into three general categories: fate, lack of work experience, and my immigration status.

The first category, fate, centers on being in the wrong place at the wrong time. This refers to the fact that, the employers of Washington, DC, knew that I was a foreigner, black, and had an accent. I was therefore not considered to be important and relevant in the American job market. It was hard enough for American citizens graduating from college to get a job. How much more difficult would it be for a foreigner with student visa like me? The second factor negatively affecting my professional job hunting was the lack of professional work experience in the field of communications. This leads, inevitably, to the question: How can one acquire work experience, unless he or she is given a chance to work in the field? The third and final factor was the lack of permanent resident visa or green card which authorizes foreigners to be employed in the USA. I need not spend any more time discussing the difficulty of nonresident immigrant employment. Most of it is self-explanatory.

Although I have outlined the three urgent needs that I had to deal with, it was the second of the three priority needs—identified as getting married—that received my immediate attention. That is because I got married the week of my first college graduation. Just as I was struggling to complete my graduation requirements, I was also getting ready for my wedding, which eventually took place at the Kay Spiritual Life Center of American University on August 23, 1975. In fact, my best man, Dr. Paul Reuben (now in Miami, Florida), and some other friends not only assisted me with the wedding plans, they also helped transport me to drop off the last class assignment in the mailbox of my communications professor, Mr. Ronald Sutton. So, while the marriage question was easily answered, it still presented new problems, as will be seen later.

The third conflicting priority, identified as the need to gain admission to a graduate school, actually became more complicated because of certain questions that needed to be addressed. The questions posed were how would I fulfill my desire to enter a graduate school, and where were the resources to help me get there? Other issues that I needed to deal with included deciding where I was going to attend graduate school, where I was going to settle while starting a family, and how to get a handle on the economic resources that would sustain my subsequent ambitions. Unless a person is directly involved in resolving issues of this nature in his or her life, it may not be possible to comprehend the turmoil, the storms, and the stresses that can be induced by situations like what I have described here. I will attempt to address these questions and related issues in the next sections dealing with my departure from Washington, DC, and eventual enrollment in graduate school at the University at Albany.

CHAPTER 7

ARRIVAL IN ALBANY

Among all the major moves that occurred in my life heretofore, history will probably prove the move from Washington, DC, to Albany, New York, as the "mother" of all the moves. This is based on the number of years that I have lived in Albany, from 1976 to the present date of 2011, without moving to any other metropolitan area. It is also based on the amount of changes that have taken place in my life during this past thirty-four years. Although I obtained a bachelor's degree before coming to Albany, I have also seen a great change in my educational level, in my family life, my economic position, and in my social standing. I should venture to mention that my change of status from a none-immigrant to legal permanent resident (LPR), all the way to becoming a citizen of the USA, took place while in Albany. As far as I am concerned, I consider the phrase, "a great change," to refer strictly to those changes that are positive, with minor hills to mount and valleys to walk along the way. In this chapter I will do my best to capture the stories surrounding my move from Washington, DC, to Albany and all the changes that I have highlighted above. Others will be a full coverage of the hills and valleys I have climbed and walked thus far, the restless nights and hectic days I had to endure both at school and at work, and a look at my unparalleled, highly esteemed social and family dynamics in Albany.

THE PROMISED LAND

Based on the above-described life changes, regardless of all the tribulations that I have encountered, including the graduate school struggles, the endless immigration fights, family and employment issues, and the controlling politics of the Albany City Hall, it is safe to say that Albany boldly wrestled the title of being my "Promised Land" from Washington, DC. By "Promised Land" I am referring to the concept of Albany becoming the arena in which all the good and bad things combined to propel my life from point A to point B.

Whereas Washington, DC, played the role of being the incubator city for my intellectual and academic development, Albany became the principal environment, not only for completing my advance studies, but also for subsequently integrating all of my learning into a more practical framework and shaping my life as a family man and a respectable member of the society.

My move to Albany from Washington, DC, on the sixth of January, 1976, capped an extensive period of soul searching and decision making regarding where my wife and I were going to set-tle following our wedding. Loading up my Globe Taxicab to get ready for the road trip to Albany was a very somber and uneventful act compared to my previous road trips to Albany from Washington, DC. Prior to this final move, I had made repeated road trips to Albany from Washington, DC, immediately before and after my marriage to Elizabeth Okon Bassey on August 23, 1975. The most hectic and risky of those road trips took place just a few days before the wedding day, when I drove all night to pick up Elizabeth and return to Washington, DC, without much sleep or rest.

On the day of the actual move, it was just a matter of loading my Globe Taxicab with my personal belongings and taking the trip. Those of my friends who heard of my intention to move to Albany thought I was out of my mind because, in their opinions, my wife should have been the one to move and join me in the nation's capital. But I needed to move to Albany to be with my wife and to start a new life in a new environment.

So I was not bothered by the impending change of scenery. I was not even terribly worried about the snow in Albany which was quite heavy that January. There is no doubt that, by the time of my move to Albany, I was already a veteran of moving from place to place and living through chaotic situations. I would like to think I was psychologically and physically ready for this particular relocation after all the other moves.

As already alluded to in the above narrative, I completed my move to Albany incrementally because of the recurring needs to return to Washington, DC, to drive a taxicab which was my only known source of income in those days. In one of those trips while I was on my way to DC from Albany, my Globe Taxicab, a 1972 Plymouth, broke down at exit 15 of the New York State Thruway and, of course, this was not going to be easy for me to handle. I waited on the road side for approximately one half hour. Then there was a New York State road patrol trooper stopping to offer an assistance by calling a road emergency tow truck for me. The tow truck came and picked me up and towed my car to Havel Motors in the town of Monroe, Orange County, New York, where I left the 1972

Plymouth for repair and took a shuttle bus to New York City to join another bus to Washington, DC.

After I arrived in DC, my next urgent task was to rent another Globe Taxicab and start driving around the city picking up and dropping off passengers. I was determined to work as hard as possible to make enough money to be able to recover my car back in the town of Monroe, New York. Indeed, going back to drive a taxicab in Washington, DC, was not a problem because I already mastered the area while I was there as a student, and I was still in possession of my DC cab driver's license long after moving to Albany from DC. With the undeserved help of the Lord, over the next two weeks, I was able to make enough money driving a rental taxicab in Washington, DC, before traveling back to Monroe, New York, to claim my car and drive back to Albany. Havel Motors charged me the sum of seven hundred dollars (us$700) to cover the cost of repairing a bad engine rod in the 1972 Plymouth.

The 1972 Plymouth automobile was the car I purchased with the financial assistance of the Globe Cab Company of Washington, DC. I had the car for three years driving for the company on contract basis. The arrangement was such that I paid monthly car loan, my insurance, and membership dues to the company. Whatsoever was left of the income after all the payments constituted my earning. It was the best possible arrangement for a self-supporting foreign student that I was. That is why it was not an easy decision for me to leave DC for Albany, but it was time to make a change in my life.

Considering all of the problems that I encountered in the process of moving to and settling in Albany, many would like to ask if I would do it again were the opportunity to present itself. My answer is most certainly yes, simply because I would not possibly have any new tool at hand to predict the possible outcome and, therefore, make a different choice. I still consider my decision to move to Albany to be a sound decision that has benefited me greatly. All of the experiences have been both challenging and rewarding. The experiences might have taken different forms and rigors due to time and space, but they all contributed toward making me the man that I needed to be.

SETTLING IN WITH MY WIFE

Nothing more deserved a special attention in this book than the experience of starting life with my new wife, Elizabeth. I want to open this section with a direct reference to the book of Ecclesiastes chapter 4, verses 9 to 12 (USCCB-NAB), which states as follows: "Two are better than one: they get a good wage for their labor. If the one falls, the other will lift up his companion. Woe to the solitary man! For if he should fall, he has no one to lift him up. So also, if two sleep together, they keep each other warm. How can one alone keep warm? Where a lone man may be overcome, two together can resist. A three-ply cord is not easily broken." I consider this to be the best biblical text that supports all my decisions, first my decision to marry Elizabeth Okon Bassey and, second to move from Washington, DC, to join her and start a family in Albany.

As we were beginning to get to know each other a little better after we got married, it became necessary that we should openly discuss our future, with specific reference to how we were going to work within our means to ensure our survival in Albany. As we began our deliberation, it became obvious that I would need to make a major decision regarding our family housing. As I was con-

The author, Dr. Bassey E. Essien, with wife, Mrs. Elizabeth B. Essien.

fronted with this task, I could not help but try to draw from my previous resettlement experiences. This meant that, instead of relying too much on scientific logic in my decisions as would be expected in modern intellectually-rich society, I had to draw on my basic survival instinct which has been the hallmark of my survival in the past. I was able to explain to my new wife that it was not necessary for us to move out of her existing low cost studio apartment to a more expensive one, due to our poor financial situation. I persuaded her that it was more important to look at the big picture as we were starting out together. It was not how low we started life that mattered. It was how we would end up in the future that we should be concerned with. Luckily for me, my wife agreed with me after just a brief deliberation. This agreement offered me the peace of mind I much needed at that time to proceed to other important items, such as preparation to register in the graduate program at the UAlbany—State University of New York.

I am sure my new wife had expected that when I arrived in Albany we were going to move into one of those ultra-modern apartments in town, but it was not going to happen just yet as nature would have to take its course. We then continued to occupy the second floor studio apartment on Central Avenue, Albany, for approximately one year before renting a second studio apartment on the third floor of the same building. The third floor apartment allowed us to utilize extra space, as the children began to come into our lives. It also enabled us to conveniently receive my mother-in-law, Mrs. Patricia Bassey Okon, who came from Nigeria to visit with us during the period of 1977 and 1978. At this time, our daughters, Eno Essien and Ime Essien, were already born, and that presented a baby sitting challenge to my mother-in-law who quickly realized it was different to care for babies in America than it was in Nigeria. Even then, she was extremely pleased with having to play a much appreciated role in the children's lives.

Our daughter, Anniedi Essien, was the last baby born during the family's stay at the studio apartments, where we lived well into the middle of 1981 when we bought our first home located at 352 Orange Street, Albany, New York. Our daughter, Iquo Essien, was the only baby born right after we moved into the Orange Street house.

ENTERING M.SC. PROGRAM AT UALBANY

Similar to most of the previous endeavors and adventures in which I became involved over the years, I went into the graduate program in educational communications with a very high set of expectations. In my effort to get into graduate schools following my successful completion of a bachelor's degree at American University in Washington, DC, I had applied to and was accepted into Howard University's African Studies Program, the University of the District of Columbia's Library and Information Science Program, the Towson State University in Baltimore, Maryland's Speech Communications Program, and, finally, the UAlbany's Educational Communications Program. After carefully reviewing all of the admissions, I opted for UAlbany—State University of New York.

Considering the fact that my wife was studying for her Master of Science degree in educational administration at UAlbany—State University of New York, in addition to the prospect of receiving a one year fellowship, it was more logical for me to choose UAlbany—State University of New York for my Master of Science degree in educational communications. It was just like killing two birds with one strike: that is to say I had to commence my graduate education while starting a family as well. In a way, it was also a double-blessing for me.

Starting graduate education classes at UAlbany—State Universit of New York did not present any particular shock to me. The overall atmosphere at the campus, including the School of Education, was a very friendly one. The standard of seminar discussions and instructions was quite uplifting to me. I do not recall any specific discomfort in any of my classes or projects. However, finding my way around the city of Albany as a newcomer was not as easy as I had thought it would be. It took me quite some effort before I became more confident driving around the city, using Central Avenue and Washington Avenue as my points of reference. The city of Albany, New York, is uniquely situated geographically at the center of the State at the intersection of Interstate Highway 87 (I-87) and Interstate Highway 90 (I-90). Albany is located about 150 miles north of New York City and about 250 miles south of Montreal, Canada, on I-87. It is approximately 280 miles east of Buffalo, New York, and about 170 miles west of Boston, Massachusetts, on highway I-90. As the capital city of New York State, Albany is also the administrative headquarters of the county of Albany, surrounded by the counties of Rensselaer, Saratoga, and Schenectady, which make up what is known as the Capital Region.

I consider my experience of graduate education at UAlbany—State University of New York to have been very rewarding. The main source of the reward came from the class discussions, seminars, and the opportunity to demonstrate mastery of subject matters through various independent research and group projects. This is not to say that my undergraduate education did not challenge me.

Graduate education raises the bar on the student's maturity level and opens new avenues to one's professional future.

At UAlbany—State University of New York I quickly began learning about the function and benefits of graduate education. I developed the feeling, among others, that graduate students were supposed to know what they wanted from their education and that they knew how to go about getting it. This knowledge meant so much to me as a late starter in the field of academia. I also found the professors to be very supportive and interested in their students and what their goals were in life. As a graduate assistant, I found it very challenging to be given the opportunity to assist other students with their academic work under Robert Hedges in the Educational Communications Laboratory. Perhaps the most serious challenge to me in my graduate education at UAlbany—State University of New York came not from the classroom but from the outside. It was the uncertainty of day to day survival. It is no secret that no one can attend any school in America without having a reasonable financial support. In my case, my history of being a self-supporting foreign student did not end with my arrival in Albany. Self-support remained a constant problem that I could not really get rid of at that time. Having started a family while in graduate school did not help the situation at all.

During my first year of graduate school, I was awarded a graduate fellowship from UAlbany—State University of New York, as I mentioned earlier. After that first year, I was given a stipend of only two hundred dollars a month as a graduate assistant to the chairman of the Curriculum and Instruction Department. This stipend ended immediately after I became successful in my doctoral comprehensive examination in 1979. From 1979 to the date of my doctoral graduation in 1981, I received no stipends and had no real income of any kind. My family depended mostly on the meager income my wife was earning from working as nurse's aide at Eden Park Nursing Home in Albany. Summer employment for me was not always easily obtainable, and whenever a job came, the wages were not usually adequate. It was not the easiest time for me considering the high cost of travels to and from school and the added cost of completing a doctoral thesis; however, I was determined to complete the program by whatever means necessary.

MY FIRST UALBANY GRADUATION
The month of May, 1977, was perhaps the most important month and period in my academic and personal life in Albany, New York. Not only was this my birth month which I was beginning to learn to celebrate, but it was the month of my graduation from UAlbany—State University of New York with the degree of Master of Science in educational communications. With my new graduate degree in hand, and with the encouragement of my wife, I had to celebrate my birthday by cutting a cake—for the first time. Learning to celebrate my birthdays at middle age might come as a surprise statement to some people, but the fact of the matter is that starting a family with children whose birthdays must now be celebrated made it instantly imperative that my birthday should be celebrated as well. There is no doubt that my wife Elizabeth was responsible for bringing this about. In my growing up years in Nigeria, including the years in the village and Lagos, in addition to the years I spent living in Washington, DC, I never celebrated my birthdays.

My timely graduation with a master's degree, coinciding with my birth month, would have been considered a great blessing and a period of immense happiness, if only I was assured of where to go and what kind of work I was going to do. Under the circumstances, what then was I expected to do in order to resolve my financial problems? The answer was, simply, nothing much unless there was a professional job for me to do. There was no professional job for me, however, even though I was qualified to work. No, I was not eligible to work with my qualification because I was still on student visa.

Indeed, this was such an uncertain period that I was seriously considering returning to Nigeria. If that were to happen, then I would still be facing even more critical uncertainties, since I would have had to start searching for a job again. However, without actually making a clear decision regarding what direction I was going to take to avert this worst case scenario, I attended an interview at the Consulate General of Nigeria in New York City, in an attempt to join one of the Nigerian universities as a lecturer. Within a few months from the date of the interview, I received an employment letter from the Institute of Management and Technology (IMT), Enugu, in Enugu State of Nigeria. Unfortunately, however, the job offer came long after I had already signed up for the Doctor of Education (Ed.D.) program at UAlbany—State University of New York. I had to turn down the IMT opportunity in favor of continuing in the Ed.D. program. Many African graduates, such as myself, who do not return to their homeland after completing their education are afraid of impending hardships that would face them after arriving back home. My situation was no exception.

Most developing countries are not well prepared to resettle their returning graduates. The result is that returning graduates may face a more difficult time in their countries than those who never went anywhere to study. In my case, as a Nigerian returning home right after receiving a degree and starting a family would have meant the hardest time of resettlement and adjustment. I could not even afford the money to buy travel tickets for myself and my family to return home at that time. By the same token, I could not imagine arriving back home with my family only to be asked to pack my bag and report for service at a campsite of the National Youth Service Corps (NYSC). By law each Nigerian university graduate is required to fulfill one year in a youth service camp as a service to the country, before seeking employment. My decision to remain in the USA was the only viable option for me. Since it was not possible to immediately obtain a professional employment in Albany, the idea to continue in school became more attractive.

By the time I received my master's degree in 1977, I had virtually no financial resources. My wife had been working at night as a nurse's aide, while working in the day as counselor at the City of Albany's Human Resources Center. Her combined income was in the neighborhood of eight thousand dollars (us$8,000) a year at that time. I had virtually no income, except the two hundred dollars a month stipend as graduate assistant.

This income was by no means sufficient at any point to sustain my family, even if children were not yet in the picture. For this reason, by the first three years of my stay in Albany, I used to travel back to Washington, DC, during extended school breaks, to drive a taxicab and make some money, since my DC taxicab driver's license was still valid for that period of time. However, it was impossible to make enough money from driving just a few days, considering the cost of traveling to and from Washington, DC, and paying the cost of taxicab rental. More importantly, the practice of going back to Washington, DC, was becoming a serious distraction to my academic work as it was a very risky venture. My wife, for instance, considered the risk level to be so high she could not be convinced of my safe return to Albany after driving a taxicab in Washington, DC. Beyond the perceived danger itself, her fears were well-founded, especially since it was known to her that I lost a dear friend in Washington, DC, as a result of an armed robbery attack while he was transporting passengers. Personally speaking, cab driving in big cities is a great act of courage as no one knows what might happen at any time. It is always difficult for me to deal with situations or settings where my personal safety is not assured, particularly when I remember the way I used to feel during my fishing expeditions with my father in the mangrove swamps off the Atlantic coast of Nigeria and the Cameroons. Considering the dangers and very low level of benefit of traveling from Albany, NY, to drive a taxicab in Washington, DC, for a few days to meet financial needs, I found myself virtually in a no-win situation.

Taxicab driving was my last serious part-time job in the nation's capital. Since coming to Albany area the list of my mini-occupations expanded beyond driving to include titles such as a substitute school teacher, a family and youth counselor, a civil servant, and an adjunct college instructor. Although working as a civil servant became my permanent employment in Albany, each of these job experiences presented something of memorable interest to me, opportunities for growth, and unique challenges. More than any of these things, they also enabled me to appreciate the importance of individual strength and endurance—the ability to successfully utilize survival instinct and abilities with which we are endowed by our creator. That is the way I see it as far as I am concerned.

On the hind side, it is quite clear now that my desire to seek a more respectable level of education was more and more stifled by my continued financial problem. However, it was always my determination never to give up pursuing my passion. That is why I was always ready and willing to engage in various little adventures and occupations I have had to undertake in my life. Every one of these "survivalist" occupations, such as working as taxicab driver or hotel porter, was the result of my effort to resolve a financial problem in order to be able to advance my passion to the next level.

Throughout my life, the nature of experiences that I have had, as narrated above, has brought me, not just to tears and chills, but also to ask more questions: *How* was I psychologically and spiritually able to handle my school or survival job situations? *What* kind of emotional condition and strength did I muster to get past each day? *How* did I know that it was possible for me to carry on the way I did, and for how long? Finally, *why* did it have to be me and not someone else? I have raised these questions, not to confuse but, to invite, the reader into my ever-bubbling thinking processes and into my continued struggles to see my mind through a mirror. Apart from all I have already described, my shortest answer to the questions is that, in my life, all things happened for my own good.

ENROLLMENT IN THE DOCTORATE PROGRAM
Although I considered getting into a doctoral program to be a significantly logical step for me to take after completing my Master of

Dr. Bassey Essien
Graduation from U Albany, 1981

Science degree, getting started in the application process did not come quite so easily. I suffered a tremendous amount of nervousness, while trying to follow several uneasy steps to establish myself and complete the degree program in a timely fashion. Weeks after I had completed the complex application process, Dr. Joseph Leese, Chairman of the Department of Program Development and Evaluation, invited me to his office in the School of Education to inform me I was accepted into the doctor of education (Ed.D.) program, effective beginning the fall of 1977. He then added that he wanted me to wait to see if "an accommodation" would be made to offer me some financial assistance.

After waiting the longest ten days of my life, as the Lord would have it, the Department of Curriculum and Instruction extended to me an offer of graduate assistantship with a tuition waiver scholarship. This was one of the best pieces of news I had ever received in my life since coming to UAlbany—State University of New York. This action effectively confirmed my entry into the Ed.D. program at UAlbany—State University of New York. I completely welcomed all the challenges that my entry into the program was going to bring my way. For example, due to my short-term entry into the world of academia, I needed to continue to work extra hard to fulfill my strong desire to reach the top in education. Moreover, I needed to be sure that I did not relent on my effort to pursue my goal of educational achievement with all the zeal and determination that I could muster.

My area of concentration was in Curriculum Planning, with a foundation area in sociology. The academic program consisted primarily of three major segments—completion of classroom instructional assignments, successful completion of the terminal or comprehensive examinations, and completion of a doctoral thesis. Completing a doctoral thesis consists of first developing an acceptable proposal, writing an acceptable thesis, and successfully defending the thesis. Of course, all these requirements are now history to me as I was able to complete them all in due time for my graduation in 1981. Readers may want to check out my doctoral thesis, Perceived Effects of Achievement Factors on the Curriculum Decision Making Process, (UAlbany—State University of New York, 1981).

There is no doubt that completing the requirements for the doctor of education (Ed.D.) was a very challenging and rewarding experience for me. The program gave me the motivation and the opportunity to learn about education theories, teaching methodologies, curriculum theories, and theories of educational leadership. It also gave me the chance to get to know the university professors well. Perhaps the most inspiring curriculum planning theoretician in the department was none other than Dr. Maurice Johnson whose book, *Intentionality In Education* (1977), was considered to be the "programming language" of the profession, because of its emphasis on curriculum planning and evaluation.

It was an unwritten rule in the Department of Curriculum and Instruction that Dr. Johnson's book should be used as a yardstick for measuring any other book on curriculum theory. Johnson defined curriculum as a "structured series of intended learning outcomes." He distinguished between curriculum development and curriculum. Specifically, Johnson described curriculum development as a process and designated curriculum as the output or the product of curriculum development. He contended that the process and product nexus could not be complete, until both have been fully evaluated to determine their effectiveness (Johnson 1977).

Many other authors, including John Bobbit and Joseph Tyler, also occupied the focus of the department's curriculum theories. For example, Bobbit characterized curriculum as "a race course" or a "race." He describes this race as "…that series of things which children and youth must do and experience by way of developing abilities to do the things well that make up the affairs of adult life; and to be in all respects what adults should be" (Bobbit, 1918: 42). Tyler, on the other hand, argued that school testing conditions must be made similar to learning conditions in order "…to check the validity of the basic hypotheses upon which the instructional program has been organized and developed" (Tyler, 1950: 69). Personally, it will be an understatement to say that my experiences at UAlbany—State University of New York strongly reinforced my desires, efforts, and struggles, not only to obtain a meaningful education, but to become a productive member of society.

I am grateful to UAlbany—State University of New York for the opportunity given to me to learn so much and to improve myself intellectually and socially. As a result of the very genuine interest that I observed on the part of the professors, I cannot recall any specific academic pressure—or bad memory of any sort—that was ever unbearable for me to endure, except in the areas of finance. Even though I was financially struggling and sometimes terribly frustrated, I still was able to complete my subject course work, the comprehensive examination, the thesis writing and its defense within the shortest possible time. Of course, I recall the time my wife Elizabeth went to my thesis committee chair, the late Dr. John Ether, who was also the chair of the department responsible for curriculum and instruction program, and another committee member, Dr. Joseph Bosco, to appeal for more humane attention to my thesis situation. My wife, Elizabeth, wanted to explain to the committee members the dire financial situation of our family and how difficult it was for me, personally, to meet my family needs. She told them that keeping me much longer in the program was not in the best interest of the Essien family. The action of my wife came about after she observed evidence of some frustration on my part. Pregnant with our last baby girl, Iquo Essien, it was Elizabeth's idea to intervene on my behalf, and I could not stop her from doing so, especially since she knew most of the professors. Most men learn quickly not to argue with their wives, much less when they are pregnant, for the interest of peace and progress.

Having completed the writing and defense of my thesis, and for the cooperation of the committee members and other professors who impacted my life positively during the period of my graduate studies at UAlbany—State University of New York, I want to publicly, though belatedly, thank them. I also want to extend my gratitude to all my teachers starting from Armstrong High School to DC Teachers College, to Howard University and American University—all of Washington, DC. This group of professionals jointly helped awaken and nurture my "lost voice" from the mangrove swamps. I want to more specifically mention those professors who got me started vigorously at the District of Columbia Teachers College (the counselors and especially Dr. Lebedorf of the history department), Howard University Professor Samuel Yette, author of *The Choice: The Issue of Black Survival in America*), and two professors from American University, Professor Sutton of the

Film Department and Professor Poliski of the Journalism Department. If these professors did not get me on a firm footing, I would not have even thought of continuing my education to graduate level in Albany, New York.

MEETING PROFESSIONAL CHALLENGE

Now that I have obtained a doctor of education (Ed.D) degree in Curriculum and Instruction, in addition to a Master of Science degree and a bachelor of arts degree, the burning question then was how was I going to make a living from this point on? How was I going to respond to the challenge of being a professional? How about the impact of being a foreigner in a strange land? Finding answers to these questions is one of the reasons why I added this section of the book. From the look of things, it appeared that having advance college degrees did not bring an instant end to my struggles. Indeed, having degrees might very well have started me up on a different kind of a race. As I prepared myself to start job search in Albany, I quickly found that my long sought-after college degrees have left me in the mental state that almost made me question the benefit of my education in America.

The story that I am presenting here is really the story of witnessing a rude awakening, the realization that it is one thing to have a graduate level college degree, whereas it is another to use the newly acquired knowledge in a rewarding and self-satisfying employment setting. As I have covered in different sections of this book, we all have different experiences, depending on the type of environment and circumstances that we find ourselves. My particular circumstance, when it comes to job search in Albany, was heavily impacted by many factors, some of which were systemic, others environmental and, still, others personal. With regard to systemic reasons, I have to go back to the first major hurdle I had to face after completing my Ed.D. degree in Albany. It was the apparent barrier placed over my job hunting effort by reasons of having been in possession of student visa. There is no doubt that my Washington, DC, experience was repeating itself all over again in Albany.

As a foreign student with an F-1 visa, I had to apply for, and obtain, an immigration permission to work one year for practical training purposes, following the completion of my studies. To nobody's surprise, the official US Immigration position regarding practical training authorization is not for a person to earn a living, but to prepare himself or herself for eventual return to his or her country of origin. Unfortunately, however, employers in the US did not then, and still may not now, honor practical training permissions for full time employment. My experience showed that prospective employers wanted to see my green card or evidence of citizenship before offering me a job. I can imagine the situation I have just described has now been further complicated by new homeland security regulations, including requiring employers to complete Form I-9 on every potential employee. I suggest that readers interested in learning more about that should contact the United States Citizenship and Immigration Services (USCIS) now under the Department of Homeland Security.

Another system-induced hurdle that hindered my job searching effort at that time was New York State's requirement that qualified foreigners who wish to teach in public schools must not be given State teacher certification to teach in public schools of the State, unless they have declared their intention to become citizens. In my case, I could not declare to become a citizen because I was still on F-1 student visa status. Indeed, immigration regulations require that one hold a green card for five years before declaring the intention to become a citizen. In the final analysis, this is also interpreted to mean that non-citizens should not hold important job positions.

Frankly speaking, I find the whole concept to be ironic because, as much as citizenship may be required to hold certain types of job, becoming a citizen does not seem to increase one's chances of being given a better job in America, especially for black Africans. A good percentage of foreign-born citizens, especially Africans, are still considered to be second class citizens, especially in work places, no matter what their levels of education may be. This statement may not necessarily be true of those Africans who major in the areas of medicine, engineering and other sciences.

My entire postgraduate employment struggles, as described above, forced me to confront all of my mental dissonance and contradictions, especially at such times that I have had to talk to my children or other young people about the importance of their education and when being absolute and self-assured become paramount. People who have seen the kind of trials and tribulations that I have seen in my life have found it to be very rewarding in the end, when they stand firm and share their experiences truthfully and with an open mind. This is the kind of message that I want to get across through this writing.

What I considered to be mostly an environmental limitation to my job search was the fact that Albany area of the 1980s was a very isolated area to foreigners, especially people of African descent. This made it virtually impossible to circulate freely and to choose from a variety of employment opportunities. How much this situation has improved in 2010 is still debatable. My feeling is that there have been significant changes for the better, judging from the number of foreigners who are now in the capital region. It was not easy for me in those days simply to pack up and leave Albany to go somewhere else, due to my concern for the welfare of my children. Contrary to all of the advice that many of my friends gave me, I still thought Albany offered my young children, at that time, the best opportunity to attend school. That is one thing about which I strongly believe I was correct, based on their educational performances at all levels of their schooling.

Having to deal with the system-induced and environmental-induced problems that confronted me during my search for professional employment contributed to personal limitations as well. After careful reassessment of my actions and reactions, I found that it was too risky for me to pay undue attention to things that tended to retard my progress. I am referring to emotional concerns and fears of failure. I believe I might have fallen prey to that condition in some ways. Apart from that, my intense feeling of disappointment after completing my education was not very helpful to me. I think I mustered more energy studying in school than out of school, in terms of professional job search. Looking back, I can now see I was just beginning a journey that would take days, weeks, months, and even years, to arrive. My best self-aggrandizement in the circumstances is that I have come a very long way. I may not be there yet, but I am much closer to arriving there. I have made significant progress. I am still walking the walk as I am talking.

Even though the famous Chinese proverb states that a journey of one thousand miles begins with one step, I have found myself taking so many steps to complete one journey and, in each case, I always seem to be at the beginning of the journey. I even came to believe that a different set of rules was written for me such that I would always have to take ten strokes just to complete the first step. It was my conviction that most of these complicated situations and difficulties were due to my unsettling immigration status. The complications of my immigration status served to hold me back at the time that I could have moved in record speed. This forced me to redirect my effort and to seek employment in other areas of related experiences. That inevitably set a pattern for what was to become my professional life in Albany, New York.

Between the period of 1981 and 1985, I worked on jobs that paid salaries that were significantly below what would match my training and experience. This was the period when my wife, Elizabeth, and I battled the United States Immigration and Naturalization Services (INS) for our green cards. The INS unsuccessfully sought to deport my wife back to Nigeria while I was still working on my doctoral program at UAlbany—State University of New York. Over this period, we acquired the services of at least three immigration lawyers to defend us against INS. Imagine the stress and drain on our family's limited resources. The only positive outcomes have been the highly valuable experiences I have acquired in the process. These experiences only helped to make me stronger and more resilient.

The resolution of our immigration problem came with the appeal of our case to the immigration appeal tribunal in Washington, DC, in 1983. That was the year my wife was finally granted her green card, which enabled me to file for my own green card afterwards. I finally received my own green card in 1985 and declared my intention to become a citizen five years later. Ever since that time, I have achieved two related milestones—becoming an American citizen and obtaining two New York State teaching certificates, one in social studies and another in library media services. I will forever live to relish, and thank the good Lord for, this level of achievement in my life in the New World. Indeed, this and many other accomplishments, including my family life and children's education, constitute the triumph that is part of the subtitle of this book. It is also a testament to Albany as the land of promise.

It is difficult to state whether I have effectively addressed the questions of surviving as a professional after my education. I think the main point that needs to be restated more clearly is the fact that the story of my successful completion of three college degrees could be misleading when one considers the employment position in which I found myself following my schooling. In order to understand the reasons for my apparent lack of professional progress, one need to look at intervening conditions outside of my control. For example, my struggles with immigration, which impacted on my employment opportunities, must be examined, on the one hand.

On the other hand, the many challenges also forced me to chart a slightly different course of action, such as working for nonprofit agencies as a case worker, a counselor, and a program specialist, in Albany and Orange counties of New York State. After putting in my time working in these positions from 1981 to the early part of 1985, I finally joined the government of the State of New York as a civil servant. Considering it to be another miracle of my life, the year of publication of this book marks my twenty-sixth year working for New York State government. Again, considering where I came from, this is a milestone in my life that will remain indelible in my heart. Although I have not had the satisfaction of working in the professional area for which I obtained my degrees, with just one exception, it would seem as though I have made progress in different ways.

To explain the one exception alluded to above, while I was still working on this book, I was offered a position as adjunct instructor in the department of education at Siena College in Albany, NY. A year later, I was offered a similar opportunity at UAlbany—State University of New York. The experience I have gained and shared in these positions have been intrinsically and extrinsically very rewarding, not for the financial benefit alone but for the intellectual stimulation I have enjoyed. The professional and support staff of these institutions were very helpful and friendly to me during my brief tenure. I will continue seeking to renew my academic skills through teaching. This is because after twenty-six years of work in the New York State civil service system, I still feel unappreciated and even mistreated by the State Office of Temporary and Disability Assistance, by its practice of isolation of minority staff. Teaching, therefore, renders to me an instant feeling of achievement as I watch the changes that take place in the life of my students.

In scientific analysis, one has no choice but to compare certain conditions against each other in order to extrapolate some hypotheses from which to draw informed conclusions. Having said that, I am compelled to briefly reflect on the dilemma of African people and other minorities in the USA. I am referring to the issue of employment and economic security. As a struggling black man in America with all my education, I am still trying to determine where and how I fit into the class or caste system of America.

Though there is the appearance that I have been successful in my endeavors, I personally have very mixed feelings about that, considering what I have been through in obtaining my job of choice. In his book, *American Education* (2002: 102) Joel Spring addresses this point:

"No matter how high a person's status or income, racism is still a problem. However, social-class remains important. Opportunities are quite different for an African-American or white child growing up in poverty. Social-class lines are as sharply drawn in the black community as they are in the white community. Therefore, it is important to consider social-class as it intersects with race."

Spring made this statement in his book as an attempt to shed light on the age-old phenomenal conflict of race and social class in America, but he falls short of suggesting a solution to the problem. In any case, whether my success or perceived failure is related to my race, poor decision-making, or imperfect timing, I leave the final judgment to the reader to make. Suffice it to say my experience has shown that too many African intellectuals have suffered immensely from the pains of not being given equal access to employment in their respective professional fields, especially in regard to promotion to management and leadership posts, based on their academic qualifications.

CHAPTER 8

FACING MARRIAGE AND CHILDREN

Subsequent to several references that I made to my wife and children in different sections of the book, it is my intention to fully discuss in this chapter their specific contributions to my progress as a family man as well as a member of the community. Of course, not all family experiences are positive, even though we always want to keep them that way, and I am no exception, as you could see from reading this chapter. There is no doubt the story of my life would not be complete without adequate reflections of my family life in Albany as well as my early beginnings back in Nigeria. At every point in time during my stay in Albany, my wife and children played significant roles in my struggles, apparent successes and even failures. For the record, I believe my family contributed more to my success than otherwise. I'd like to say right from the top that the only negative aspect of my family life, from my own perspective, could have been possible tensions and heartbreaks caused by financial difficulties, especially at the early stages of our lives in Albany.

As stated elsewhere in this book, I began my married and family life with my new wife, Elizabeth Okon Bassey, in Albany early in 1976. Albany became our host residential city after nearly four months of living separately following our wedding in Washington, DC, on August 23, 1975. At that time, no final decision was made as to where we were going to settle as a couple. It took a period of soul searching for me to finally decide it was a good idea to move from Washington, DC, to Albany, New York.

It is appropriate to mention that while Elizabeth arrived in Albany from Nigeria in 1971 to study at UAlbany—State University of New York, I arrived in Washington, DC, in 1969 to launch my quest for an education, details of which were presented in the section dealing with Washington, DC. Guided purely by fate and faith, Elizabeth and I met each other at Columbia University in New York City in 1974, when we attended the annual colloquium of the Association of Students of South Eastern State of Nigeria (USA). This organization has since become known as the Akwa Ibom State Association of Nigeria (USA), Inc., and the annual colloquium has also been upgraded to a convention status. Elizabeth was introduced to me by Mr. Mathias Essien, a native of the Village of Mbak Etoi, which is also Elizabeth's original hometown in Akwa Ibom State of Nigeria.

Because of the location and time that Elizabeth and I met, there was no doubt that we were both desirous of long term companionship, while struggling inwardly to control our strong desires to get married. This point is supported by the fact that we met in August of 1974 and got married in August of 1975. Obviously, this short time of courtship did not allow us much time for companionship or to get to know each other much better. Being newly married, it became imperative that we should move in together and, even after starting life together as a couple, we were bound to have some rough times in the process. These became evident early on when we tried to stabilize ourselves economically as struggling foreign students in America.

The period immediately following our wedding was particularly uncertain, largely due to the fact that we had not yet chosen our place of domicile. The most concrete choices were either Albany, NY, or Washington, DC. The final choice, however, was to be determined by the location of my graduate school. As we were trying to decide on the matter, Elizabeth was helping me in talking to the graduate admissions office of UAlbany—State University of New York to secure an admission for me to start my graduate studies. Before I actually moved to Albany, not only was she persistently talking to the Admissions Office personnel on my behalf; she convinced me to apply to the UAlbany for my graduate admission. It was without any hesitation that I went ahead and completed all the applications and ordered my undergraduate college transcripts sent to the UAlbany—State University of New York. She then stayed on task with the graduate admissions office directly to be sure they received from me any required admissions information, such as teacher recommendations and transcripts.

At this point, I still had serious conflicts since I was already accepted at Howard University in Washington, DC, as well as at Towson State University outside of Baltimore, Maryland. After all was said and done, it became imperative that I move to Albany, not only to pursue my graduate education but also to firm up my new family life. As much as I would like to claim that I was ready for the new life, it was not the easiest thing for us as a newly married couple trying to start life together without any concrete source of income. Therefore, we were starting out on very shaky grounds. My wife was completing her Master of Science degree program in educational administration, while I was starting my own graduate studies in educational communications. My wife had a part-time employment and I had nothing, except the promise of graduate fellowship. I also returned to Washington, DC, to drive a taxicab during extended school breaks. So, our first year in Albany together was not a very palatable one; however, there was a remarkable sense of cooperation between the two of us and that seemed to have conquered any unpleasant feelings.

An example of our cooperation was demonstrated by our decision to remain in my wife's studio apartment, following my arrival in Albany. Though Elizabeth was hoping to move to an ultramodern apartment after getting married, we ended up living in her apartment for nearly five years before buying our first home on Orange Street, Albany, in 1981. Even being able to buy that first house was, to me, a miracle, due to the fact that we had no reasonable family income, except what was brought in through part-time employment.

In order to ensure our self-preservation in dealing with the family's poor financial situation, we had to adopt an unwritten code of conduct. We carefully managed our scarce resources while maintaining a near average lifestyle with some dignity. There was no room to compete with the "Joneses." If there was room for competition, we could not qualify to enter. There was no significant change in our financial condition when our first daughter, Eno, was born in December of 1976. The real change I can think of was the fact that the family was growing larger in size, and we the parents were getting older and, perhaps, more mature. After all was said and done, considering all that we had to deal with, the state of my marriage to Elizabeth remained progressive.

THE BIRTH AND GROWTH OF THE ESSIEN GIRLS

The fact that our daughters were born during the period that the Essien family was at the lowest point of economic and social status is a testament to the basic theme of this book. That theme seeks to emphasize my subsequent triumph in the new world after years of struggles and often desperate experiences stretching from my early to middle years. In fact, one of the most salient indicators of the recent "loudness" of my previously lost voice has been the gift and presence of my four girls—Eno, Ime, Anniedi, and Iquo Essien. I have already alluded   elsewhere in this volume to the fact that the impetus for writing this book began with class essays first initiated by Ime Essien at Cornell University and later followed by Anniedi Essien who also interviewed me for a class essay while she was at Brown University. In the section that follows, I will describe how each of the girls came into our lives, by following the order in which they were born. The role of the Essien girls in shaping my emotional state and maturity levels need not be over-emphasized. Of course, most of the credits for their overall intellectual growth and achievement must also be given to their dear mother and my wife, Elizabeth Essien.

THE BIRTH OF ENO BASSEY ESSIEN

Eno Bassey Essien was the first child to be born into our family while we were still living in the studio apartment on Central

Avenue, Albany. She was born at Albany Medical Center Hospital on December 30, 1976. During my wife's pregnancy, we both attended Lamaze childbirth classes in preparation for her natural delivery; however, she ended up delivering by Caesarian section due to what the doctor described as a narrow pelvis. Doctor Donald Swartz was the physician who handled Eno's delivery and all subsequent deliveries, assisted at one time by Doctor Brown. Eno was such a bundle of joy for me and Elizabeth; we were both very pleased to receive counseling and instructions as to how we were going to care for our baby.

The idea of undergoing a Caesarian section for child delivery was inherently scary to us. Admittedly, this was not a common practice in our place of origin. Even when and where medical facilities were available, and a Caesarian section could save the lives of mother and child, our people back home might not seek such medical assistance because they erroneously believed that either God would save the woman or the woman was cursed or afflicted by a demon if she could not deliver her child naturally. These ignorant beliefs continue to this day in many parts of developing world. Those who did not believe in prayers would engage in various acts of native medicine to ensure a safe delivery. As a result, many women who could not naturally deliver their babies lost their lives and do so even to this day. In our case, we needed to be well-informed of what was involved and how to prepare for it. Appreciation is hereby extended to all those who assisted and supported us throughout the entire process.

As a result of the Caesarian section delivery of Eno, my wife became sick with a blood clot two weeks after returning home from the hospital. She was admitted back into Albany Medical Center Hospital while I cared for the baby at home. We did not know how bad the situation was until the doctor explained it to us and assured us that Elizabeth would come out of the condition successfully.

We had great confidence in Dr. Donald Swartz and his team of assistants. My wife was in the hospital for about one week and recovered fully before returning home to be with the baby. During her hospital stay, I was the lucky dad taking care of the baby at home. I do not recall having any significant problem, including feeding and routine clean up activities. I was told by the baby care experts to concentrate in caring for the baby at home and leave Elizabeth in the hands of the hospital staff and the doctors.

After that initial period of fear and uncertainty, we were able to hold our own and went on to raise a happy, beautiful, and well baby girl that was Eno Essien. She was baptized by Father Paul Roman at St. Paul's Roman Catholic Church, Albany Street, Schenectady, New York. Her Godmother was Mrs. Catherine Eneh, who lived in Albany then with her family and later returned to work as examinations supervisor at the West African Examinations Council in Lagos, Nigeria. Catherine has since moved back to the USA where she is currently living and working in Dallas, Texas.

Apart from having been diagnosed with asthma which required routine medication, Eno Essien was generally a healthy baby as she grew up to become a very successful student from kindergarten through high school to college. There were, however, a handful of notable physical conditions and injuries that required in-depth medical testing and/or surgery. The first and probably most serious illness occurred when Eno was still less than one year old, and we took her to Albany Medical Center Hospital. I recall my wife screaming profusely until she had to be restrained by hospital staff, after the doctors told us that they were going to conduct a spinal tap on Eno to investigate what type of infection she might have. My wife could not stand the sight of doctors passing a needle into the baby's spine to draw fluid for testing. As it turned out, the test result proved negative; Eno did not have any infection and she recovered from her discomfort within a few days.

While growing up, Eno had scary incidents involving some injuries that were quite disturbing to the family. Beginning at about the age of two, we had returned home from a family outing as I parked the car, got Eno out of car seat and stood her up to wait on the sidewalk beside the car. In a twinkle of an eye, Eno ran across Central Avenue, a major traffic highway in front of our building. As I noticed her running across the street, I quickly ran across to pick her up, while she kept on giggling without acknowledging the danger she was facing. This was such a shocking scene, and we thanked God no car was passing through at the same time. Another very disturbing incident occurred on the playground of Washington Park on State Street and Northern Boulevard, Albany. Eno had fallen off a jungle gym at the park and sustained a deep cut on her lower lip. That injury required major stitches by an orthopedist and the healing lasted about three weeks.

The second major injury occurred at a privately operated roller skating facility on Route 9, north of Albany. Eno was taken by a friend to Guptills Skating Rink during which she slid under a bench while she was skirting, hit her left foot against the wall, and the left foot was either broken or the ankle was badly twisted. This injury also required wearing a cast for a period of about three weeks before recovering fully and returning to her second grade class at Our Lady of Angels. Finally, at about the age of twenty, Eno also had a corrective surgery to adjust her left and right toes, which were causing her severe pains.

All in all, the Essien family has been blessed with Eno Essien being the first born out of four daughters. She has been the trend-setter and the guiding light for all the other girls as they all grew up following in her footsteps in terms of personal growth and academic accomplishments. As a father, I have always gotten a kick out of observing the girls relate to, honor, and protect each other. It is also personally rewarding to see a child grow up to be a responsible and contributing member of the family, particularly, and of society in general.

THE BIRTH OF IME BASSEY ESSIEN

Ime Bassey Essien is the second of the Essien girls and was born on May 16, 1978. Both my wife and I thought that Ime was conceived too close to Eno, but there was nothing we could do about it then. After Ime was conceived, we also continued to think that she could be delivered naturally and continued to participate in Lamaze childbirth classes in preparation for her natural delivery. However, that did not happen. Ime was born by Caesarian section. In addition, she received a blood transfusion and required being in an incubator with special lighting for a twenty-four-hour observation. As a father, I was very nervous about what was going on with her since my wife was also recovering in the critical care room at Albany Medical Center Hospital. Luckily for us, however, both Ime and mother Elizabeth recovered fully and were able to come home in due time.

The period immediately following the second baby was quite unsettling for us as a young family in a one room apartment. On many occasions, we had to choose between food and medicine on behalf of the family. With one infant and a toddler on our hands, we had to decide, quickly, which of them deserved the day's attention. As we all know, no parents should ever be forced to make this sort of decision, even though this sort of situations continue to occur in the life of poor people here in the USA and in many parts of the world. The problem is that, time after time, there are parents who simply cannot make ends meet. All of our children deserve the best of our attention, no matter the condition of the parents. In our case, as the praying hands would indicate, "thank goodness" that Elizabeth and I gave the children our best attention and love, without regard to any form of difficulties we were facing. We did the best we could, and we praised the Lord for being on our side.

It is quite interesting to note how children grow up and learn to observe and understand the ambience and the body language of their families. This probably begins even when they are in the womb, but we may never know. This phenomenon became apparent in the behavior of Eno Essien right after she began to walk. We observed that she began to act as if she were no longer a baby and came close to thinking that she herself should participate in caring for Ime. Eno exhibited this behavior one day when she attempted to lift Ime from her crib only to drop her on the floor when she sighted her parents. This was the only really scary incident involving Eno and Ime together that I can remember.

Ime was baptized in the Roman Catholic Church at 125th Street, Manhattan, New York, by Father Silas Bassey, who was studying for a Ph.D. at Columbia University while serving in the Diocese of New York City. I remember that on the night before the day of the baptism, we drove to New York City under a heavy snow making the roads very treacherous. We arrived later to spend the night with a very good family friend who hosted our family and also accompanied us to the church for the baptism service. My wife wanted the Rev. Father Dr. Silas Bassey to baptize her baby, having known him in Nigeria long before coming to the USA. The actual baptism was the highpoint of our New York City visit. Ime's Godmother was Dr. Rose Udonkim-Ebana who was then living in Brooklyn and had since returned to Nigeria where she completed her Ph.D. in chemistry at the University of Calabar in Cross River State. Ime was named after Mrs. Ime Akan-Etuk, who died in a Greyhound bus accident on her way to West Virginia in the summer of 1998. May her soul rest in perfect peace. We continue to be proud of our community members for their strong support, love, and good will.

Although she needed blood transfusion at birth, Ime grew up to be a healthy baby and never exhibited any other serious medical problems, except when she and her little sister, Anniedi, underwent outpatient surgery to remove umbilical hernia. Ime was five years old then and Anniedi was three years old. Ime has been a very competitive and goal-oriented child based on the way she has handled herself in the community and in her academic and professional activities.

THE BIRTH OF ANNIEDI ESSIEN

Having had Eno Essien and Ime Essien back to back between December of 1976 and May of 1978, you might think that we were not going to have yet another baby in less than a three-year period. That was not the case. Anniedi Bassey Essien was the very next child born into our family on June 2, 1980. That made it exactly two years after Ime was born.

Again, Anniedi was delivered by Caesarian section as my wife was found still not capable of natural delivery. Although Anniedi was born a well baby, her mother required massive blood transfusion as a result of having bled profusely during delivery surgery. Elizabeth's post-delivery condition caused us serious concerns, although the doctors would not raise any unusual alarm while she was still receiving treatment.

Anniedi was also the third and the last baby to be born while we were still living at the Central Avenue address in Albany. Before we moved to our first home on Orange Street, we had all three babies in the two studio apartments. At this point it was becoming more and more difficult for us to take care of the children. We needed the assistance of friends and relatives, and since Eno began growing stronger, it was quite manageable. I remember a very frightening incident involving Anniedi one night in the apartment. She fell down the steps at about the age of one and a half. Apparently, she was climbing the stairs behind mother who was going up the steps at the same time, but without noticing Anniedi. Suddenly she turned around and instantly noticed that Anniedi was attempting to climb the steps to the next floor; she got excited and screamed lightly. Hearing her mother's sudden voice, Anniedi became afraid and decided to turn back to go down suddenly. She did not realize that turning quickly and going down the steps required the ability to manipulate her way safely on the steps. That was the time she accidentally rolled down the steps, while her mother kept on screaming. How else could a mother react to such incidents? Only God knows—and we thank God that Anniedi was not seriously hurt.

Anniedi was the first Essien child to be baptized in a church in our immediate neighborhood, Our Lady of Angels Church of Albany, led by Reverend Father Giles. By diocesan action, the church has since merged with St. Patrick's Church and adopted a new name of Holy Family Parish, now led by Reverend Fathers Tony Kall and Joseph Angolini. Anniedi's Godparents are Dr. Tom Okure and Mrs. Josephine Jones, both of Albany.

As a baby and a growing child, Anniedi also had a few medical episodes of her own. The most notable among them were her recurrent ear infections, her late bout with asthma, and her scary illness in 1988 during a visit to Akwa Ibom State of Nigeria. With regards to the ear infections, my wife has confirmed that she counted a total of eighteen incidents of ear infection in a seven-year period that required doctor's prescriptions for antibiotics. At one point the doctor came close to requesting parental approval for the installation of a tube into Anniedi's ear to help drain out excessive fluids. For some reason, this did not happen because Anniedi began to respond well to treatment, and the ear infection episodes finally subsided.

Anniedi's bout with asthma was most surprising to us all because she did not show any symptoms as she was growing up. It was one day when she was either six or seven years old that she exhibited the symptoms of asthma. In fact, when we first noticed the symptoms, we did not take them seriously, and she never indicated having a problem, except that we saw her wheezing. It was when the condition failed to go away that we finally took her to the doctor who ended up diagnosing her with asthma, to our surprise, and was given Ventoline Spray to be used for treatment. Anniedi used the Ventoline Spray only for a short period of time and did not need it any more after the symptoms disappeared.

Another one of Anniedi Essien's scary illnesses was the one that occurred in 1988 in Akwa Ibom State of Nigeria during a short visit at the age of seven. Anniedi and her sister, Eno, traveled with their mother to visit their grandparents in Nigeria in the summer of 1988. According to the report, Anniedi developed breathing difficulties while there. Thank God that Anniedi's mother quickly noticed the condition and sought medical help for her at a local hospital. I suspect this was a touch of asthma for Anniedi, having been exposed to extremely dry and dusty condition in Nigeria. With the available treatment given to her, she was able to come out of the condition and return to Albany safely. Anniedi's illness was not the only incident on that home visit. It was on the same trip that my wife and the two Essien girls ended up representing me at the funeral of my dear father, the late Mr. Edet Essien Asuquo. May his soul rest in perfect peace. Immediately before his death, my wife and the two Essien girls visited with my sick father and took him to the nearest hospital for treatment. Unfortunately, my father was too far gone in his sickness which had begun one year earlier due to a mild stroke. I remain forever grateful to my wife and the girls for representing me at my father's funeral in 1988 during their short visit to Akwa Ibom State of Nigeria.

THE BIRTH OF IQUO BASSEY ESSIEN

We have now come to the last, but not the least, of the four Essien girls to be born into the Bassey and Elizabeth Essien household in Albany, New York. Iquo was born on October 14, 1981, also by Caesarian section at Albany Medical Center Hospital. Being the last of the four girls could inevitably imply that she would be the weakest link of the lot; however, the reverse turned out to be the case. First of all, Iquo was born at the time we thought we were not ready for her, considering the condition of her mother during Anniedi's birth. Our experience with excessive bleeding that required blood transfusions left us with a sense of insecurity as to having another baby.

Ironically, however, Iquo's birth turned out to be the most peaceful, especially as Elizabeth was under the care of an experienced nurse in charge of the maternity ward. Ms. Dulcie Bishop, the nurse in charge of the maternity ward of Albany Medical Center Hospital, excused herself from her regular duty just to personally care for my wife during delivery. Ms. Bishop took this considered action because of the love she had for Elizabeth and since she was particularly concerned about the bleeding episodes suffered by Elizabeth during Anniedi's birth. Because this last time was such a success we had to give all the credit to Ms. Bishop for what she did. We had a reason to believe her presence and care made all the difference in calming down Elizabeth, and that helped her to undergo the entire delivery procedure without any serious physical reaction. As any one could tell from Ms. Bishop's contribution to the welfare of the Essien family, particularly her medical care for Iquo and Iquo's mother, Ms. Bishop was nominated Godmother for Iquo Essien during her baptism at Our Lady of Angels Church, which was then led by Reverend Father Giles.

Iquo ended up exhibiting her own medical conditions that

Dr. Bassey Essien with wife Elizabeth and children.
Standing, L-R, Eno Essien, Anniedi Essien, Ime Essien, and Iquo Essien.

would follow her from infancy to adolescence. For example, Iquo Essien was diagnosed with having eczema or irregular skin condition. The treatment required special care to keep the skin moist and normal. She also has serious allergic conditions and has had to undergo various diagnostic tests by doctors. Among Iquo's range of allergic conditions is her allergy to peanuts. In fact, this particular condition once manifested itself in a very life threatening and scary way, when Iquo reacted to some peanuts she had eaten. We have been as guarded as we can be in dealing with this condition.

Iquo's worst medical condition that has required more medical treatment and occupied most of our time in care has been asthma. Her asthma condition has been the most serious one among our daughters and has resulted in at least two different hospitalizations prior to her adolescence. Iquo learned quite early how to properly use her doctor-prescribed medications and how to manage herself at home and during rigorous activities. We all continued to do our best in keeping up with the changing mode of treatment for asthma for the interest of all our daughters. We continue to pray for their success as they learn to take full control of their medical conditions.

CHAPTER 9

BEHOLDING THE CHILDREN'S EDUCATION

I begin this chapter by citing from chapter twenty-two, verse six, of the book of Proverbs (New International Version), which gives us the following directive: "Train up a child in the way he should go, And when he is old, he will not turn from it." This is probably the best of the many verses of the bible that deal with parental obligations to take care of their children's training and education. I could not avoid citing this biblical text to highlight the importance of the effort that my wife and I had to make in raising our children to be sure they were receiving the best education to prepare themselves for a better future.

My wife, Elizabeth, and I had four children in a five-year period, while I was still in graduate school and she worked on a very low paying job. This situation presented a tremendous amount of stress on us as a young family trying to survive in Albany. Not only were we struggling to complete our graduate education with very little or no reliable sources of income, the children themselves were also placing additional demands for our attention and tender loving care that only parents can provide, just to be sure that they remained healthy at all times. Indeed, it is fair to say that caring for the children constituted a major part of the burdens that we had to carry in our struggle to make ends meet in the city of Albany. To be very candid, there were those who wanted to know why we did not choose to delay having children, as we were working on finishing our graduate education. The best way to explain our actions is that we did not and could not knowingly and deliberately create hardships for the family. We started a family with an open mind, with no crystal ball to predict the outcome of our actions. It was our attitude to remain positive for the best outcome of our every venture, including having children, and we remain forever grateful to God for blessing us with the gift of all our children.

Whatever our children would have become thus far, they are the product of our past activities and labor. We know that in order for our children to grow up and become useful members of the society of which we as parents and the entire world can be proud, they have to be nurtured both intellectually and physically. Otherwise, how can we claim credits for their success? The problem comes when the parents' interests and ability to adequately care for their children are clouded by poverty and other personal issues. In such cases, personal sacrifice has to be brought to bear in order to save the children. Certainly, my wife and I could not, and would not, consider our situation to be the most reasonable or the best example of meeting parental obligation for their children's education.

When it comes to the necessity of beholding unto our children's education, we must institute our own style, adorned by efforts and commitment. In our case, our actions strictly reflected our parental love of the children, care, and empathy. Simply stated, we followed a slow and an incremental process in fulfilling the obligation of our children's education. That means we always tended to pay greater attention to what works and de-emphasize that which does not work. Mind you, we never boasted of having a house full of educational toys. We accomplished our approaches simply by being very sensitive to the issue of the children's education and welfare. We always exercise extreme care not to allow our children to experience turbulence and stress, similar to what we experienced as parents in our early days.

First of all, my philosophy is that we are not educated, until we are all educated. This philosophy speaks to the obligation of all capable parents to ensure that their children receive the best possible education. It also empowers the society to make sure that all children are educated, without regard to their parental social and financial status, and none are left behind. Second, it is my belief that parents, especially minority and low income parents, should be sensitive to the daily needs of their children's education and pay close attention to issues affecting their academic performances on a routine basis. Finally, judging from my experiences in the past as I have narrated in this book, parents' past turbulent and difficult beginning should serve more as a motivating factor for beholding their children's education, not a reason to succumb to the whims of failure and inferiority complex. In many ways, my untiring effort to promote my children's academic successes was, in part, the results of my past turbulent experiences and difficulties of getting an education. In the following sections I will do my best to illustrate our local experiences as they affected my children, beginning with the Albany experience which began in the city of Albany from early to mid 1980s. At the end of the narrative of the Albany experience, I will turn my attention to the South Colonie experience which will cover the period of late 1980s to later part of 1990s.

THE ALBANY CITY EXPERIENCE

Our initial direct experience with the education of the Essien girls began in the city of Albany, New York. It was here that Elizabeth and I were first brought into the limelight of raising school-age children. Albany, therefore, became the first stage of the Essien girls' education, covering the early childhood experiences of Eno Essien, Ime Essien, and Anniedi Essien. Our daughter Iquo Essien's early childhood experiences were interrupted by the family's move from Albany to South Colonie. It was the combination of Albany and South Colonie experiences that contributed to the educational progress of the children.

Over the years friends and well-wishers alike have made it a habit of praising me and my wife for all the work that we have done in the education of our children. Some have gone out of their way to recommend that we write a book on the subject of the parental role in their children's education, particularly our children. My usual response to such statements has been to chuckle over them and move on. I mean "chuckle over them" because I am not the type who believes in miracles to get things done, even though it seems much like miracles have been in charge of my life history.

As I mentioned already, my philosophy on the subject of children's education is that *we are not* educated until *we are all* educated. By the same token, it will make no sense to expect my children to go through the same difficult experiences that I went through—or their mother went through—growing up in Akwa

Ibom State of Nigeria. Consequently, my wife and I considered it our obligation to make sure our children received the best possible education we could access and could afford.

Like most of the experiences and phenomena I have narrated in different chapters of this book, it was not so much a matter of sitting down and planning that our children were going to attend the best schools and receive the best education on earth. Where the heck would I or my wife have that sort of planning time and knowledge? The truth of the matter is that all of the work that we did to ensure our children's education were our spontaneous actions and reactions to the children's needs and demands of the moment and location.

Spontaneity meant that we maintained the operational attitude that parental actions or response to the children's educational needs was our primary responsibility and, therefore, the children's educational needs were given precedence over all other matters in the family. It was not a question of worrying about physiology or genetics as the most influential phenomenon on learning. It was more of the positive parental instinct and desire, not only to make sure that our children received the best parental support, but also that they received whatsoever could be described as the best education in Albany and in South Colonie. In fact, it was really a question of trying to put in our best efforts to make the best of any educational opportunities and resources that were there for our children. This, in part, is how the entire educational activities and routines came together to yield a meaningful result for our children.

THE INITIAL CONTACT WITH HEAD START
Our initial contact with the Albany County Head Start resulted from

our effort to get our children into a preschool program in the city of Albany. Due to the fact that we were at the lowest point of economic ladder, we needed to register our children in a preschool program that was well managed, reasonable, high quality, and also affordable. As our fate would have it, the only such early childhood educational program in town was the Head Start, a preschool program that was then, and is still, sponsored by the Albany County Opportunity, Inc., a community action program that provides assistance and various forms of community and social services to the poor and low income families. Head Start Program was, and still is, a federally funded educational program geared toward laying strong educational foundations for four-year-old children of poor families. The Head Start Program's emphasis includes, but is not limited to, nutrition, health, and a very strong parental involvement in the educational and policy making processes.

We had to take our children to the Head Start Program and prayed that they be accepted into the school, for the first time. Yes, we prayed that our children be accepted into the program because we simply had no other means of starting the children on their educational path. In fact, any different idea of taking the children to other regular preschools was out of the question for us, because we could not afford to pay for such programs. For that reason, it was simply not the right time for us to be too selective about the type of preschools that the children should attend. It was a very critical period in the life of the Essien family as I was still undergoing my graduate studies at UAlbany—State Universit of New York.

The Albany County Head Start Program was extremely accommodating of our needs through their flexible schedules, highly diversified programs, and friendly staff. The program also had what was called a "home-based component," designed for families who could not take their children to the center due to either their physical condition or location of their residence in the county. The Essien family was never considered suitable candidates for the home-based program.

Having to take our children to the Head Start Program was not just a lesson in humility; it was such a great learning experience for me and my wife as well. Head Start was, and still is, noted for having outstanding programs for parental training and participation. In order to be effective in helping to train our children, we were all required to complete parental training programs, which were, perhaps, the strongest component of the nationally acclaimed preschool education program. In many instances, Head Start parents were encouraged and sponsored to attend national conferences on early childhood education, and those conferences became one of the main sources of educational information for parents.

As a result of the program's active parental involvement and training, my wife, Elizabeth, was elected president of the Albany County Head Start Advisory Board for a period of two years (1980-1981). In 1982, I was nominated and sponsored by the Albany County Opportunity, Inc., to undergo a Head Start's train the trainer certificate program at Elmira College in Elmira, New York. The training helped tremendously to enrich my knowledge of different techniques for training parents and managing Head Start's educational programs. Head Start also had a program in place to encourage low income parents, who complete Head Start programs for certification, to use their training credits and work records as the basis to enroll in college to work toward a bachelor's degree.

Parents who do not have high school diplomas are encouraged to enroll in school for their general education development (GED).

All of the skills we as parents acquired from the many Head Start training programs helped us to provide the best early education to Eno and Ime, who attended the Head Start Program between the years of 1980 and 1984. Although the third and fourth of the girls, Anniedi and Iquo, did not attend the Head Start preschool program, the parental training we received from Head Start equipped us, in parts, to better assist them in all subsequent educational program in which they .participated.

We considered ourselves to be fortunate that the first two of our four children, were accepted into the Head Start Program, offering us a tremendous opportunity to receive very high quality parental guidance, motivation, and training that have remained with us for the rest of our lives. One of our prayers has been that our parental contributions toward the education of our daughters will be rewarded with lasting academic achievements and subsequent life accomplishments that can only be the envy of the civilized world. Considering my irregular educational beginning, it has been a pleasure observing the educational successes of my children, as described in the following section.

ENO AND IME ESSIEN
As the first-born among the four Essien daughters, Eno Essien was the first child to start her preschool education at the Albany County Head Start program. She was joined at the Head Start program after one year by Ime Essien, our second daughter. Both Eno and Ime spent a total of two years each in the Head Start Program between the period of 1981 and 1984. Having been the first daughter to enter

Head Start, Eno became her baby sister, Ime's, early coach as they used to share their reading exercises together. Anniedi and Iquo, the third and fourth daughters, attended the United Methodist Society's preschool program, and that will be discussed in detail later.

As described in the opening section of this chapter, Head Start was very good for Eno and Ime Essien and the family. This was because of the program's emphasis on human touch and parental training and involvement. Throughout the two years Eno and Ime were at the Head Start Program, nearly every staff person working there, ranging from the van driver to the dietician, knew us parents and the children by our first names. In fact, over the years since leaving Head Start, I have come across many former Head Start staff members on numerous occasions who eagerly recognized and greeted me with fun memories, as a former Head Start parent.

Head Start's preschool programs consisted of early nutritional and health maintenance component for all the children. During the feeding time, there was a strong reliance on trained parent volunteers, in addition to paid staff supervision. Following the early morning nutritional and health programs, regular classroom instructions were conducted to help the children's development in different cognitive, intellectual, and psychomotor skills.

Head Start parents were always encouraged to participate in their children's early childhood education. This meant that if it was a parent's wish to accompany his or her child on a field trip or to sit with the child during the morning feeding or during classroom instruction, such a parent would be welcome and given proper guidance to boost the parent's confidence. The general rule governing parental participation has been that parents must take part fully in all of the children's activities, including all physical and reading activities. This is due to the fact that such activities have been known to be significant contributing factors toward children's intellectual, spiritual, and physical growth and development.

In the case of our daughters, Eno and Ime, my wife and I used to alternate our participation in their educational and physical activities, with my wife taking the brunt of the parental involvement. Up to and including the time that she served as President of the Albany County Head Start Advisory Board, Elizabeth did more than oversee our children's progress. She helped to ensure that needed resources and programs were in place for the ultimate improvement of the overall Head Start educational program for all families in Albany County. Elizabeth also helped to institute a stronger parent-driven home-based program for Head Start families. The program called for parents to practice and follow schedules of weekly reading and other activities for their children. With this concept in mind, Elizabeth put in place a schedule of weekly trips to the local libraries to give each of our children an opportunity to borrow and read up to ten children's books per week. Different forms of reward, including special outing and special evening treats, were employed as positive reinforcement to the children whenever they completed their weekly reading assignment. There is no doubt that the weekly reading assignments contributed a great deal to our children's love of books and their subsequent academic performances.

Routine field trips were also made a major part of the Head Start Program. For preschool children, field trips were planned on the basis of the children's domain needs, explained in the following examples: If the teacher's intention was for the children to enrich or improve their cognitive development and the skills in object recognition and recall, a field trip was planned and undertaken to emphasize sightseeing of historical things and events, including museums, theatres, and musical concerts. Early childhood education teachers would attest to the importance of cognitive development and the importance of exposing young children to many external stimulants, such as pictures, sounds, and meaningful objects in the learning environment.

Head Start was a good way for Eno and Ime to jump-start their paths to educational leadership and human resource development. This is mainly due to the fact that Head Start helped them, in my opinion, not only with developing cognitive skills, but also in recognizing the importance of health and general development of the human mind.

My conclusion is based on personal observation and the feedback that I gathered from Eno and Ime themselves. It is amazing how our childhood experiences can remain implanted in our memories. These two girls have already demonstrated in their subsequent educational experiences that they are up to the tasks of not only going after their educational goals but also of trying to bring their friends along with them, as shown in their working with other children in the Science and Technology Entry Program (STEP), a summer school program for adolescents, sponsored by Union College in Schenectady, New York. Eno and Ime were regular participants at STEP which provided various challenging summer activities to them and other children.

After graduating from Head Start, Eno and her sister Ime were registered in Our Lady of Angels Church Elementary School on Central Avenue in Albany, New York. Eno was registered in 1983, one year before Ime. Eno went on to complete her first, second, and third grade education at Our Lady of Angels School. Ime later completed only her first and second grades at Our Lady of Angels School before the family moved to the Colonie Central School District in 1986.

We decided to transition Eno and Ime to Our Lady of Angels because of our long-standing faith in religious education. Our faith goes back to our village beginnings. For example, I was baptized in the Apostolic Church at Ifa Ikot Idang prior to leaving the village in 1959, while my wife was raised a Catholic in the village of Mbak Etoi, just three miles from Ifa Ikot Idang. Both of us grew up with, and maintained, strong Christian religious values that have guided us in raising our children. Consequently, it was inevitable that we sought to enroll our children in a religious school. However, our daughters' experiences at Our Lady of Angels School in Albany were far below our expectations. Our Lady of Angels School lacked the kind of human relationship and parental training and outreach components to which we became accustomed in the Head Start Program. The two teachers mentioned here made it a habit of complaining about our children each school day.

It is also possible that the school's teachers were not well versed in the technique of child behavioral management and in dealing with cultural differences. For example, whereas Eno and Ime were not considered to be bad students at Our Lady of Angels School, their classroom teachers chose to emphasize their mistakes and misbehaviors to the exclusion of positive reinforcement. It was a common practice for us parents to receive complaints from the teachers for one form of behavior problem or another. However, most of the teachers' complaints usually lacked cogent solutions from the teachers, and they were not open to our suggestions as to how to better resolve the problems.

As a graduate student in instructional technology and curriculum planning, I desperately attempted to reach out to the teachers at Our Lady of Angels to suggest ways of dealing with their classroom problems. I was not even given an audience by the teachers. I always believed that I could combine the child development techniques that I learned from Head Start teachings with some of my professional knowledge to help both the children and their teachers at Our Lady of Angels. Unfortunately, my professional and parental ideas were not even tried by Our Lady of Angels in their curriculum and instructional approaches. Fortunately for the Essien family, we no longer needed the help of Our Lady of Angels in teaching our children because we moved out of Albany to the South Colonie Central School District. Our overall reaction regarding Our Lady of Angels could be summed up in a rhetorical statement made by one of the Essien girls during our brief discussion of the issue: "Sometimes we wonder how different things would have been if we never moved out of Albany." All in all, my family considered our final move from Albany to South Colonie to be a great blessing because it offered us an opportunity for a fresh and serious start in the process of the children's education.

ANNIEDI AND IQUO ESSIEN
Our third and fourth daughters, Anniedi and Iquo, did not attend the Head Start preschool program. Anniedi was registered at a preschool program run by the United Methodist Society (UMS) on Clinton Avenue in Albany. She later attended Our Lady of Angels'

kindergarten program prior to our moving from Albany to South Colonie. Iquo was also registered in the UMS preschool program, one year after Anniedi in 1985. The UMS preschool was not as sophisticated and well equipped as was the Albany County Head Start program, however, the preschool program had a group of very highly committed staff members who showed a remarkable dedication and devotion to serving children.

The principal supervising director of the UMS program was the late Reverend Dr. Carl Taylor, whose daughter, Mrs. Barbara Weber, was the director of the preschool program. Prior to his death, Dr. Taylor was the principal area administrator for the United Methodist Church Society in the Capital District of New York State.

The other body of support for the program was the church's board of advisors, made up of parents and other important members of the Capital District community. The performance of the UMS board of advisors was a good example of the popular saying that, "It takes a village to raise a child." Although the preschool did not have a significant amount of money to purchase expensive instructional equipment and hire more staff, UMS tried very hard to follow the pattern of the Albany Head Start Program, by ensuring that the children were fed and well cared for while in the program. The program also organized field trips for the children, based on the importance of the site to be visited and the affordability of the transportation to the children's families.

At the time that Anniedi and Iquo joined the UMS preschool program, we had become a little more knowledgeable and aware of our obligations and responsibilities. Our Head Start experiences not only equipped us with the knowledge to help our children, but also taught us how to relate to educational staff and directors, including those of the UMS program. At this point both Eno and Ime were already either completing or beginning their kindergarten program at Our Lady of Angels School.

Creativity and resilience became part and parcel of our continued effort to help the children and see them get ahead in their learning. For example, it was the persistence and creativity of my wife, by taking the children to the local libraries and by fostering good reading habits through positive reinforcement on the children, that enabled them to start reading books at a very early age.

THE FAMILY'S MOVE TO COLONIE

My family's move from the city of Albany to the suburban section of the town of Colonie capped months of sleepless nights for me as I worked tirelessly to secure a safer and more comfortable living accommodation for the family. The process began sometime in the middle of 1985 when I received information to the effect that there was a single family house on Grounds Place, South Colonie, whose owner lived in California and would like to sell. Upon further inquiries, I found the house was not in good shape due to lack of maintenance. With the help and permission of the owner's attorney, we were able to arrange for a professional inspection of the property. The result of the inspection came back satisfactory, with the exception of all amenable items. The interior of the property was full of pieces of old furniture and the wallpaper was in poor shape. On the outside, the lawn was full of overgrown bushes and trees, in addition to messy soil and dirt. The walking path to the front entrance was full of weeds and sands; the back and sides to the property were full of overgrown and tall trees; whatever was left of the old stockade fence were broken and in very poor condition. Notwithstanding all these problems, and after carefully considering their future ramifications, we reached the conclusion that we should be able to conduct a thorough clean-up, as soon as we sign the purchase contract and close on the property.

The purchase price of the property was significantly lower than it would have been, due to the fact that the house was not in the best condition. As soon as our purchase offer was accepted by the owner, we proceeded to apply for a mortgage at the Albany Savings Bank—years later Charter One Bank and now Citizen Bank. After our loan application was approved and we closed on the property, the next immediate task at hand was to figure out how to clean up the place and fix it up to some extent in order for the family to move in. For a period of about three weeks, I made it a routine duty to go and work on the house late in the evenings after returning from work. On some nights, I would be there as late as two o'clock in the morning. We also sought the assistance of a handyman to help us remove the wallpaper and repaint the entire house. At least two overgrown trees were taken out of the front yard at a cost of two hundred dollars. For another two hundred dollars, we acquired the services of truckers to remove all of the old furniture. Eventually the house was put into good shape for the family to move in.

Our physical move from Albany to the South Colonie School District was, in itself, a life-changing experience for the family—especially for the children—as it seemed to heavily account for most of the subsequent events and actions that followed. These actions either contributed to, or directly shaped, the education of the Essien girls since 1986. It was the stage at which we had children of different maturity and grade levels collectively participating in an unsettling situation that can only be likened to my early life experiences.

As an example of the type of psychological and emotional chaos that the move created for the children, Mercy Essien transferred from Albany High School to South Colonie High School. Eno and Ime transferred from Our Lady of Angels School to South Colonie Schools at the fourth and third grade levels, respectively. Anniedi started at the first grade level, and Iquo started at the kindergarten level. The task for the family was how to find a common ground for the children to adapt to in our new community. Considering our immediate past disappointing experience with Our Lady of Angels School in Albany, we did not anticipate the luxury of having any of the kids in any classroom, in any school, that we could consider to be safe and more accommodating. We were not able to determine what was a safe or reasonable level of confidence for the children, when it came to the question of who would be their teachers, who would be their next best friends in class, and what would be their comfort levels in the new school environment.

To describe the transitional period of January to March, 1986, as a battle royal would be an understatement, but suffice it to say that, when all the phenomena are considered, it became clear there was a tense feeling of nervousness on the children's part regarding the family's move from Albany to South Colonie. We did not know whether the children were going to attend private or public schools. The children's nervousness could be described as the fear of the unknown and the fear of isolation. The girls did not think they would make any new friends, and they did not know whether they would be well received into the South Colonie classrooms. In some cases, the children's fears were not well-founded, as it did not take too much effort to make new friends after getting into the South Colonie schools.

Another factor that dominated the move to South Colonie was the fact that our economic base was beginning to get stronger and better than what it had been in the previous years. Having to move from a two family house in Albany to a single family Cape Cod cottage in a suburban neighborhood in a different school district was a major change in the life of a young African immigrant family. It was the beginning of the period during which my wife and I began to bring in a more steady income through professional employment with the government of the State of New York.

In an attempt to rationalize all of these experiences and transitional turmoil, I could not help but reach the conclusion that the situation was a result of our effort to adjust from one social stratum to another one. In other words, the so-called "American Dream," an apparently illusive concept of family self-sufficiency and self-actualization, was beginning to knock on our doorstep and was waiting for a positive response. We still had a long road to travel, however, not only on the economic and social track, but also in keeping a more perfect balance and in making decisions about our future actions. This was the point at which we needed help to deal with the agony of transferring to South Colonie Central School District.

For the benefit of the reader, I want to provide a brief background of why a move that outwardly appeared to be a sign of progress could have created such untold turmoil in the family, particularly for the children. First of all, the period that we moved the children from both the United Methodist Society preschool program and Our Lady of Angels School to South Colonie was not the easiest time of our life in Albany. Not only did we have to go through changes and the agony of moving to what is considered the suburb of the city of Albany, we had to register the children in new schools as well.

Second, the challenges we faced after moving to South Colonie presented us with numerous choices, none of which appeared to be the best one at that material time. In fact, just like many parents trying to oversee their children's education or health, nobody told us what we should have done or in which school district we should enroll our children. If anyone tried to tell us what to do and where to go, we probably were not even equipped to follow such advice. The thorny question was whether to take or not to take our children to another Catholic school after our negative experiences with Our Lady of Angels School in Albany.

As a matter of fact, despite our frustration with Our Lady of Angels School in Albany, we were still bent on registering the girls in another Catholic school, and the school of record then was St. Pius School in Loudonville, about four miles northeast of our residence. We actually started action to get the children registered at St. Pius School, but we were delayed by the conditions and requirements that were imposed on us. There were two sticky issues, however, the school fees to be paid and the transportation arrangements.

It was after a period of frustration in setting up the children's program at St. Pius School that I decided to contact the South Colonie Central School District to find out what we could do to register our children in the public schools. To our surprise, the South Colonie Public Schools became the easiest thing for us in terms of all grade levels and the transportation set-up. We were told to visit appropriate elementary and middle schools to meet the principals and staff to discuss our needs. With the kind of easy reception that we had in the South Colonie School District, it was inevitable that we register the girls in their respective classes in South Colonie Public Schools.

THE SOUTH COLONIE EXPERIENCE

In January, 1986, the Essien girls began to deal with a new system of instruction, make new friends, and became part and parcel of the South Colonie experiences that would subsequently prepare them for college. Details of their activities and performance will show magnificent efforts on their part to meet and surpass all forms of new academic and social demands that came their way. In keeping with the same method that I adopted in presenting their educational experiences at the top of this chapter, I will continue to do so by first narrating the stories of Eno and Ime, followed by Anniedi and Iquo's experiences. I have also decided to add the girls' college experiences to the list of items to be narrated in this section. It is my hope that this approach will shed more light on my story, as I consider my children's academic achievement and subsequent accomplishments to be an extension or raising of my "voice" that was once lost in the mangrove swamps.

ENO AND IME ESSIEN

Eno started her classes in the fourth grade at Sand Creek Middle School. She was recommended for, and registered in, the Talented and Gifted (TAG) Program one year later. At the same time, Ime Essien started in the third grade, also at Sand Creek School. Unlike

Eno, Ime was not recommended for the TAG program. However, in sixth grade she entered and won a black history month essay contest in 1989 and was given a chance to read her essay on local television. Ime's video reading her essay was broadcast repeatedly on Channel 6 during February black history month. Both Eno and Ime continued to study hard with each other all through high school. Eno entered high school in 1991 and Ime in 1992, but the one year separation did not appear to affect their progress or relationship.

While in high school, both girls were also in the NYS Board of Regents's Honors Program, and they registered for and completed advanced placement (AP) classes. On the basis of their successful performance in the AP classes, the girls were allowed to take a state examination for advanced placement during college admission. Unfortunately, however, many colleges and universities, especially the Ivy League schools, did not grant advance standing for those credits. The children, however, enjoyed the benefit of advance instructional activities while still in high school, as this subsequently enabled them to perform well in college.

With regard to their assimilation in Sand Creek School, Eno and Ime might have enjoyed the advantage of being able to adjust faster to a different and more sophisticated school system because of their maturity levels. Eno particularly enjoyed learning in the middle school classes taught by Mrs. Nancy Jonas in the Talented and Gifted (TAG) program. She also liked Mrs. Lynn Vaccaro in the English Department. Anniedi and Iquo later followed in Eno's footsteps as they, too, were accepted into the TAG program. Unfortunately, Sand Creek School subsequently decided to abolish the TAG program and replaced it with technology classes.

Both Eno and Ime made tremendous efforts to participate in activities, including high school basketball and orchestra. Ime in particular participated in the Area All New York State Music Association (NYSMA) annual concert, sponsored jointly by different school districts. The concert is usually conducted by a professional musician invited by NYSMA and called for an intensive weekend-long group practice before the actual concert event.

Eno and Ime Essien were responsible for setting up the human relations club for the South Colonie Central School District, to foster the assimilation and understanding of diversity and multicultural issues among students of different races. The idea of forming the human relations club resulted from the two girls' 1994 summer participation in the Ella Baker Academy at UAlbany—State University of New York, which took them to Morehouse College, Atlanta, Georgia. The summer program was sponsored by the New York State Martin Luther King, Jr., Commission on Nonviolence, under the then Governor Mario Cuomo. Both Eno and Ime used the platform of the human relations club to encourage other high school students at South Colonie High School to learn and assimilate issues of diversity among the races.

Eno and Ime were also heavily involved in other extra-curricular activities, including the Student Theater Outreach Program (STOP), sponsored by the New York State Martin Luther King, Jr., Commission on Nonviolence in Albany. STOP provides a creative outlet for youth while offering them lessons in the Kingian principles of non-violence, performing art, drama, voice development, and African dance. Using their knowledge, strong interest and leadership qualities, Eno and Ime provided valuable African dance and cultural lessons to other youngsters who were members of STOP.

During their senior years in high school, Eno attended a special summer public policy program at Georgetown University in Washington, DC, and Ime attended a special summer science program for high school students at Roswell Park Cancer Institute in Buffalo, New York, on a Westinghouse science research grant. She completed a research project titled: "The Involvement of Protein Kinas C in Cell Cycle Progression." The research report was later published in the B Section of January 10, 1996, issue of the *Daily Gazette*, Schenectady, New York.

As they battled their ways to new beginnings, Eno Essien graduated at the rank of eight out of a class of four hundred students from the South Colonie High School in 1995 and went on to the Massachusetts Institute of Technology (MIT), where she earned a bachelor's degree in mechanical engineering in 1999. Ime graduated in the year 1996 at the rank of twenty out of a class of four hundred students and went on to Cornell University where she earned a bachelor of science degree in human development, with emphasis in biological sciences in the year 2000.

ANNIEDI AND IQUO ESSIEN

As mentioned before, Anniedi started her classes at the Shaker Road Elementary School in the first grade because she had already completed two years at the United Methodist Society (UMS) preschool program and one year of kindergarten at Our Lady of Angels School in Albany. Anniedi was at Shaker Road all the way through the fourth grade before being moved to Sand Creek Middle School in 1990 at the fifth grade level. After leaving the UMS preschool program, which coincided with the family's move to Colonie, Iquo spent a brief time at Mrs. Kospa's Family Day Care Center, located two blocks from our new residence on Grounds Place. She then went into the kindergarten class at Shaker Road Elementary School in 1986 and stayed there through the third grade when she was transferred to Roesseleville Elementary School on California Street. Iquo completed fourth grade at Roesseleville before moving to Sand Creek Middle School at the fifth grade level in 1991. This was the same year that her big sister, Eno, was transitioning from Sand Creek Middle School to the Colonie Central High School.

It is important to note that Anniedi moved to Sand Creek at the fourth grade level, while Iquo moved there at the fifth grade level. The reason was purely administrative. As part of the school district reorganization, it was decided, right after Anniedi had started classes for the school year at Sand Creek, that elementary school students should complete their fifth grade years prior to registering at Sand Creek. I do not think that either Iquo or Anniedi suffered any adverse consequences from that new policy. On the contrary, my observation is that, having to start afresh at South Colonie and being below their more mature sisters, Eno and Ime, gave them two advantages. The first advantage was that they more fundamentally benefited from being introduced early into the rigor of South Colonie's system of teaching from the ground up. The second advantage was that they also stood to gain from the experiences of two older sisters who had already completed most of their elementary educational experiences in Albany and could help them out with reading and homework whenever that became necessary.

These advantages could have, quite possibly, far outweighed any possible traumatic shocks that the family's move might have caused them when one considers the latent fear and uncertainties that permeated the family during and after the move to South Colonie. Indeed, for Iquo, the fact that Sand Creek Middle School abolished the Talented and Gifted (TAG) program did not matter much. She was one of the first sets of Sand Creek students recommended to participate in the technology program managed and run by Mrs. Sally Heritage.

The Technology Program was designed to challenge the bright students to engage in more advanced academic work and independent projects, guided by the class teacher. Without a doubt, Iquo made the best use of every opportunity offered to her in the Technology Program and she excelled in all her assignments. Iquo was also placed in the advanced mathematics class while she was in seventh grade, skipping the equivalent of two years of mathematics classes. Her participation in that class eventually resulted in starting her morning classes at the high school and ending them in the afternoon back at the middle school. The end result of her acceleration was that Iquo completed her high school science and mathematics requirements ahead of time, thus allowing her to attend the University at Albany part time before high school graduation. This also paved the way for her to take advantage of placement above her freshman college mathematics requirements.

A basket full of appreciation buttons is due to some of Iquo's teachers who trusted her so much and consistently recommended her for more challenging courses. Her excellent academic performance resulted in numerous awards that she received from the school district. Iquo received one special award together with her teacher in 1997, after she was asked to nominate her chosen teacher of excellence to have lunch with her at the award ceremony. Without any hesitation whatsoever, Iquo nominated her former sixth grade English and technology teacher, Mrs. Sally Heritage. Mrs. Heritage was such a positive influence on Iquo throughout Iquo's tenure at South Colonie Central Schools.

Anniedi's most significant achievement at the middle school level was being recommended two years in a row by her teachers to attend a special summer science program at Clarkson University in Ogdensburg, New York. During her first year in high school, Anniedi applied for, and was accepted in, the University of Pennsylvania's Summer Science program in Philadelphia, where she was first introduced to the subject of biomedical ethics under the renowned Dr. Arthur L. Caplan, professor of bioethics. In her sophomore and senior years of high school, respectively, Anniedi attended a summer science program at the University of Massachusetts at Amherst. Just like their two older sisters, both Anniedi and Iquo took part in numerous extra-curricular activities which greatly enhanced their growth and achievements.

Among some of the activities in which they participated were the Student Theater Outreach Program (STOP), the church choir, the Science and Technology Entry Program (STEP) at Union College, and the Summer Science Program for high school students, sponsored by the University of Massachusetts at Amherst. Both Iquo and Anniedi were heavily involved in the technology program at Sand Creek Middle School. That program enabled them to engage in independent projects and take advantage of computer applications. Iquo even won a school district award for being the best student at all levels of computer technology education.

It is becoming nearly impossible to separate Anniedi's and Iquo's middle school experiences from those of the high school.

The fact is that the differences might not have been great. For example, while Anniedi entered Colonie Central High School in 1995, and Iquo followed in 1996, they both were already part and parcel of the high school scene on the bases of their academic performances. The greatest challenge at the high school might have been in the area of sport for Anniedi, who did not care to participate, while Iquo was involved in both track and field and basketball. Both girls also attempted to take nearly all of the required advance placement classes, like their older sisters.

In her final year before graduation, Iquo suffered what the family considered to be an injustice at the hands of school officials who passed her over as class salutatorian, even though ranked second brightest student in the graduating class. The reason given for this action was that Iquo scored a fraction of a point below the student chosen as valedictorian. The family resented this action, considering the fact that Iquo had an overall superior record throughout her tenure at the South Colonie Central School System.

Anniedi graduated from the South Colonie High School in 1998 and went on to Brown University from where she earned a bachelor of science degree in biomedical ethics. Iquo graduated from South Colonie Central High School one year later in 1999 and went on to Stanford University from where she earned a bachelor of science degree in premedical science education. During Stanford University graduation, Iquo was nominated to deliver a speech at the University's 2003 Black Graduation celebration night. By being nominated to give that speech to a much larger and diverse audience, Iquo did not just make up for the disappointing graduation experience of South Colonie Central High School; she also made the family very proud. I have been, and will always remain, very proud of my daughters. I pray that God continues to shine bright lights on them and their future endeavors and families all the days of their lives.

The Essien girls (L-R): Iquo, Ime, Eno, and Anniedi Essien

CHAPTER 10

REFLECTIONS AND RECOMMENDATIONS

As I stated in several sections of the book, I am not writing this memoir for personal aggrandizement; it is virtually a dramatic incursion into what hitherto has been a family taboo in my neck of the woods. Indeed it was a family taboo that was never written down and placed in any family rule book but by pure ignorance and fear. For this reason, it is quite possible that my writing of this book may set off a wave of secondary traumas or discomfort that might still leave some wounds on the author and within the family circle. That is the reason I have decided to embark on this reflection as an attempt to more objectively look at the little issues that have the potential of joining together to create lasting effects.

I consider my writing of this book to be an invitation to my reader, not just to virtually travel along with me, but to also conceptually share in my experience working in the farmlands of my village in Nigeria. From reading the book you will have been able to mentally travel with me through the rough seas of the Atlantic

Ocean and the rugged mangrove swamps of coastal Nigeria and Cameroon on the Gulf of Guinea. Indeed, you would have joined me on the bumpy lorry rides along Nigeria's Trunk A Roads from the village to Lagos in 1959, from Lagos to Washington, DC, in 1969, and from Washington, DC, to Albany, New York, in 1976. These were the roads, the arena and the segments of my story. Without traveling these routes, it is impossible to rediscover and hear my lost voice. On that note, please accept my deep appreciation for your patience and understanding.

HEARING MY VOICE AT LAST

In many ways, writing this book was an attempt on my part to share the joy of hearing my voice which was lost, literally, in the mangrove swamps. I used the analogy of having heard and found my voice that was lost in the mangrove swamps to illustrate the joy of discovering the benefit of getting an education as an adult after what amounted to a lost opportunity during my early youthful days in Nigeria. I also employed the concept of hearing my voice to joyfully articulate how much I appreciate the opportunity to belatedly enter into the academia and what that entry has meant to me and my family in America. Among all that I have said about painful memories and trauma in my life, the phenomenon of finding my voice symbolizes my triumph in the new world. Losing my voice was closely associated with extreme isolation and painful experiences, as narrated in the book. By the same token, hearing or finding my voice is a strong evidence that whereas I was once lost, I have now just been found. For that I am forever grateful to God.

I want to believe and hope that there will be at least one important rewarding lesson in this book for that one reader who finds himself or herself in a similar situation that I found myself during my childhood. The message from this book is that such a person should persist and continue to do what he or she has to do, with hope and prayers. A day will come when the state of despair will turn to hope and success.

The Reverend Dr. Martin Luther King, Jr., said in his famous "I Have A Dream" speech in 1963 that we are "Free at last; Free at last." In the same vein, I am pleased to use this phenomenal occasion to shout "Heard at last; Heard at last." Yes, I am happy I am heard at last, even if it took fifty-five years of my life to get there. This is because there is nothing else in this world that better ensures a person's happiness, self-esteem, and dignity than being given a chance to be heard. Of course, even when the chance is not given for you to be heard, it is quite possible to carry on your own battle up to the point at which you may be heard at last. The freedom and joy of being heard remains fundamental to an individual's expressive power, especially when that expressive power yields a loud voice such as this one now in progress.

Psychologists suggest that an individual's capacity for vocal expression is, perhaps, the single most important determinant of personality. Many other personal traits are also explained through vocal power—articulated in words, inflections, and gestures. Yet, words mean more to our senses when they are written down. It is amazing and personally rewarding to me to see how possible it has been for me to develop my own frame of reference around vocal power and the written word. In my opinion, vocal power and written words are integrally and positively related. Thank God I have been able to write down what I could not articulate vocally over these many years. It is now possible for me to be heard loud and clear.

To be heard loud and clear means that I had to virtually think out loud and conceptually reproduce my voice by means of written scripts. That is why I decided to take a few moments in this section to reflect on the processes that led to getting this voice out in print so that it may be read and heard at the same time. To begin with, I want to thank the good Lord for giving me the ability to start and complete this mammoth memoir which covers my experiences from the fishing port to the farm and to the main streets of Lagos and Washington, DC. It has been said that a person to whom much is given, much shall be expected of him. I strongly believe that it is the Lord who saw me through the many experiences, some of which were bitter and painful, that also gave me the courage and character to write this book. I could not help but characterize the entire processes of compiling this story as phenomenal and life changing.

As indicated in several sections of the foregoing chapters, not a single successful action of my life achievement was a function of any long-term plan. For the most part, I take the liberty of describing my earlier achievements as a matter of happenstance in the face of hopelessness. This is simply my way of saying that my only long term plan had been to do whatever it would take to educate myself. To be clear, my reference to "long term plan" does not mean that I had a written statement of goals, broken into objectives and tasks. Everything was taking place within my mind, and my daily movements. This is why I would submit that the achievements I am now celebrating is the result of hard work, commitment and sleepless nights, even though I did not start out with a formal work plan to follow. That was also the case in writing and producing this book, since I never really thought, at the early going, that the experiences of my life deserved to be compiled into a memoir. I could not be more wrong!

So without having a formal plan drawn up to guide me in doing all these things, how is it that I was able to assemble and carry out all of the tasks that needed to be executed to bring the projects to success? My humble answer is that I was able to meet the daily demands of my writing tasks, by setting priorities. For example, I usually took a moment to select the priority level, high, medium, or low, that I would need to place on writing or investigating, depending on a typical day. In most cases, priorities one (high) and two (medium) were very rarely chosen, except at the beginning of the writing a few years earlier. In retrospect, I might have utilized medium and low priorities more often than not. I worked on writing the book as a high priority much more at the beginning and close to the period of final editing.

While I had to put a tremendous amount of time into writing, it would not be fair for me to blame the book for taking away all my attention from tackling other important matters affecting my family. For the nine-year period that it took to start and complete this memoir, there were many events that occurred in my household which significantly affected my writing tasks. In the course of this work, we suffered losses of family members, celebrated marriages, and a few college graduations. These events occupied a large chunk of my time and significantly interfered with my normal work routines. It took a lot of re-energizing and strategizing for me to get myself back to the condition that I could let go the worries and resume the task at hand. That is how I have been able to attend to my writing tasks, while also spending time in dealing with urgent family matters. The end result of all that I have done can not be anything less than my personal satisfaction and pride.

Personal satisfaction and pride call for a person to be both psychologically and physically ready to talk or write about himself, especially in a book form such as what I have done. But doing so also calls for personal discipline that is not easily attainable by many. Indeed, until I tried my hand in writing this book, I would not have known what it is like to write a book, much less writing about myself. I have found that it is not so easy for anybody to just get up and write, especially when they have to struggle day in and day out to put food on the table for the family. Even for someone like myself, who dreamed of being a writer, as time went on and the pressure of life set in, I discovered that I could not become a writer unless I began to sit down and write.

It was a combination of many things that brought me face to face with the computer screen and keyboard to start my writing tasks. Certainly, it was the call and urging of important friends and family that forced me into action. I am grateful to the almighty God for seeing me through all my trials and tribulations at the early going, and for being my constant guide in all subsequent endeavors, including writing this book. It is nice to finally be able to do this for myself and for my family. It is nice to hear my lost voice come back to life. Even with this, I am convinced that this effort is not the best as yet, because the best is yet to come.

THE SOUND AND TONE OF MY VOICE

One of the difficulties I encountered in preparing this book has been how to deal effectively with its many angles. From the way I have presented the story, this is a story that has links in the woods, swamps, seas, towns, hills, and valleys. For this reason, writing it involved an arduous task of explaining the nuts, bolts, shape, and form of the links, in order to more truly capture the fundamental concepts and themes of the many chapters. Indeed, the statements I have made in each chapter of this book represent an attempt to explain the sound, the tone, and the pitch level of my newly found voice which was lost, conceptually, in the swamps. It is my hope as well as my pride that I have presented each segment of the story in a clear and understandable way. That is the kind of result with which I will be very pleased. Having said that, I now want to take a few moment to explain how I remembered so much of the past events and incidents in my life, without which I would not have been able to complete the story. Parts of what guided my memories of the past were the sounds and the tones of all those things with which I came in contact. As we all know, the meanings of different languages of the world are determined and controlled by their sounds and tones. All that I want and pray for is for the sound and tone of my voice, tendered herewith in written form, to be forever positive and inspiring to all.

At the beginning of this story, I took you on a journey through four distinct settings upon which all of the narratives are anchored. They are my birth place, the fishing port location of the Atlantic coastal swamps, the rat races of Lagos, the arena of Washington, DC, and my family life in Albany, New York. The essence of recounting these many settings is to reconfirm the fact that, though we go through despair and toil, with confidence and determination we can always hope to see light at the end of the tunnel. Mine is a story of life because, while the story came out of a personal traumatic struggle and absence of educational opportunity in my youth, my eventual triumph in the new world sends a powerful message of hope to those who may find themselves in similar situations, especially the neglected and disadvantaged children of the ghettos of America and the so-called third world. The message is that, though the doors may have been locked, the avenues to hope and determination are never forever closed to those who persist and who stand firm in plotting and exploring their ways to the future.

One does not need to have any talent to be persistent and determined, but you do need to have some level of energy and endurance to maintain your persistence. By my own assessment, energy and endurance helped me to stand firm on my goals, written or unwritten, to move forward and improve myself, especially at those times when I found myself on the rough edges. When you stand firm with endurance, the battle is half won. When you are persistent and determined to succeed, you most certainly will succeed. It is my definite hope that reading this book has opened your ears to hear my voice, and that the voice that you are hearing through your reading of this book is the voice of life, liberty, courage, and progress.

Again, looking back at all the chapters covering the early days of my life and upbringing, I cannot help but remain tremendously impressed by the wonders of nature and the miracles of God in protecting and seeing me through those difficult times. Not only was I born and brought up under the most untenable conditions in the village, with no known childhood immunization against deadly diseases, I was placed in what can be described by today's standards as brutal work environments. This was manifested in the intense physical labor on the farmland, at the fishing ports, and in the mangrove swamps. My reference to "brutal work environment" should not be interpreted to mean a direct condemnation of the age-old practices of poor families who had to use their children to perform all forms of work to ensure the family's survival. Although these practices may continue even to this day in many parts of the world, that does not make it right. That is why these families must be helped. Unless they are helped, the children will continue to suffer, and not too many of them will live to write books about it.

WHITHER THE NEXT STEP?

Now that I have completed the painful narrative of my childhood struggles and how I managed to emerge from isolation to take my place in the community of survivors, I seriously wonder where we go from here, in terms of setting new goals and taking on new challenges. Judging from how I began my struggles, the next destination, in my humble opinion, is not going to be any closer or easy to reach. It will still require a lot of work and determination. The roads may not be any easier to navigate. For this reason, it is necessary for us to be prepared by taking cues from all of the foregoing experiences that I have already narrated. I wish that this new challenge of mapping out new destinations would be free of storms and stress along the way, but that would not be realistic. For that reason, I have taken the liberty to identify and present the following important questions:

The first question is what impact will publication of this book have on my life, my outlook, and my support environment in the near future? The second question is how will publication of this book affect members of the Essien family? The third question is what will be the impact of this book on my immediate social circles in Nigeria, the USA, and in the Diaspora? By "Diaspora," I am referring to all those who share similar backgrounds and interests with me, but who are scattered around the globe. Finally, the fourth question, a very critical one, is how will the experiences gained from publishing my book be applied toward solving future intellectual and physical (health) problems of the heretofore neglected and "rejected" children of Nigeria and the Diaspora? I will endeavor to address each of these questions separately.

IMPACT ON THE AUTHOR

I would be less than candid if I failed to acknowledge the overwhelming impact that writing this book has had and will continue to have on me, personally. Even if I were not the subject of the book, the mere fact of the enormous amount of energy I have spent in writing the book should affect me directly, and it has. A few of the most obvious impacts I can identify consists of the urgent need to improve my self-esteem, to reshape my outlook, to feel a strong sense of satisfaction, and to feel generally happy that I have been able to write a complete book about my life.

Self esteem, positive outlook, sense of satisfaction, and happiness are inevitable outcomes of my education, age, and sense of freedom. They are also the imperatives of the time. There is no way I could sit down to write this book, unless these qualities were intact. Naturally, there are those who would wonder and ask why I am reflecting on these sorts of impacts and where the indicators might be found. The answer is that the indicators may not be so obvious to the naked eyes, and they may not be something on which you can lay your hands. You need to measure these impacts by counting the many years it took me to get to the point of even beginning to gather all of my stories into a book form. It is my hope and prediction that the same positive impact should be felt by members of my family, including even those who may not be able to read the book as it is written in the English, not the Efik/Ibibio, language.

Of course, I am aware of the fact that, by taking the trouble to describe my own feelings and reactions, I am stepping ahead of myself to do something that should be left to the critical eyes and views of the reader. However, I am still hopeful that my story will evoke in the reader either a constructively critical review or a well-thought out action that will reflectively address the issue of basic education programs for disadvantaged children. As Paulo Freire stated in his famous educational philosophy book, *Pedagogy of the Oppressed* (1970): "Every human being, no matter how 'ignorant' or submerged in the culture of silence he or she may be, …is capable of looking critically at the world in a dialogical encounter with others."

Based on the above idea from Freire, I look forward to more constructive criticism, not just a critical acclaim from the readers and reviewers. I believe critical response has its benefits. It is, in the first place, evidence of learning, involvement, and participation, but these should not be the ends of the game. The solution to our children's education is not accomplished by the knowledge of the problem alone, but by the positive action taken to address the problem.

The content of *Voice From the Mangrove Swamps* addresses only a small part of the problem; however, the solution lies in future actions that will be taken to address this problem. When the pieces of the story in this book become the beacon of hope for hopeless children, the searchlight for the short-sighted power players, and the impetus for action for the discouraged, then and only then shall

I feel truly at peace, even after I shall have departed the earth.

IMPACT ON THE FAMILY

Just as I reflected on the impact of the story on me as the author of the book, the same, or more severe, level of impact will be the case with regard to all members of the Essien family. They include my wife, the Essien girls, my brothers, and my sisters. Additionally, the list extends to cover all of my nieces, nephews, grandchildren, uncles, and all of their families. Most of these people who consider themselves to be extended or nuclear members of the Essien family stand a better chance of being impacted by my actions. However, the possible impacts may come in different forms and to the surprise of some observers. It is not all those family members impacted, especially the extended family, that will be cheerful, positive, and appreciative of every bit of the story narrated in this book. This is due to the obvious reasons of fear and self-preservation. It is my hope, however, that there will be at least a faction of the family members who will read and understand the story and, in turn, serve as a resource to help those who may not be able to read and understand. I am aware of the fact that my analysis of every possible impact may be flawed in some way, based on my past experiences. The point is that there are too many factors that may prevent any form of understanding and cooperation, unless the resource person maintains a strong sense of mission and determination to overcome the revulsion.

As an example of the point I am making here, only recently my older sister, Iquo Essien, was actually afraid of what she perceived as a negative impact of my bold act of writing a book that provided so many intimate details of the Essien family, especially regarding those family members who are either dead or still living in Akwa Ibom State of Nigeria. You could tell from the tone of her voice that, inwardly, she was happy for my effort, except she wanted me to limit my narrative to certain aspects of the home situation. My sister, Iquo, was simply apprehensive of the consequences of "poking my nose" into an unknown territory, an area we were supposed to avoid—writing our history. She was concerned over the mention of the names of village chiefs in Chapter I, because she could not trust that the village chiefs would appreciate that very much—and she did not think that such a narrative mention would be well-received by some, especially the extended and nuclear family members both in Nigeria and in the diaspora. You could say this particular encounter gave me the reason to include this reflective chapter in the book. At least one such impact has already manifested itself.

My older sister's fearful reaction to my work is a typical example of the kind of unexpected impact the writing of this book can, and likely will, have on the Essien family. These reactions, in most cases, manifest themselves as fear, which deserves our attention. I see this form of fear as consisting of three layers—perceived, real, and incidental. By whatever form it manifests itself, fear can be damaging. I wish this were not the case. Unfortunately, it is not within my control, but it is my hope that this book may instead help my people to wipe out these fears as they begin to more positively interact and commune with each other.

The reality of fear is something with which we all have to reconcile, whether it be fear of success or fear of failure. It is even possible that, unless well-informed, one can be afraid of how others will react to his or her actions. This is the situation that will face members of my family, especially in my homeland. For this reason, part of the challenge that now faces the Essien family will be working on the "damage control," so to speak. "Damage control" can be more effective if it is conducted proactively. This means that those family members who can read and understand the contents of this book should take it upon themselves to explain things to other family members to help them enjoy the stories rather than be afraid of the unknown. The alternative may be more damaging and is not recommended.

IMPACT ON MY SOCIAL CIRCLES

For a person who considers himself to be an important member of society, a person who very much values his friends, relatives, and family, it is my belief that my actions are impacted directly or otherwise by the thinking or reactions of my immediate social peers. The question that must be asked, therefore, is whether this impact is positive or negative in the long run. Perhaps the first and most salient aspect on my social circles is the aspect of communication sharing. I am referring to the simple act of exchanging ideas and viewpoints with friends and significant others. For example, I have found that it became more and more important for me to start writing this book as I became more and more willing and open to share my viewpoints and ideas about my early days.

It was through the open sharing of my inner thoughts with others and the feedback I received from them that I developed the much needed impetus that propelled me to start writing. Another source of strength and encouragement for me to start writing emanated from two of my daughters, who interviewed me and subsequently wrote lengthy papers for their college class assignments. Needless to say reading those papers gave me more than stomach butterflies— enough to get me flying to "the promised land." In other instances, it was the way certain serious-minded friends reacted to something I said or wrote in my electronic mail communications that made me stop and think maybe it was time to start writing.

I have also noticed in my other social circles that there have been certain levels of expectation that began to filter their way to my attention. I simply thought it was time to try to make some sense of these impulses. After all, I am the same person who usually talks about writing this and writing that. Consequently, I concluded that the number one social impact on my work has been in getting me to buckle down and start writing the book. The very fear of disappointing those who expect me to complete this book is an enormous impact, a different kind of peer pressure, that I can feel and appreciate. It is my hope that, with this work completed, these people will not be disappointed in me.

The final aspect of the impact to which I look forward and would like to describe will probably be more impetus for more writing, especially when all of the criticisms and suggestions begin to arrive from readers. That is what I have to prepare myself for, and it will not be easy. I am already beginning to feel this impact simply by thinking ahead of the game. I am also looking to dealing more directly with the general public in the effort to market the book. From my observations, this is as much a difficult job as writing the book, but I feel I am ready and prepared to do that as well. Of course, I know this is not going to be easy to get done—and neither should it be—but I am still the same person who has been preaching, advocating, and even exhibiting patience, determination, and endurance. I like to think I am psychologically prepared to handle all forms of difficulties and disappointments that are likely to result from being described as an author by society. As the saying goes, "uneasy lies the head that wears the crown."

A CLARION CALL: SAVE THE CHILDREN

I have decided to devote this section of my concluding statements to the issue of children's welfare. With all of the energy I have put into telling my story, I find it debilitating for me to recall and recount the type of difficult conditions that governed my life as a youngster. While I thank God for giving me the energy and zeal to be alive and write my story, the fact is many children in my native land and other parts of the world, who happen to face childhood deprivation and neglect, do not live to tell about their experiences. That is why I am devoting this section to the clarion call for action to save our children who are still being deprived of opportunities to learn and grow. I want to call the attention of the world to the persistent and hardened conditions that continue to afflict children in the developing countries of Africa and many other parts of the world. I am referring to inadequate medical attention, lack of clean water, poor sanitation, inadequate food, and lack of functioning electricity. As an example, in my place of birth and in many developing countries, poor road conditions and poor means of communication combine to impede the ability of petty traders to conduct business. Many African children attend schools that have no libraries or books. The school buildings are poorly maintained and teachers are poorly paid. The condition of hospitals, if and where they exist, still leaves much to be desired.

This clarion call for action to save the children is directed to those who have both the means and the knowledge to change the life of a child wherever he or she might be. It is for those who care and want the world to be a better place for all our children. It is indeed a pleasure for me to devote this concluding section of my book to the issue of saving or rescuing children from impending destruction. I am doing this because of the painful memory of how I started my life in isolation, suffering, and turmoil. Growing up in poor and unsafe conditions, without medical care and educational opportunity, is not something that should be allowed to continue anywhere in the world. Although I have since left my village and have significantly changed my life, the conditions in my village and in many developing countries of Africa have not changed much.

I am sure many readers may be surprised to learn that some of the above mentioned conditions still persist in Nigeria, the so-called giant of Africa. There is no reason to be surprised. After peacefully achieving independence from Great Britain in 1960, Nigeria embarked on an effort to transform the country from savagery to civilization. Efforts to improve infrastructure were classified under rural development projects. Rural development encompassed all kinds of plans to build roads, provide electricity, install water pumps, etc., to selected towns and villages. The problem is that this efforts are not noticeable in many small towns, including my village.

Unfortunately, after fifty years of independence and a series of untold political and social changes, my birth place of Ifa Ikot Idang, Akwa Ibom State of Nigeria, has not changed from the time I was born. Women still give birth to their children at home, except in rare cases of emergencies when a medical doctor may be involved. The few local hospitals around the area are extremely poorly equipped to handle childbirth necessities. The village still has no clean water supply, the electricity does not stay on more than two hours a day, and there are no safe roads. The average family is still struggling with the pressure of raising its children in the same way I was raised more than fifty years ago. There are more people dying each year in my village today than even while I was there. The sad message I am sending here is that the same or worse situations are taking place in several parts of Africa, especially with the prevalence of HIV AIDS crisis. While I am proud to write about my voice having been heard loud and clear from the mangrove swamps, thousands of children are losing more than their voices by the minutes—they are dying.

In 2001, as I began writing this story, the Unitarian Universalist Association of the United Nations organized a conference in Dublin, South Africa, to address racism and other issues affecting poor nations. In his remarks, the secretary general, Kofi Annan, referred to racism, slavery, reparation, and debt relief as the burning issues that the world needed to face urgently. Although Kofi Annan was attempting to highlight the sufferings of poor people on this our planet earth, the real question is whether anybody out there is listening? Is any authority out there trying to do something to bring about changes to the lives of the suffering people?

At one time in my life, I was in the same situation as those of our suffering brothers and sisters on the African continent. Maybe I was not afflicted with a deadly disease, but I came close to succumbing to ignorance and sometimes personal injury. Maybe I did not suffer racism, but I came close to being totally isolated from the rest of the world and, as a result, being shut out of opportunities that several other well-placed and dominant tribes enjoyed in Nigeria. Needless to argue, it is not every one of the suffering people that will emerge victorious on their own without outside help. I am hoping, therefore, that the United Nations will work with each country to find a permanent solution to the sufferings of poor people wherever they may be.

I realize that, in the previous chapters of this book, I referred to persistence, endurance, determination, and energy as the necessary qualities that would almost guarantee success when going through hard times and struggling to survive. I must admit these qualities alone would not have been sufficient to save me from destruction if I were too malnourished to be able to function or if I were to succumb to any one of the deadly, but preventable, diseases that were prevalent in my growing environment. Diseases such as mumps, rubella, whooping cough, tetanus, typhoid, yellow fever, etc., are all preventable with appropriate immunizations. Diseases resulting from hunger and starvation have the potential of damaging the mental and cognitive capacities of children, yet they can all be prevented in a very simple way, by providing the children with the necessary amount of food. This is not happening, but it should. That is why I am submitting this clarion call to save the children.

When I remember the roads I have traveled to where I am today, I cannot help but be convinced that we are never educated, until we are all educated. I want to also add that, in the present circumstances, we are just not a healthy people until we are all in good health. Every one of us has a job to do to fight the diseases of poor health, ignorance, and hunger. The concept of "to each its own" must be changed to a new and more demanding one: "to all our own." Let us all be involved in order to make a difference. Let us save the children!

Below are suggested resources and websites to access world-wide information to save the children:

Save the Children (also International Save the Children)
54 Wilton Road, Westport, Connecticut 06880, USA
Telephone: 1-203-221-4000; 1-800-728-3843
Website: http://www.savethechildren.net
This website has links to local offices in different countries.

United Nations International Children's Education Fund (UNICEF)
Headquarters: Avenue Appia 20
CH-1211 Geneva 27, Switzerland
Telephone: 41-22-791-2111
Website: http://www.unicef.org
This website has links to many local offices in many countries.

United States Fund for UNICEF
333 East 38th Street
New York, New York 10016, USA
Telephone: 1-800-486-4233
Website: http://www.usfundforunicef.org
This website has links to many local offices in the United States.

United Kingdom Committee for UNICEF
Africa House, 64-78 Kingsway
London WC2B 6NB, United Kingdom
Telephone: 020-7405-5592; 020-7430-0162
Email: webmaster@unicef.org.uk

World Health Organization (WHO)
United Nations Plaza—DC-2 Room 970
New York, New York 10017, USA
Telephone: 1-212-963-6132
Website: http://www.who.org
This website has links to local offices in different countries.

World Vision (also World Vision International)
P. O. Box 9716
Federal Way, Washington 98063, USA
Telephone: 1-800-423-4200; 1-800-777-5777
Website: http://www.worldvision.org
This website has links to local offices in many countries.

Christian Children's Fund (CCF)
(International Headquarters)
2821 Emerywood Parkway
Richmond, Virginia 23294, USA
Telephone: 1-804-756-2700; 800-776-6767
Website: http://www.christianchildrensfund.org
This website has links to offices in different countries.

Global Fund for Children (GFC)
1101 14th Street, NW Suite 420
Washington, DC 20005
Telephone: (202) 331-9003
Website: http://www.globalfundforchildren.org
This organization will gladly attend to an application from an

organization requesting funds for the purpose of serving children in different countries of the world, including developing countries.

CHAPTER 11

REMEMBERING MY LOVED ONES

In the course of compiling the stories for this book which actually started in 2001, I have suffered and untold amount of losses of my loved ones in such a way that it became almost unbearable and impossible for me to continue writing. One of the reasons why I managed to control myself and continued writing the book was the fear in my mind that if I failed to complete this book, and I happened to join the line of the dead, then death would have gained the upper hand and, therefore, become the biggest winner of the silent battle. If this happened, my story and my voice would be lost forever. Now then, I am so grateful that the good Lord did not allow that to happen.

Since I managed to struggle through my multiple bereavements and complete my writing, I thought it is appropriate to attach the final words of acknowledgement and remembrance in honor of the souls departed. It has been a terribly difficult task for me to complete writing my story that references close relatives who would not live to the end of the writing assignment. In fact, many times as I was working on the chapters that required mentioning their names, especially my wife, I came close to losing my focus. Again, something held me up and I was able to go on. Below are the special requiem to my dear wife Elizabeth and a special remembrance note to my two sisters, Iquo and Nkoyo, and my nephew Ita—all of whom passed away while I was still writing this book. May their souls rest in perfect peace.

A REQUIEM TO MY DEAR WIFE ELIZABETH

With the deepest sense of loss, regret, and sadness in my heart, I wish to attach this special requiem to my dear wife, Elizabeth Okon Bassey Essien, who was called to rest by the Lord on October 3rd and was buried on her birthday, of October 12, 2002, right after I had begun writing the first few chapters of this book. Having actually started writing in the middle of 2001 and having even sought her assistance along the way to clarify certain factual information in some sections of the book, her passing forced me to suspend further writing, until such time that I could feel psychologically and physically more able to resume.

The untimely loss of Elizabeth, my dear wife and the mother of my daughters, left me and the children in a total state of disarray. Prior to her death, she and I were looking forward to celebrating the girls' educational achievements, after many years of hard work in their respective institutions of higher learning. As has been referenced repeatedly in sections of this book, Elizabeth worked the hardest in ensuring that the children received a better, if not excellent, education. Unfortunately, she only witnessed the college graduations of Eno, Ime, and Anniedi Essien. She also witnessed Ime's marriage in the summer of 2002, an event she was always praying would come to pass. As we struggle to reconcile our loss, it is our belief she has been looking over the subsequent academic successes of the girls ever since. As far as I am concerned, her death leaves me with the worst possible situation I have ever faced in the recent memory. I have so far not yet quite succeeded, after several years, in getting myself ready to start over.

In several sections of this book covering the Albany experiences, I have made references to my dear wife and her tireless work to get us settled as a family, raising the Essien girls, and working to build up the family. At the onset of my work on this manuscript, I sought, and obtained, counsel and input from Elizabeth on specific factual pieces of information, and she responded well to help me make sure I was on the right track with the data involved.

It was not just the assistance I received from her that will remain indelible on my mind; my wife was a power house of ideas and actions regarding whatsoever it takes to improve one's life, wherever a person finds himself or herself. She was sought out by many in the Capital District of Albany and many parts of the USA. Five years after her passing, my four daughters, my nieces and I still have a very difficult time forgetting her and her vibrant personality.

Personally, I still find it difficult to watch the Black Apostolate Choir rendering the communion meditation hymns on Sunday afternoons without her in the Choir, with her signature liturgical dance moves. Elizabeth was always the one choir member who would start dancing all the way from the altar down to the pew. The congregation would always come alive with some excited members joining her in the dance and bringing joy to all. Our daughters all join me today in praying that her soul continues to rest in perfect peace, till we join her in heaven. The obituary that is reproduced below was originally published in the *Albany Times Union* the week of October 6, 2002.

"Mrs. Elizabeth Bassey Essien was born on October 12, 1950, in the village of Mbak Etoi in Uyo Local Government Area of Akwa Ibom State of Nigeria, West Africa. After graduating from the Cornelia Connelly Secondary School, Uyo, and having obtained her high school certificate from the West African Examinations Council in 1969, she came to Albany, NY, in the autumn of 1971, and enrolled at the Hudson Valley Community College in Troy, NY. She later transferred to the State University of New York at Albany, where she obtained her first degree in English education in 1975, and a master's degree in Educational Administration in 1977.

"Mrs. Essien was certified by the New York State Education Department as an English teacher. Throughout the years that she lived in the Capital District of New York State, Mrs. Essien touched the life of many people, black and white, through her places of employment, religious circles, family and social circles. Among the places that she had worked are Eden Park Nursing Home; NYS Education Department—Summer Food Program for Children; Our Lady of Angels School; Milne High School—all of Albany, NY. Elizabeth was also always so proud of her previous experience teaching at the Loreto Girls Secondary School, Abak, Akwa Ibom State of Nigeria.

"With regard to her religious circles, the Black Catholic Apostolate at St. George's Church of the Diocese of Albany must be mentioned. Elizabeth was the first president of its Advisory Board between 1986 and 1992. She was the first and only founding president to be publicly honored by the Apostolate in 1992. It is fair to state that Elizabeth's family, extended family, and social support systems constituted the center of her life. She was a bridge builder for the family members who were considered hard to integrate.

"She made numerous trips to the motherland in the company of her American friends and children, and extended family members for the purpose of helping them know where they came from. Mrs. Essien is survived by her husband, Dr. Bassey E. Essien of NYS Office of Temporary and Disability Assistance (OTDA), Bureau of Refugee and Immigration Affairs, four daughters—Eno Bassey Essien, Ime Bassey Essien, Anniedi Bassey Essien, and Iquo Bassey Essien and many nieces, nephews, aunts, and cousins.

"Mrs. Essien was employed by the NYS Office of Mental Retardation and Developmental Disabilities (OMRDD) from 1981 to the time of her death. She started in her job position as Project Assistant and was subsequently promoted to the position of Program Operation Specialist 2. Her responsibilities in these positions included ensuring statewide uniform application of community-based ICF/DD programs and working with Home and Community Based Services waiver. She later became the principal spokes person and great advocate for OMRDD in the area of statewide waiver and Self Determination of the mentally retarded persons. Mrs. Essien was highly respected by her coworkers and recognized as the OMRDD's authority in the dissemination of information to circle of Support team members and providers throughout New York State.

"One of the most outstanding contributions of Mrs. Essien to the Capital District of Albany, NY, was her persistent and untiring work in spreading African culture and heritage. In this regard, Mrs. Essien set up the Center for African Fashion and Cultural

Awareness, through which she was able to promote African fashion, African dance, and African cultural Education throughout the Capital Region and beyond. There is hardly any school district in the immediate counties that has not availed itself of Mrs. Essien's extensive knowledge.

"With the assistance of the OMRDD staff, the family set up a Circle of Support Scholarship Program in the name of Mrs. Elizabeth Essien. The family also requested that all contributions, in place of flowers, should be sent to Fleet Bank, 25 New Scotland Avenue, Albany, NY 12208. Fleet Bank has since become Bank of America, but the address remains the same. Elizabeth Essien's Scholarship was meant to target students from Cornely Cornelia Secondary School or Loretto School in the Akwa Ibom State of Nigeria, The qualified student or students will demonstrate a strong interest in art, science, and religion, in addition to being in above average or better academic standing in class. These criteria are based on Elizabeth's qualities, which included ability and love of literature, dance and culture; practical sciences such as biology and chemistry; a strong devotion to Christian life. The family has final decision, and may have additional information, on the scholarship awards, if requested."

REMEMBERING SISTERS IQUO, NKOYO, AND NEPHEW ITA

It is with a very heavy heart that I have to write this statement of remembrance in honor of my older sister Iquo Edet Essien, my stepsister Nkoyo Edet Essien, and my nephew Ita Edet Ekpo, all of whom passed away in the year 2008. Of course all these deaths followed the death of my wife Elizabeth Essien who passed away in the year 2002. When I began preparation for this book, all of these important sisters, my wife and my nephew, were alive and well.

Indeed, I mentioned their names in the appropriate sections of this book dealing with my siblings and my spouse. I know that there is no amount of remembrance that will bring them back to life.

My intent here is to console myself and all of my other relatives who join me in the prayer that their souls may forever rest in peace. We miss all of you dearly. We also pray for the good Lord to take care of the children that you all left behind, as they are now venturing their different ways in search of salvation and economic survival. Again and again, may your dear souls rest in perfect peace!

Printed by Publishers' Graphics LLC